201.11

"Robert William Jenson's book is the first and only major work that analyzes the logic of the language of hope. . . . We could say this is the needed epistemology for an eschatological view of the world's meaning, of my personal existence and of world history. Jenson moves into the sphere of the Continental 'theology of the future' with the Anglo-Saxon tools of logical and linguistic analysis [and] . . . takes the best of both worlds into an imaginative synthesis of his own. Those interested in the logical and linguistic credentials of the new theology . . . will welcome this book."

Carl E. Braaten,
Lutheran School of Theology, Chicago

"At a time when theology has been fragmented into many schools, Professor Jenson crosses frontiers, and around the central problem of God-language he considers the views of analysts, existentialists, representatives of the new hermeneutics and the theology of hope, and such giants of the past as Origen and Aquinas. The result is to throw much new light both on the central problem and on the state of theology today."

John Macquarrie,
Union Theological Seminary, New York

Robert W. Jenson is Professor of Systematic Theology at the Lutheran Theological Seminary, Gettysburg, Pennsylvania. He holds a doctorate in Theology from the University of Heidelberg. He is an editor of *Dialog*, a contributor to many theological publications, and is the author of *Alpha and Omega: A Study in the Theology of Karl Barth*, and *A Religion against Itself*.

THE KNOWLEDGE OF THINGS HOPED FOR

THE KNOWLEDGE OF THINGS HOPED FOR

The Sense of Theological Discourse

Robert W. Jenson

NEW YORK

OXFORD UNIVERSITY PRESS

1969

theology - terminology
language and languages
Religious
aspect -
Christianity

For Peter Brunner
Emeritus Professor Ordinarius at Heidelberg
my revered "doctor-father"

Foreword

The following essay will no doubt be taken as an example of "the theology of hope." I have the usual antipathy for being labeled and doubt that "the theology of hope" exists. Yet the conclusions of this essay do indeed enforce that concern for the reality of promise which is the common motif of such otherwise very different theological programs as those of Pannenberg, Moltmann, Braaten, Altizer, Sauter or—for that matter—myself in my other work.

If this investigation enforces a theology of hope, it is still true that I arrived at the position by a different way than that taken by the others. The order of the book follows the order of my reflection, which began, as the book begins, with puzzlement about the logic of theological discourse over against the demand for verifiability. For me, *this* was the pressure which led to acknowledging the centrality of promise and hope for Christian faith and discourse.

There are many I must thank. Professors Peter Brunner, Gerhard Ebeling, and John Linnell read and criticized various parts of the manuscript. My wife read and criticized the whole, several times. The manuscript grew in bits and pieces over a period of years, and I owe the time spent on it to Luther College at Decorah, Iowa, for generosity while I taught there and for a sabbatical during which decisive parts were written; to the Lutheran School of Theology in Chicago, where the first draft of chapter five was taught; to Mansfield College in Oxford where the final work was done; and to the Lutheran World Federation, who support the Oxford post. I should also thank Mr. J. K. Cordy of the Clarendon Press; the editors of Oxford University Press, for truly remarkable expedition; and Basil Blackwell and Harper and Row, for permissions to quote at length from John Wisdom's "Gods" and Ludwig Wittgenstein's *Blue Book* respectively.

R. W. J.

December 1968
Gettysburg, Pennsylvania

Contents

THE KNOWLEDGE OF THINGS HOPED FOR

1. The Problem about 'God'

That Christianity's language about God has become unintelligible to its hearers is finally apparent also to us who speak it—in that we find it increasingly unintelligible to ourselves. The nasty and deadly question of the twentieth century, "What do you *mean?*" is now heard even in the religious ghetto. We sit in the pew, to our own annoyance ask, "But what does the preacher mean?" and are unable to discover an answer. We climb the pulpit with despair of the words we must utter—a despair present for a generation at least, but now become explicit. We suspect that this is why those "outside" stay there so stubbornly: it is not that they have rejected the message, but they have been unable to make out what the message is. Worse yet, what if those "inside" stay there only because they, too, have never understood what is being said?

If this question is put with sufficient intensity, it tends to acquire a codicil: "What do you mean—*if anything?*" For if we once admit that we are uncertain what a given use of words means, we are no longer in a position to assume that it has any meaning. We have disclosed the uncanny possibility that our words are nonsense. Then suspicion poisons all speaking. Who knows what innocent utterance may not on closer inspection turn out to be like 'Ixplies are dingle' or 'The piano is two-thirds altitudinous'? If 'The absolute descends into nature' is clearly a case of this sort, why is 'Water runs downhill' not a similar one? It is not, we are sure, but *why* not? [1] Once this question is raised, we have to try to answer it. Then we are responsible to the intended meaning of our words only if, when challenged, we reflect on and try to point out how what we say works. Otherwise our utterance is legitimately met with the nonresponse, "Oh well, who knows what *that* means?"—exactly, that is, as the Christian talk is now met.

This account of the matter is, of course, oversimplified. Utterances that are nonsensical in the straightforward way of that about the altitudinous piano are rare. Any combination of words that people actually use must do *something,* or they would not have created it. But the horrid possibility now exists that once we respond to the questions of our time and dig out the actual meaning of one of our uses of words, we will no longer be interested in that use. A whole body and style of utterance may be received—and properly so—with "What does that mean?" in the sense of "So who cares?"

We can engage in any number of pursuits using words. We state facts, make promises, give commands, posit values of various kinds, etc. We begin new language activities for special purposes as needed. Wittgenstein gives as an example[2] the language of the mason and his apprentice: "Brick," "Mortar," "Brick," "Mortar," "Mix," etc.—all one-word sentences that are not statements, not yet quite commands, not yet anything but what they are: elements of a language activity with its own categories and rules. And in general each language activity has its own purposes and rules and is not to be judged by those of some other. If commands are not discredited because they do not convey facts, may not a language activity be played with a key piece 'God'? May not a language-activity be concerned with positing and manipulating the relation to this key piece of such words as 'me,' 'future,' 'salvation,'? May we not have a game with

1. That this question is itself a confusion doesn't alter the point.
2. Wittgenstein, *Philosophical Investigations,* Part I, § 2 ff.

its own rules, by which its sentences are meaningful in their own way, so long as we follow these rules? Why not a "language of Canaan," if there are those who need it?

Why not indeed? For those who need it. But who needs it? Obviously not the vast majority of men—at least, not any more. I do not mean only that the majority reject what the Gospel says about God. The majority of those who hear the Gospel have always rejected it—as predicted. But even to reject the Gospel one must hear it. The language in which the Gospel is said must be comprehensible; one must be able to play the game, whether as protagonist or as opponent.

Languages are born and die, old ones are abandoned, and new are created. Who now actually speaks the language of the Greek myths? Or that of a prewar statesman? Of the unlimited number of possible language activities, most, at any one time, *we simply do not care to pursue.* Or rather, most we may not and ought not pursue. For the abandonment of old languages and the adoption of new is not accidental: it is identical with the direction and movement of history.[3] Thus the Greek creation of logic, of a formalized language, was perhaps the main event of Western history; though the seventeenth-century creation of a materialist language, with all its consequences down to and including its petrification as Marxism, is a close second. The abandonment and creation of languages *is* history. For every age, therefore, there are languages that it is historically irrelevant, impertinent, and impious to speak. Those Greeks who chose the logic of the philosophers could not simultaneously continue to speak the language of myth in the old way, at least not for long. To have done so would, then, have been to opt for darkness and illusion. And their choice remains decisive to this day.[4] Again, having opted for science, we do not, whatever we pretend, speak seriously the language of supernaturalist metaphysics. Whatever languages may be in themselves possible, we rob our lives of

3. Cf. below pp. 11–12, 195–201.
4. Here is the point where, for all his great service, Heidegger may, by his empty dream of a return to a prelogical "evocation of being," be a seduction from the very abyss—especially for theologians.

their historical reality and abandon ourselves to chaos if we seek to move all directions at once in history.

Here is the deepest sense of our "What do you mean?" with its skeptical overtone. A whole elaborate enterprise of speech may be unintelligible to the men of a culture or a period by being a language that they are no longer or not yet called to hear. When those who use this language receive no reply but a plea for elucidation, they should be moved to investigate what they do mean; and then they may find that when they know what they are saying, they, too, no longer wish to say it. The question that history will not let us ignore is: Is the Christian activity of utterance about God one in which we are permitted any longer to engage?

We must not answer carelessly. The punishment for a false move will be great. A language activity pursued in defiance of history, with ears stopped to the question of meaning, will pervert and distort all of life. The language itself that is thus made a weapon against sense and honesty will disintegrate inwardly until its utterances arrive at that point of logical chaos where they are nonsensical even in the primitive sense of 'Ixplies are dingle.' A life that sought its religious reality through such empty words would be what is meant by hell.

II.

At this point let me insert two necessary specifications.

First: Our topic is God-language, the group of utterances containing the word 'God' or some of its many near equivalents. By "theological language" we mean the class of such utterances. We ask: How do such utterances work—if at all? Whether such utterances form one logical series—that is, whether any one answer to this question will be part of an analysis of all of them—is part of what we have to investigate. Whether such utterances exhaust such a logical series, or whether there are perhaps other religious utterances not containing 'God' or its equivalents but sharing all important logical characters with those that do, we will leave unsettled. Our topic is not, therefore, theological language in the sense of the whole mixed bag of language popularly called theology. It is not theology in the narrow sense that includes only second-level reflection *about* the direct expressions of faith. And certainly it is not "religious language" in general—whatever that might be.

Moreover, by 'God' I mean the father of Jesus Christ. Whether an analysis of what is said about this God holds for all language about gods, we will leave unsettled. Still more narrowly, "utterances containing the word 'God'" are those made by Western believers. Whether our analysis will apply also to the theological language that Eastern and African Christians are developing must again be left open.

Second: The problem is not one of vocabulary. Customarily the whole matter is evaded with the relieved appraisal, "Oh, you mean the problem of communication! You're right. I, too, feel that words like 'atonement' and 'sacrifice' should be replaced with more contemporary equivalents." Now this last is quite correct. The business of translation is indeed a continual and chief task of systematic theology. But the translation is not done by providing word-for-word equivalents. When we have substituted "recovery of authenticity" for "regeneration," what, after all, has been accomplished? Theology's task of seeking the new words for each generation is never merely lexical. This is so because the historical changes of vocabulary with which theology always reckons are rooted at a level deeper than vocabulary: the level of the structure of language, of the rules by which these games are played, of logic. Our theological speech's present unique uncertainty penetrates this level deeper than ever before. Therefore the problem of vocabulary itself is now extraordinarily acute.[5] Therefore also merely lexical approaches to "the problem of communication" are now so unsuccessful: the hipster talking preacher is less understood than are his traditionalist colleagues.

III.

Faith's claim to make statements about God is not originally problematic. It is not, originally, made with fear and trembling or accompanied by difficult reflection. Faith does indeed recognize that

5. To this side of the matter, cf. my article, "Proclamation without Metaphysics," *Dialog*, I, 4.

God is not within our power in any sense, that talking rightly about
Him is not of the activities that we can simply take up at will.
Faith recognizes—rather, proclaims—that unless God chooses to be
present to us, He simply is not there for us to talk about—and that
its ability to talk about God is therefore astonishing. But this aston-
ishment is interior to faith. Faith's knowledge of God's unknowabil-
ity, its knowledge that only if God is graceful can we know Him, is
knowledge that it has *as* faith; that is, as a mode of existence which
originates in God's decision to be graceful, to make Himself present
to us to be talked about, to intrude Himself into our life stories.

We call this self-interposition of God "revelation." By it God
makes Himself the decisive pole of life. He interpolates His own
story as the climax and denouement of ours. 'Faith' is our stumbling
name for finding ourselves in this situation, for the whole posture of
life evoked by God's sudden presence. 'Faith' is, therefore, not the
name of any set of ideas, emotions, or attitudes. Nevertheless, as
faithful, I live in this situation and so think (and emote and take
up attitudes, etc.) in this situation. Thus my life of faith involves
having and expressing ideas, including ideas about God. Indeed,
speaking is the characteristic act of faith: faith exists exactly in the
act of confession. For God meets me in my history and is Himself a
person. Which is to say: He comes to me as a word and evokes
from me an answer.

It is in this situation that we come faithfully to say 'God.' Therefore our God-utterances are not originally puzzling to us. It is not
'God is love' that seems unclear and uncertain. It is rather what I
have to say about *myself* that, to begin with, becomes difficult and
reflected in the situation of faith. It is between 'I am a sinner' and 'I
am a saint' that I may be unable, for example, to differentiate.

But it is nevertheless inherent in the situation of faith that its utterances can *become* problematic for it, that they can become matters for doubt and risk and courage—and for philosophical reflection. For God's Word and our answer are not angelic or divine
speech—whatever these may be: they are human speech. They are
constituted of utterances that belong to the whole body of utterances
by which man, as he lives in history, projects and grasps and re-

ceives and loses his life. The crisis of language has been dealt with often enough by retreat from speech in the public language, with any who may listen, to the safely private communication of sectarian religion. If there is a group able to function as a group by a use of language, it cannot, of course, be denied that this language has a use, that its users must therefore have rules for its use, and that the utterances of that language are, for them, meaningful. But whatever may be true of other "religious languages," the language of Christian faith cannot be saved in this way. For by this move we deny the content of the assertions and commands that make up the body of faith's utterance: "For God so loved the *world . . .*" or, "Go ye therefore unto *all nations, teaching* them. . . ." [6] The final retreat is to "speaking in tongues," whose current vogue is a remarkable confirmation of our diagnosis. It is precisely the withdrawal from public responsibility for sense and nonsense which Paul found suspicious in this practice.[7]

Thus we assert that for faith's speaking about God to be speaking of faith, it must be in some, for the present undefined, sort of logical continuity with our other utterances. Men must be able to call its utterances into question. The unbeliever must be able to reject them.

In fact, faith's utterances are invariably so challenged. Manspeaking always finds faith's statements about God absolutely odd. He cannot in conscience repeat them or even allow them to pass unrebuked. Whenever faith speaks, there is a clash. It is out of this clash that the necessity arises for the believer to explain what he is doing when he says, for example, 'God is love'—precisely so that his speech can maintain itself as what it essentially is and must remain: the human speech of a human being speaking out of a particular human situation.

The challenge of culture to faith's language about God can take many forms. The most usual has been a claim to possess more adequate language about God than faith has: to have more accurate in-

6. An acute awareness of this is the common motif of such diverse theologians as Paul Tillich, Ulrich Mann (*Theologische Religionsphilosophie im Grundriss*), and Wolfhart Pannenberg.
7. I Corinthians 14: 1–25.

formation or to dispose of more potent cultic formulas. But the challenge may be an attempt to eliminate God-utterances from language altogether.

It is this form that the challenge to theological speech now takes—which is much of what is meant by calling this a "post-religious" age. Formulated explicitly: statements in the form 'God is . . .' are meaningless; they are pseudo-statements, improper language.

This explicit assertion is, of course, that of the logical positivists,[8] now nearly extinct. It is, moreover, easily shown to be itself a misuse of 'meaningless.' But this is by no means the esoteric matter of a diminishing sect of philosophers and their dubious dogma: the attitude this statement expresses controls most speech in our time. The denial that the Gospel now meets is not unbelief but incomprehension. Those who reject it do not do so because they find it false but because they find it uninteresting, pointless, obscure, unimportant—any or all of which may be expressed by "It doesn't seem to mean anything to me."

Moreover, the positivists have had successors, most of whom have been no more kind to theological talk. They will be major partners in discussions throughout this book.

IV.

All expressions have, if they are in fact in use, rules for when and how they are to be used. If I say, "Runs smells good," you will reply, "You can't say that." If I ask why not, you will tell me, " 'Runs' isn't a word for something that can smell good or bad." To my attempted utterance, that is, you will respond with the rules for how to use 'runs.' To take a different kind of case: If I say, "John is iggle," you will reply, "What's iggle?" If I then say, "A thing is iggle if [I am in effect saying, '. . . is iggle when . . .'] it is tall and ill-

---

8. The names of Russel, Carnap, Schlick, Neurath, and (as patron-prophet) Wittgenstein will serve to give flesh to logical positivism. The viewpoint was classically popularized in Ayer's *Language, Truth and Logic*. The more recent analytical philosophy was founded by Wittgenstein in his later period. Representative names would be Wisdom, Austin, Ryle. A first orientation in the history is given by Urmson, *Philosophical Analysis*.

tempered," you are now in a position to respond indignantly, "John is *not* iggle!" This you could not do before the rule was given.

Language rules may be put somewhat arbitrarily into two classes. Some stipulate the nonlinguistic circumstances under which an utterance is appropriate—so those for '. . . is iggle' above. Others stipulate kinds of expression and their relations *to each other*—so those against using 'run' with 'smells.'

The meaning of expressions is set by these rules. When, therefore, expressions are used contrary to their usage rules, or when a new use is posited without stipulating at least implicitly the new rules, the result is a puzzle.

The cure of a philosophical puzzle has two stages: (1) If the logic of the case can be straightened out, it may be possible to alleviate the intractibility of such questions as "Do Universals exist?" or "What is energy?" (2) The result of analysis will be a statement or a set of statements in the form "Such-and-such a type of expression is used in such-and-such a way," which then may answer the original puzzle.

An aspect of this second step will become important later. We may as well examine this aspect here—as a sort of excursus. Examples of this second step from the history of philosophy might be: " 'Being' is used primarily only of substances; when used in other categories, it is used in a sense defined by giving its primary use and then stipulating the relation of whatever is said to 'be' to the category of substance." Or: " 'Exists' should be used only of descriptions."

To both these classic examples it is perfectly proper to reply: "Who says so? Who says this expression is to be used only in this way?" Unwilling as the philosopher now is to answer, "Reason says so," or "God says so," it seems he must answer "*I,* the analyzing philosopher, say so." But then the assertion must lack some authority. It can then only be a *proposal,* a proposal for a set of rules for the use of the expression. Moreover, these proposed rules stipulate a usage somehow different from the one in fact current; otherwise, no clarification would result from adopting them.

Why make such proposals? Obviously the proposed rule or rules must be intended as an improvement over those empirically found to be in use. Moreover, the proposed improvements of language are not in these cases trivialities of vocabulary; they are alterations of the logic, that is of the structure, of language. And to make such an alteration is no small matter for the one who does it. For the structure of our language is the structure of our apprehension of reality; and to propose an amendment of logic is to say in effect: "Come, let us look at the world differently than we have been accustomed to do."

Thus the decision to accept or reject a philosophical analysis is in the life of the decider a move of the kind that used to be accomplished as an advance in metaphysical discovery. It is an existential move to a particular vantage point on and in reality.

Moreover, if an analysis is proposed as an improvement, this in itself posits some goal that determines that this change is an improvement and that some other is not. This goal is that final vantage point on and in reality toward which the life of the philosopher moves in each step of analysis. It is not fixed in advance but is articulated exactly in the course of analysis. Just so a metaphysical system has a goal, the "Absolute" or the "Ground" or whatever, posited exactly in and by the system as a whole. Thus the endless task of analysis has the same place in the life of the analyzer as the equally endless task of working out a metaphysical system has in the life of the metaphysician: it is the articulation of his search for meaning.

V.

Now there is no reason why our utterances containing 'God' should not be analyzed in this fashion. They certainly create problems enough. And such analysis has, with increasing zeal, been attempted.

The findings have been discouraging, for they have tended toward the conclusion that theological language is in logical disorder, and that it cannot be put in order without ceasing to be theological. C. B. Martin's *Religious Belief* is a good compendium of this negative view. He finds that logical disorder is inherent in religious language. Scientific language, moral language, etc., are not, he points out, typically in logical disorder themselves. We usually find logical knots only in the products of reflection about these languages. Thus in everyday life people handle 'good' and 'evil' easily and efficiently. They get into trouble only when they begin to ask, "But what *is* good?"—that is, "What does 'good' mean?" Not so with theology. Like speculative metaphysics it is possible only by lawless use of language, and so is inherently nonsensical. People do not handle 'God' well at any level. "The method of theology is that of giving a description that seems to have a perfectly straightforward meaning and then denying that it has that meaning without giving instruction as to what sort of meaning it has." [9] In speaking of God we use expressions that in ordinary discourse are governed by certain rules, we deny that these apply here, and we provide no substitutes: "God is my Father—but this does not mean that He has begotten me or that He in all cases behaves in the way fathers of my acquaintance would." But what then *does* 'God is my father' mean?

In the first period of analytical philosophy, the attack—for that is what it was—took the form of applying to theological utterance the "verifiability criterion of meaning." The logical positivists were mostly concerned with the workings of descriptive language, language used to describe states of affairs, to seek, record, and communicate information. They were concerned, that is, with the logic of the sciences. They asked the questions: How can we tell when an utterance is of this descriptive sort? How can we recognize a genuinely scientific statement? And they proposed the answer: A sentence makes a statement when it is in principle possible to determine its truth or falsity by observation. More precisely: A sentence is descriptive when it either is itself verifiable by observation or is logically so constituted that from it, together with the whole system of otherwise accepted propositions, there can be deduced propositions that are so directly verifiable and could not otherwise have been deduced. Whatever problems may be found with this criterion, it does make a rough distinction between science and pseudo-science—which is really all it needs to do.[10]

Applying this criterion to statements about God, we see at once

9. Martin, *Religious Belief*, p. 5; cf. also p. 18.
10. To the vicissitudes of this criterion, cf. Ayer, *Logical Positivism*, introduction.

that they are unverifiable: 'God' is by definition the name of a transcendent entity, that is, one unobservable in any normal sense of 'observable.' In itself this is not necessarily bad. Poetry, moral exhortation, and a great many vital uses of language consist of unverifiable
utterances—which only means that they are other-than-scientific
uses of language. But theological utterances *intend* to state facts: for
example, 'God is loving.' They fail to do so, and so are at best
wretchedly disguised poetry. They are would-be factual assertions,
pseudo-statements. They are cognitively vacuous and won't admit it.

Later analysts, led by Wittgenstein, became aware that there are
many language acts besides describing, that there are many games
with words besides the one played by scientists. They saw, moreover, that some of these might be *philosophically* interesting linguistic performances. They found the positivists' catch-all category of
other-than-descriptive[11] entirely too undifferentiated. Austin's analysis of such statements as 'I do thee wed' or 'You are hereby notified
. . .' as "performative utterances" is a paradigm case. He isolated in
the present active indicative a whole group of sentences that are not
verifiable yet are none the worse for it, as they do not merely describe a state but create it.[12]

The questions now directed at theological language are therefore:
What language activity or activities are being pursued here? What
are the rules of *these* games? *Is* there a consistent set or sets? One
specific question is: Is a *cognitive* language, which is to be used in
learning and informing, being done here? With an appropriate set
of rules? Or will religious language, theological language included,
have to be understood as, to take one possibility, purely performative—and our actual use reformed to avoid the false and bewitch-
ing appearance of making statements?

This development had a hopeful aspect and was received by some
theologians and philosophers as license to proceed without further
inconvenient reflection. But those who have actually attempted such
analysis have often found that theological language is no better off
when the matter is put this way than it was under the blunderbuss

11. That is really the only content of their term "emotive."
12. J. L. Austin, *Philosophical Papers*, pp. 222 ff.

assault of positivism. They have looked for "the rules which Christians appear to lay down for the interpretation of theological statements," and have been led to hold "that these rules conflict with each other in such a way that no meaningful statements could possibly be governed by such rules." [13] Or they have saved theology by drastic logical reinterpretations unacceptable to the actual users of this language. It is in this context that we must clarify for ourselves the logic of our talk about God—not to satisfy a coterie of philosophers but to be responsible speakers to and for a culture whose challenge to faith's language takes this particular form.

Let us get this challenge before us in the form of a list of some of the most frequently discovered difficulties in the logical workings of theological language. And let us remember that the question is not whether any particular theological statements are true, but whether any such statements can mean what we want them to mean. Thus we cannot escape by reference to "taking on faith" or to the "illumination of the Spirit." Take *what* on faith? [14] And if the Spirit interprets, then it does so either to me alone or by providing the public key to decoding the expressions in question. If to me alone, then the expressions are not interpreted as language; if publicly, it is irrelevant who gives the keys so long as they are at hand.[15] Our statement of the problems will be at this point extremely schematic.

  1. Most criticisms begin with the observation that believers do not treat their statements about God as hypotheses—that is as opinions held pending further confirmation or possible disconfirmation.

---

13. I. M. Crombie, "The Possibility of Theological Statements," *Faith and Logic,* ed. Basil Mitchell, p. 33. This is *not* Crombie's own view.

14. "To say that it is to be believed on faith and not by reason, does not face the difficulty: for the question was not how it should be believed, but what was to be believed." Bernard Williams, "Tertullian's Paradox," *New Essays in Philosophical Theology,* ed. Flew and MacIntyre, p. 211. ". . . When the meaning of religious utterance is in question, no appeal can be made to revelation or external authority. These become relevant only when the question of meaning is settled and the question of belief arises." Martin, op. cit., p. 142.

15. ". . . A special . . . grace might be bound up with finding the biblical assertions acceptable . . . but . . . not . . . in finding them meaningful." Alasdair MacIntyre, "The Logical Status of Religious Belief," *Metaphysical Belief,* ed. S. E. Toulmin, pp. 167–211, p. 176.

Believers do not say, 'God is love—perhaps.' Yet they insist that their statements are informative. The allegedly anomalous character of this situation can be approached in two ways:

(a) If a theological assertion such as 'God is love' is not a hypothesis, that is, if it cannot be refuted by objections like "But what about the sufferings of the innocent?"—then it does not function by delineating one range of possible situations in which it is true as against another range of possible situations in which it is false. It is held to be true no matter what situation obtains. But now if no possible situations in the world could fall outside the range of those evoked by 'God is love,' how does this sentence *say* anything about what situations in fact obtain or do not obtain? That is, how does it assert anything? What more do I believe about the way things are if I affirm this sentence than I would have believed had I denied it? And how are we ever to specify what 'love' means? Ordinarily we would do this by ruling: If anyone does such-and-such, he loves; if he does such-and-such, he does not love. But here we insist 'God is love' is true no matter what He does.[16]

(b) We give rules for the peculiar predicates we feel proper to use with 'God'—such as 'perfectly . . .' or 'infinitely . . .'—so that their meaning is defined by 'God.' Thus 'perfectly good' means of course simply 'good the way God is good.' But then 'God is perfectly good' simply means 'God is good in the way God is good'—which is necessarily true but, alas, entirely uninformative.

Or rather, putting the problem more precisely, 'God' may be a name, in which case 'God is good' is, like 'John is good,' a hypothesis and so possibly false. Or 'God' may be a place-marker for a description: 'the perfectly good, perfectly wise, etc., being.' In this case 'God is good' means 'The perfectly good being is good,' which is indeed necessarily, and not merely hypothetically, true but is informationally vacuous. *Theology wants it both ways at once*: it wants 'God is love' to be both informative and irrefutable; it wants to use

16. Cf. the discussion of "Theology and Falsification" in Flew and MacIntyre, *New Essays.* . . . Cf. also Schmidt, *Religious Knowledge,* pp. 3–60; I. M. Crombie, "The Possibility of Theological Statements."

'God' with some characteristic of a name and some of a description
—which is the inherent logical confusion in the word 'God.'[17]

2. Other problems grow out of the notion, evidently inseparable
from the word 'God,' that the reality so named is ontologically
different from all other reality; that is, that He is what He is in a
different way than creatures are what they are.

(a) One side of this is that although 'God' appears to be used as
a subject-word, it is not used as ordinary subject-words are used.
Their use is based fundamentally on acquaintance: If I say, "John is
clever," and you ask, "Who is John?" I will respond, "Him" and
point; or if this is not practicable, I will say, "The man who married
the Smith girl," which simply moves the pointing operation one step
back: now I must point to the Smith girl. It does not seem that we
can point to God. Then 'God' is logically different from 'John.'
Now there are, of course, subject-words that display precisely this
same logical peculiarity, the logical constructs like 'the average
man': I will never become acquainted with him either, yet I find no
difficulty in speaking of him. Yet this parallel is rather an embar-
rassment than otherwise. We surely want 'God is loving' to be more
like 'John is loving' than like 'The average man is loving'; the love
of the average man will never help anyone in time of need. What
seems to be again the case is that we want it both ways at once—or
if we want to devise some third possibility, what *is* it? What are the
rules by which we stipulate it?"[18]

(b) Since God is the Creator, all relational statements about God
relate Him not to some particular reality, but to the whole of it.
This causes difficulty, for statements about the universe are tricky.
'Universe' does not mean a thing; it means the class of all things. It
is not a thing-word. Now when we speak of 'holding up' a chair, we
know exactly what we mean. But since the universe is not a thing, it
is hard to see how 'hold up' can be used meaningfully with it. 'So-

17. Cf. C. B. Martin, op. cit., pp. 35–44, 56 f., 62 f. Cf. also J. N. Findlay,
"Can God's Existence Be Disproved?" *New Essays* . . . who tries to show
why believers are forced to adopt this self-contradictory logic.
18. Martin, op. cit., p. 41.

and-so upholds the universe' is perilously close to 'runs smells.' But how are we to speak of God at all without such expressions? [19]

VI.

As we have chosen to orient ourselves by the questions of Anglo-Saxon analytical philosophy, we have devoted most of this introduction to them. There is, however, another form of the problematization of theological utterance to which our investigation will inevitably lead us—and climactically. We must, therefore, sketch this challenge very briefly before our introduction can be complete.

It is, I think, apparent that all these objections to the attempt to talk about God are but forms of the question posed, but not answered, by the logical positivists' crude negations. That question is: What is the relation between talk about God and the kind of talk we call science? The dynamic of analytical philosophy's worry about God-language is the triumphant progress in Western civilization of science—that is, of a certain way of talking about the world, a way of talking in which assertions count as assertions precisely by their openness to correction. Where the predictions that follow from a given scientific hypothesis are not borne out by events, the hypothesis is replaced. This seems like an obvious intellectual policy, but it is in fact something new in human history. Intellectual endeavor in strict accordance with this policy is what we now mean by "science."

It was inevitable that, once this policy of constant critique of assertions had become established and self-conscious in the sixteenth century, and in the seventeenth had experienced an unprecedented series of triumphs over the once hopeless puzzles of nature, it would be applied also to our efforts to know our own past. This happened in the eighteenth century. The "historical-critical" way of knowing the past was born. Our past is given to us in the *tradition* of the past: in documents, monuments, and Great-Uncle Obadiah's reminiscences of the old days. Historical-critical study of history— that is, what we now call historical research—is the asking of the question: "I know that's what Uncle Obadiah—or Caesar's *Gallic*

19. Cf. Ronald Hepburn, *Christianity and Paradox,* pp. 169 ff.

Wars, or the newspaper accounts of a thirty-year-old election—*says* happened. But now, what *really* happened?"[20]

The scientific study of history touches a nerve that the scientific study of nature does not touch. Why, after all, are we interested in our past? Surely because it is *our* past. We seek to know history because we need to know ourselves. We watch men play out their stories in order to learn our own roles, to discover what the possibilities open to us are. The enactment of human life takes place in time. It is, therefore, only past humanity whose story can be so observed and recounted. The policy of critical openness to correction, as a policy about our knowledge of the past, means, therefore, critical openness in our understanding of our own lives. It means methodical refusal to be sure of our roles in the world—which must surely also mean methodical refusal to be sure of the author of the play.

Insofar as at least some of the statements about God that believers actually make are at the same time statements about past events— for example, 'God raised Jesus from the dead'—it is plain that extension of the scientific policy to history introduces all the difficulties of the previous section from yet a new side. Believers do not say, 'Jesus died for us—pending further evidence.' Yet if they do not, how can they claim that what they say about the past is to be taken seriously as information? And if 'Jesus died for us' is not information, is it worth bothering with at all?

Moreover, a new problem posed by historical-critical study of the past arises at a different point. The first great push of historical study in the nineteenth century was carried by the faith that the scientific study of the past and the life interest in the past which moves us to such study must be compatible. The question with which the critical historian approaches the tradition of the past is: What happened? The question that leads us in the first place to question the documents of the past is: What is to happen to me? To begin with,

20. Cf. to this whole matter Gerhard Ebeling, "Die Frage nach dem historischen Jesus und das Problem der Christologie," *Beiheft I* to *Zeitschrift für Theologie und Kirche,* pp. 14–30. For a fine treatment of the attempts to overcome historicism philosophically, cf. Wolfgang Müller-Lauter, "Konsequenzen des Historismus in der Philosophie der Gegenwart," *Zeitschrift für Theologie und Kirche,* LIX, 2, pp. 226–55.

historical study was carried by the faith that these two questions roughly coincide. This faith has been lost.

Our interest in history is now dominated by the suspicion that historical-critical study and living appropriation of the past may be incompatible. The two sides of our concern for history came to a parting of the ways at the end of the nineteenth century and have continued since as separate and sometimes hostile enterprises. The concern for critically refined knowledge of the past lives in our desperately "objective" historical sciences. The concern to appropriate the meaning of the past as the meaning of life itself lives in existentialism.

The clash arises from the relativity of the historical. We concern ourselves with the past hoping to find in the stories that men have made of their lives a plot we can recognize and appropriate as the plot of our own life. But precisely as investigation informs me that such a man or group of men believed and lived in such a way, and that they did so because, probably, of such-and-such circumstances, and that such another group, in their circumstances, believed in such another way, etc., it robs their beliefs and lives of the power to address me authoritatively as possibilities for my own life. It is the nature of historical study to put everything into a particular place in history. Faith, cultural dreams, moral absolutes, all are relativized, shorn of their possibility of universal validity—that is, of their claim to validity for me. Thus, for example, historical study tells me that Jesus of Nazareth was a wandering semi-rabbi of a type not unknown in Palestine of the time, that His message seems to have a radicalized form of the message of the apocalyptic sects within Judaism, etc. And the more Jesus is thus put into His place back there, the more implausible does it become that I should take His word as an authoritative word of my destiny.

Historical understanding, once begun, swallows everything. All that men believe, insofar as they express their belief so that it becomes a possible part of tradition—that is, of the object of historical understanding—becomes by their expression a historical item—including what we ourselves believe and express of our belief. Now whatever else our talk about God may be, it is surely expression of our belief and as such falls immediately into the historical. As soon

as we speak, our truth is part of that reality to which historical apprehension will allow no absolute authority. But talk about God is
also an absolute claim about the destiny of our life, or it is nothing.

Just as logical positivism posed the problem of the workings of
theological language insofar as that language wishes to be a me-
dium of information, so the slightly antecedent movement we now
call historicism worked out and left us the problem of the workings
of theological language insofar as it is a part of man's historical existence.

And just as Wittgenstein followed the positivists, so Heidegger
followed historicism. It has been Heidegger's endeavor to think
man's historicity, and especially the historicity of his thinking,
through to the end. Whether that end is bitter, whether the outcome
of historical understanding must be absolute relativism, nihilism, remains to be seen. It has been Heidegger's conviction that if the
thought of man's historicity is thought to the end, nihilism will be
transcended.[21] Whether *theological* speech would be rescued
thereby is another question: our question, and one we must pose to
ourselves precisely against the radical knowledge of man's historicity maintained by posthistoricistic continental philosophy.

VII.

I will approach the task with three (at least) assumptions: (1)
That theological language *is* meaningful in *some* way: that is, that
the alleged logical and existential anomalies listed above at most
show that our language about God does not work in the way we
have supposed; (2) that it is possible to speak of proposed analyses
of how God-utterances work as correct or incorrect; and (3) that I
am in a position to recognize the difference. It is apparent that if we
go to work in this way, we reject any methodological postulate of
neutrality. We are declared for theological language from the outset,
though not, of course, in such a way as to foreclose the ultimate in-
defensibility of theological language: that is, the assumptions with
which we begin may be refuted in the course of investigation. Every

21. Cf. Müller-Lauter, op. cit., pp. 234 ff. Müller-Lauter doubts that Heidegger is successful. So do I.

investigator of this problem has some theological commitment, by which his analysis of theological language is, at least partly, determined. In particular, the assumptions above restrict the analyses I will accept, and depend upon my commitments to the Christian Gospel. I do not think this is a fault.

Let me try to justify this contention that one's analysis of theology's language is—and properly so—determined by one's theology. Any proposed analysis of *how* a language means is essentially a proposed set of definitions for 'means': that is, a summary of several proposed sets of semantic rules, each of which determines a language activity, with special reference to the likenesses and differences among the sets. Now such a proposal, if accepted, is irrefutable in the language activity determined by it. But it is always possible simply to reject it. What considerations operate at this point?

Adopting or rejecting a proposed language is a metaphysical move; it is determined by and determines one's posture in the world. In the case of a religious language, accepting or rejecting is a move of one's attitude toward the goal by which his life has meaning. If, therefore, one is asked to give reasons, he can only respond *theologically,* by attempting to state his commitments.

The particular material theological commitments on which are based the three assumptions above, as well as other criteria that I will use from time to time, will become apparent in the course of this study. Those of which I am aware are the commitments which I take to be those of faith in the Christian Gospel. I can only hope that those of which I am not aware are similar. If I were asked to move one more step back and justify my *commitments,* I would shift categories on my questioner and begin to preach to him. That the need of making this move does not mean that theological language is in disorder—or even, to anticipate wildly, unverifiable—is part of the burden of the study.

VIII.

We have posed the problem that the remainder of this study will try to answer, at least partially. This is by no means the first book devoted to this attempt. Why then yet another? Because it seems to me that the most vigorous analyses of theological language have been pursued in relative ignorance of theology—that is, of that language as it has in fact been spoken. The prerequisite for really beneficial work here is historical study. We must be sure that we know, for some considerable body of Christian theology, how Christian speakers about God have in fact construed their utterances, before critique—which is necessarily always critique of theological language as people have spoken it—can be genuinely helpful to our present task. Therefore we begin with Origen and Thomas—and only thereafter do we attempt our own analyses.

The task on which this book embarks is therefore both historical and systematic, and must be both in order to be either. I am well aware that only a fragment of the whole task is even envisaged in this work. Where, if the history is essential, are Paul, Augustine, Luther, Schleiermacher? Surely all of these are key figures in the history of theological language? The only defense is that one must begin someplace, that one book can only contain so much, that this book raises no claim to be more than a beginning—and that, as will become evident, Origen and Thomas have not been chosen at random.

Finally, a word about method. In accordance with the necessity for the investigation to be at once historical and systematic, we will develop our positions step by step in conversation with the position of other thinkers. This in turn dictates a difference between the two halves of the study. In the first half, where we can look back at the tradition, we can first give a closed description of a few classical figures, and then proceed to critique. In the second half we enter directly into a discussion now in progress, in which no classical figures can yet be discerned, and must therefore work by constant alternation of reporting and independent reflection, in conversation with a great number of thinkers.

2. Origen: Image

Theology as a systematic discipline—that is, theology done in a regularized language in which reflection about the rules of that language is possible—was born in a period of history very like our own, the period of antiquity's religious crisis. The inventor of scientific theology was himself one of the great sufferers and conquerors of that crisis—and would have been whether a Christian or not. Origen was undoubtedly a heretic, yet he set the basic system and created the language for the entire high patristic theology of the East and, since the Western Fathers borrowed the technique of theology whole from the Greeks, for the West as well. Indeed, in a sense Christian theology as it has thus far existed is his invention: for theology has been a work of the Greek spirit on the soil of the Gospel —blessedly so, for how else should it have been *our* theology? And it will become plain that in nothing are we all so much Origenists as in the *way* we have gone about speaking of God.

For centuries the world created by the conquests of Macedon and Rome had experienced a crisis of faith—an ever more hopeless discontinuity between given existence and its transcendent fulfillment, between life and the world as we find ourselves living them and

God or the gods or whatever provides life with a goal and so with sense and structure. The analogy to our own time is very close.[1] The great spiritual movement of that time was that river of the wide delta and many tributaries we label "gnosticism." Whatever else gnosticism may have been, it was certainly a gospel, the gospel of the stranger God, the God who is neither of nor yet for, but against and despite this world and our life in it, the God who rescues us from this world, the God who is *totaliter aliter*. And it was law, a proclamation of the utter valuelessness of all that is worldly.[2] The growing philosophical impulse of neo-Pythagoreanism and middle Platonism was a more Greek evocation of the same spirit,[3] while the *Corpus Hermeticum* perhaps preserves the most broadly representative witness of the struggle.[4]

In the crisis of religion God appears as wholly other; the sole relation between Him and worldly existence is that of total difference and opposition. It is clear that such an apprehension must lead to renunciation either of the world or of God. Our age tends to lose hold of God; antiquity's religious crisis led more typically to despair of the world, to a desperate—and so sometimes fanatical and sometimes frivolous—religiosity. But the cognitive relation to the divine was nevertheless quite as imperiled as it is among us. For the unshakable faith of Greece is that what can be known is what is, and

1. Cf. the remarkable article by Hans Jonas, "Gnosis und Moderner Nihilismus," *Kerygma und Dogma*, 1960, pp. 155–71.

2. Cf. Hans Jonas, *Gnosis und Spätantiker Geist*. Many of Jonas' particular positions are highly debatable, but his unfolding of gnosticism as a mode of existence in the world is quite without peer. Cf. also one of the great works of scholarship, Adolf von Harnack, *Marcion*.

3. For a general rundown, concentrating on what is especially relevant as background for Origen, cf: Hal Koch, *Pronoia und Paideusis*, pp. 180–314; Peter Nemeshegyi, *La Paternité de Dieu chez Origène*, pp. 15–34; Marguerite Harl, *Origène et la Fonction révélatrice du Verbe incarné*, pp. 86–97; Eugène de Faye, *Origène: La Vie, son Oeuvre, sa Pensée*, vol. II.

Typically, Albinos: "Men are dependent on sense-impression, so that . . . they can not genuinely know pure intelligibles." "God is unutterable and grasped only by pure wordless intellectual vision (νῷ μόνῳ), for there is neither genus nor species nor differentia which apply. . . ." *Epitome*, X, 1, 4. Text that of Louis, Paris.

4. To which cf., above all, A. J. Festugière, *La Révélation de l'Hermes Trismégiste*, Vol. IV.

what is can be known. Therefore a God who is the pure negation of all that *is*, is also unknown and unknowable. He is pure mystery.

Yet God is at the same time the sole possible meaning and fulfillment of life. More, He is the *actual* meaning of life; He is *the Father*.[5] He is unknown, and yet the only purely "intelligible" being, the primary object of that fulfillment of knowledge that the men of that time called "gnosis." The transcendent—which may be "God" or a mythically well-populated realm of being—is at once a mystery and the only true object of knowledge. And this world, so visible and unmysterious, is just therefore merely visible. If we will speak, then God is "unutterable" and "unnamable"—and the only thing worth talking about.

II.

This problem is also Origen's, not only because it belonged to the cultural reality to which as a theologian he had to speak, but because he was himself one of the great thinkers of that culture.[6] He worshiped a God whose reality is "unutterable," "unnamable," and "unspeakable," [7] who is "incomprehensible" and "undefinable." [8] "If one considers the fullness of what is to be seen and known of God, a fullness ungraspable by human nature . . . , he will perceive how

5. " 'God the Father of all' signifies for [the middle Platonists] that God is essentially goodness and just therefore essentially creative." Nemeshegyi, op. cit., p. 103.

6. The following analysis is based primarily on *Commentary on John* and *First Principles*. (In the area of our problem we have little to fear from Rufinus' translation methods.) The Greek texts are in the volumes of *Die Griechische Christlichen Schriftsteller der ersten drei Jahrhunderten* or, where this series is still incomplete, in Migne. Where I have used Migne, I cite as "P.G." English translations of the *Commentary on John* (Books I–X only) and *First Principles* are in *The Ante-Nicene Fathers*. I have relied especially on the researches of: Henri Crouzel, *Origène et la "Connaissance Mystique"* and *Théologie de l'Image de Dieu chez Origène;* Walter Völker, *Das Vollkommenheitsideal des Origenes;* Harl, op. cit.; Koch, op. cit; Nemeshegyi, op. cit.

7. *First Principles*, IV, 4, 1.

8. Ibid., I, 1, 5.

there is a darkness about God. For he will find no word worthy of His fullness." [9]

God is beyond the reach of our knowledge and our language because He is ontologically different from all other reality, because He has a different *way* of being what He is than does other-than-divine reality.[10] Origen makes a clear distinction between two modes of being, a distinction stated exactly in terms of knowability. Commenting on "No man has seen God at any time," he explains: "There are two modes of beholding, sensory and intellectual,[11] i.e., there is a beholding of bodily things and a beholding of unbodily things. Nor do we call those realities which present themselves to and are beheld by intellectual intuition 'unseen'[12] merely because they in fact are not seen but because it is their nature to be unseen." [13] The gap between the two realms is specified: God's intelligible and invisible reality is given only to the intellectual vision of one "who is . . . perfected in virtue." [14] This condition is identified with the further condition of liberation from time; in the perpetual not-yet of time there can be no perfection: "Therefore the intellect still bound to becoming, that is, to time, cannot properly see God." But we are, in this life, those who still strive in time's becoming toward what we shall be. "Therefore we cannot see God by a direct confrontation of the intellect." [15] The break between the ontological mode of God and that of the realm in which we are captive is the eschatological boundary between history and the transcendent goal and meaning of history. If we are to know God it will be across this final barrier.

Thus no skeptical analyst could feel more clearly or fully the hopelessness of our attempt to talk about God than did Origen: "Of the chief and most divine of the mysteries concerning God, some a

9. *Commentary on John,* II, 28.
10. *First Principles,* I, 1, 5.
11. αἰσθητικοῦ τε καὶ νοητικοῦ.
12. ἀόρατα.
13. οὐ τῷ μὴ ὁρᾶσθαι ἀλλὰ τῷ μὴ πεφυκέναι βλέπεσθαι.
14. τελειωθεὶς κατ᾿ ἀρετήν.
15. *Fragments to John,* XIII.

written Scripture cannot contain and some even human speech—functioning normally—and human language cannot contain." [16] Moreover, Origen is aware that it is the rules of our language that fail when we use that language of God. Thus, for example, he defines the Son as God's "wisdom in the mode of substance," stipulating by "in the mode of substance" that we are to disregard the usual rule by which "wisdom" is a power or capacity of a person, and yet hastening to add that also "substance" is misleading since ordinarily we call "substances" only entities with a material substratum.[17] Or again, when confronted with Christ: ". . . the narrow human intellect . . . does not know what to let go of, what to hold on to or in general where to turn. For if it thinks of God, it sees a mortal; if it supposes a man, it sees him returning from the dead with the spoils of the realm of death. . . ." [18] The criteria that tell us when to use the word "man" are confounded by the evangelical history. And likewise with "God."

This failure of the normal rules by which we stipulate the use of words and so make them useful—that is, meaningful—is traced by Origen to the ontological difference between God and the realm in which our language usually operates. Thus the Word adequate to God is *one,* while our words are necessarily many.[19] The publicly established meanings of our words are said to be inappropriate to God, in that they all are part of a language whose rules presuppose time as the horizon of reality, whereas God is timeless. "It is not possible to take words in their authorised meanings [20] when used of eternal realities . . . Words used of [the eternal Son] are not to be taken with their co-reference to time,[21] since that which is signified by them when so used is not subject to time." [22] These two specifications of the ontological difference between God and creation are really the same. The plurality of the world is the plurality of

16. *Commentary on John,* XIII, 5.
17. *First Principles,* I, 2, 2.
18. Ibid., II, 6, 2.
19. *Commentary on John,* V, 5.
20. Origen is fully conscious of the public character of meaning. But he sees just this as the problem, when it is God we want to mean.
21. μετὰ τοῦ προσσημαίνειν χρόνον.
22. *Fragments to John,* I.

succession in time; the oneness of God is the oneness of eternity's *nunc simul.*

Yet Origen did speak of God. Indeed, he kept a staff of stenographers busy recording the immense volume of his speech about God. For there *is* a language in which to speak of the unspeakable God, the language of symbols and types, the language of images.

With the word "image" [23] we have the key word of Origen's theory of language and of his ontology and soteriology as well. For Origen's solution of the problem of theological utterance is metaphysical; it is identical with a total ontological analysis, with his grasp of the difference and relation between two great levels of being. His ontological problem was so to describe the levels of being as to preserve the total difference between them, which was the fundamental religious experience of his time, yet maintain their contact, without which atheism or acosmism would be the only alternatives. He did this by describing reality as a descending series of *images*. It is this image ontology that we must first investigate, for his theory, explicit and implicit, of language is posited in it and has "image" and a series of near synonyms—"shadow," "type," "symbol"—as its operative metalinguistic terms.

III.

On the one hand, an image is an expression of that of which it is the image, of its prototype. Yet on the other hand, it is not its prototype. Thus, in the case of what we will see to be the primary prototype-image pair in Origen's system, the Father and the Son are "two entities as to existence, but only one in likeness and harmony and identity of will—so that he who has seen the Son who is 'the reflection of his glory' and the 'stamp of his nature' as seen in Him, since He is the Image of God, God Himself." [24] Operating with this two-sided notion in which difference and sameness are both posited, Origen accomplishes the metaphysical task of at once sepa-

23. εἰκών.
24. *Against Celsus,* VIII, 12. This unity of *will,* etc., is not so nonontological as it might seem. For in Origen there is a near equivalence of "being" with "quality of existence" in the case of persons. Cf. Nemeshegyi, op. cit.

rating and joining the ontological levels by constructing a hierarchy
of image realities from God at the top to physical creation at the
bottom. This can be done since an ectypical image can be in turn a
prototype by the reflection of which yet a new image subsists—and
so on to any desired number of hierarchical levels, to "the image
and the images of the image." [25] Thus *what* hierarchy of being—
how many levels, for example—is established is not fixed by the notion of image in itself, which provides only a conceptual apparatus.
But before explicitly stating the content of Origen's particular image
hierarchy, we must develop the notion itself more precisely.

There are two principle aspects to the concept of image. First,
calling one reality the image of another states its ontological dependence on that other. Again with respect to what we will find to be
Origen's principal image: "Since the Firstborn of all creation is an
image of the unseen God, the Father is His ground of being.[26] In
like fashion Christ is the ground of being of those created after the
image of God." [27] The one entity is nothing but the reflection of the
other. Were it not for the existence of the prototype, the ectype
would not exist. And the characters of the ectype are determined entirely by those of the prototype, being again simply their reflections.

Second, an image reality reveals its prototype. It is a mirror in
which is visible its prototype, which may itself be hidden. "In the
Logos, since He is God and the Image of the unseen God, we see
the Father who begot Him, so that He who looks into the Image of
the unseen God is able to intuit also the prototype of the Image, that
is, the Father." [28] Here the notion of a mirror image joins with that
of the image as the work of art which makes visible the invisible
ideal that was before the eye of the artist.

We must further note that the prototype-ectype relation works
two ways in both of these aspects. When it is used as an ontological
category, both a creative-expressive procession from the transcendent
to this world and a soteriological-cognitive return to God are posited. The prototype originates the ectype; the ectype fulfills its then

25. *Commentary on John,* II, 2.
26. ἀρχή.
27. *Commentary on John,* I, 17.
28. Ibid., XXII, 29.

originated being in reflecting the prototype. The prototype expresses itself in the ectype; therefore the ectype is the means by which the prototype may be known. An image hierarchy is thus a circulation of being and of knowledge from the transcendent to this world and back, which can bridge yet not deny the complete difference of onto-logical mode of the two poles.

It is already obvious that for Origen the notion of "image" and of a hierarchy of images provides merely the framework for expressing a christological doctrine of creation and redemption. *The* image of God is Christ. The creative-expressive procession of images is crea-tion and revelation in Christ. The soteriological-cognitive return to the Prototype is redemption in Christ. Origen's particular hierarchy of images is therefore as follows. The Image of God is Christ, God's Son. Origen describes the birth of the Son variously. It is, of course, the cosmogonic begetting of all myth that is in the background. In the conceptualized version the starting point is an Aristotelian motif: "God does not have knowledge of himself through a me-dium, but by virtue of his self-relatedness,[29] being himself both act of knowing and object known." [30] In the act of knowing Himself, God posits a self-relatedness. In this act there therefore is posited God-as-content-of-His-own-knowledge as an in some way distinct entity: "The Father does not repress His visions of truth but utters them and so posits their model in His Utterance,[31] who is thus called the image of the unseen God." [32] For God's act of self-knowledge is also self-expression.[33] Correlatively, the Son as Image returns into God in that He knows God. He exists as Himself God precisely in his contemplation of God: "The World who is with God . . . is an image. He maintains Himself as 'God' precisely by being 'with God.' . . . He would not remain God, if He did not persist in the unbroken contemplation of the abyss of the Father." [34]

29. οἰκειότητι τῇ πρὸς ἑαυτόν.
30. *Fragments to John*, XIII.
31. τὰ τῆς ἀληθείας θεωρήματα οὐ συνέχων ὁ πατὴρ ἐρεύγεται καὶ ποιεῖ τὸν τύπον αὐτῶν ἐν τῷ λόγῳ.
32. *Commentary on John*, I, 38.
33. Cf. *Commentary on John*, I, 38, above.
34. Ibid., II, 2.

Thus all other beings exist through the Son. For in knowing Himself in the Son, God knows Himself as origin of all things: that is, He thinks the original pattern of all that can be. The origin of all those creatures below the Son in the hierarchy of being is therefore described: ". . . just as a house is built or a ship constructed following the pattern of an architect, the patterns [35] and reasonings [36] in the builder's mind being thus the ground of being of the house and the ship, so the universe has come into being following the reasons of things which God has made clear in advance in his Wisdom [synonym for 'Word']. 'For He made all things in Wisdom.' Having created . . . a sort of living Wisdom God delegated it to give shape and form, indeed I believe, being itself, to beings and matter —following the patterns which Wisdom has in itself." [37] The Word is "the bodiless and living single subsistence of the varied divine beholdings which make up the reasons of all things. . . ." [38] The Word is identified with the Platonic realm of Ideas, in their at once originative and exemplary function—but now as the ideas of a Person.[39]

But the Son is not alone as image of God. There are many "gods formed according to the image of God." These are the "images of the Image," [40] of which He is "the archtypical Image." [41] There is a whole society of rational beings who are on God's side of the great ontological divide between intellectable and visible beings. All are images of the Son-Image: "The reason [42] in each rational being has the same relation to the Reason [43] who was in the beginning . . . as He has to God himself." [44]

Of these images of the Image, one, the human soul of the man

35. τύπους.
36. λόγους.
37. *Commentary on John,* I, 19.
38. ἀσώματον ὑπόστασιν ποικίλων θεωρήματων περιεχόντων τοὺς τῶν ὅλων λόγους ξῶσαν. Ibid., I, 34.
39. Ibid., XIX, 23.
40. Ibid., II, 3.
41. Ibid., II, 2.
42. λόγος.
43. λόγος.
44. Ibid., II, 3.

Jesus of Nazareth, is in a special sense the image of the Son. That is, *Jesus' personal human existence,* the historical act by which He grasps his future and so is who and what He is (for so we may here explain "soul"), is the image of the Image of God. "There is . . . an image of the Son of God. This is, I believe, that human soul which the Son of God assumed, become by its virtue the image of the Image of God." [45] Or again: ". . . that soul of which Jesus said, 'No one takes my soul from me' inhered from the beginning of creation inseparably and indissolubly to [the Son] . . . , in its totality receiving Him fully and standing in His light and splendor. And thus it was made in principle one spirit with Him. . . ." [46] That is to say, between the Logos and Jesus' soul there is a perfect mystical union [47] such that the one is image of the other.

The bridge across the ontological abyss between God and the world is now almost complete. "Soul" had since Plato been the bond between this world and the transcendent; here Jesus' soul performs the function. Yet there is one step to go. For the soul, the personal act of existence at the center of life, is an "intelligible" and not a "sensible" entity; it is itself a transcendent, a mystery. Thus the rule holds also for the soul that ". . . it is impossible for man living in the flesh to know any of the . . . invisible realities . . ." unless he "derives some image and similitude thereof from visible things." [48] We arrive finally at the visible and audible behavior of Jesus, at His life and teachings, His death, at all that Paul and Origen called His "flesh." This is the image of His interior life, of His soul—as this interior life is in turn the image of the Son. In a remarkable passage Origen says, "Our Saviour cast out the merchants bodily from [the temple], *thus making symbols of his inner spiritual deeds.*" [49] The history of Jesus that a historian could record is the image of that other history of his inner self-transcending existence. And these taken together, Jesus' life in both its hidden and its visible reality,

45. *Fragments to Romans,* P.G. 842A.
46. *First Principles,* II, 6, 3. For a plastic and dramatic account of the mirroring, cf. *First Principles,* II, 6, 5–7.
47. Cf. Völker, op. cit., pp. 110 ff.
48. *Commentary on Song of Solomon,* III.
49. *Commentary on Matthew,* XVI, 20.

His "soul . . . with its works and motions," are fully responsive to the "impulse and hidden will" of the Son; they are the Son's "shadow, in which we live. . . ." [50] The life of the Son is the reality, "of which Jesus' deeds are mirrors." [51] The revelation of God is, therefore, the Son as He exists "on earth and not as He is in heaven. For He has become flesh and thus speaks through a shadow, in types and images." [52] Christ, in His divine-human reality, is in His own person the entire hierarchy of images by which the ontological abyss is bridged, by which the invisible God is visible in His creation. Or, seen from below: ". . . just as in the temple there were stairs into the holy of holies, so our stairs are the Only-Begotten. And just as one stair is first from the bottom, then one next higher, and so to the top, so the Saviour is our entire series of stairs. The bottom rung is His humanity. Mounting it, we follow the whole path of stairs, the hierarchy of what He is." ". . . He who sees the Word of God sees God, mounting up from the Word to God." [53]

IV.

Where did Origen get this key concept of image? In one sense this is an idle question, since image or some functional equivalent is a fundamental myth, is therefore probably co-extensive with humanity, and was especially inescapable in the mystic air of Alexandria.[54] But the historical source was Plato as mediated by the second-century Platonic school tradition.

Plato uses 'image' in a variety of nontechnical ways which need not concern us. We are interested in his use of 'image' as the name for a certain kind of being and for the mode of language appropriate to speaking of being of that kind. Plato lays down a primary

---

50. *First Principles,* II, 6, 7.
51. τὰ τε πράγματα ὧν αἰνίγματα ἦσαν αἱ πράξεις αὐτοῦ. *Commentary on John,* I, 7.
52. Ibid., II, 6.
53. Ibid., XIX, 6.
54. In pure mythological form: "First . . . the eternal and unborn, God the demiurge of the whole. Second the cosmos after his image. . . ." *Corpus Hermaticum,* VIII, 2, 5.

ontological distinction between *copied* reality and *copy*-reality. The language used of either mode must be "akin" to that of which it is used.[55] Thus "the language which speaks of copied . . . reality, that reality which is itself an image, is, analogously thereto, imaging language."[56]

In this technical usage, 'image' comes from the language of craftsmanship and artistry. In that language it has its meaning in conjunction with three other words: The 'craftsman'[57] 'imitates'[58] a 'pattern'[59] and so produces an artifact that is an 'image'[60] of this pattern. Thus 'image' and 'imitation'[61] are synonymous.[62]

The great problem to which Plato turned this language was the relation between our life and the perfection from which and to which it goes. Our present existence is real precisely in that it is drawn to its own perfection; yet compared to that perfection it is worthless and unreal. It is this ambiguity of our present existence that Plato struggled to grasp, and for which image proved the increasingly satisfactory myth: an image both is and is not what it imitates.

An image does not have its meaning in itself. Therefore it has the fleeting being of that which comes into being only by virtue of the other reality that is its meaning. An image is not nothing—but is something only in and for its model.[63] An image is, therefore, midway between being and nonbeing: "Then what we call an

55. *Timaeus,* 29B.
56. Ibid., 92C.
57. δημιουργός.
58. μιμεῖσθαι.
59. παράδειγμα.
60. εἰκών.
61. μίμημα.
62. The basic passages for Plato's aesthetic are: *Republic,* VI, X; *Sophist,* 235; *Timaeus,* 28–29, 48–49, 92; *Laws,* II, VII. To the δημιουργός-παράδειγμα-μιμεῖσθαι-εἰκών complex, see especially *Republic,* 595–604, and *Timaeus,* 28–29C. To the image as a product of *imitation,* see *Cratylus,* 430E–431D. For an example of the pervasiveness of the δημιουργός-εἰκών pairing in Plato's use of εἰκών, see *Philebus,* 39B. For a detailed analysis of this whole complex, and to the following as well, see above all: Hans Willms, *EIKWN: Eine begriffsgeschichtliche Untersuchung zum Platonismus,* pp. 1–24.
63. *Timaeus,* 52C.

image, though it is not, yet is? Answer: It does seem that nonbeing
has involved itself with being—which is paradoxical." [64] Such a
halfway mode of being is conceivable, asserts Plato, if we once un-
tangle the Parmenidean logic games with 'is' and 'is not' and see
that there is a plurality of meanings for 'is.' Specifically, there is a
kind of beings that *are* in that they are "imitations of what absolutely is." [65]

Here Plato had a mode of being to assign to present reality.
'Image' expressed perfectly the ambiguity of present reality over
against its ground and goal. At first the negative side of the image
concept was most important to him. The things of this world are
only images.[66] But in *Timaeus* image "celebrates its triumph." [67]
Here the image concept allowed Plato to grasp the specific reality of
this world. All visible reality is seen as the image of eternal perfection, an imperfect yet true expression of that perfection. God is the
eternal Craftsman who fixes His attention on the eternal realities as
a pattern and crafts the cosmos as an image of that pattern.[68] Thus
the cosmos is a great work of art, an imitation, and so an expression,
of the ideal.[69] So also the value of this world can finally be affirmed.
The cosmos is a "sensible god, image of the intelligible god"; it is
"most great and noble and beautiful and perfected." [70]

In Plato, 'image,' as the designation of a kind of being, was re-
served for empirical reality as the ectype of spiritual reality. But later
platonizing thought, under Aristotelian and Posidonian [71] influence, broke down the strict two-level ontology of Plato. Thereby the
way was opened for a level of reality ectypical to the level above also
to be archtypical to a level below. Such a mediating function is,
after all, already present in the platonic notion; empirical reality is

64. Οὐκ ὂν ἄρα ὄντως ἐστίν ὄντως ἦν λέγομεν εἰκόνα; Κινδυνεύει τοιαύτην
τινὰ πεπλενθαι συμπλοκὴν τὸ μὴ ὂν τῷ ὄντι, καὶ μάλα ἄτοπον. *Sophist*,
240B–C.
65. Ibid., 264D.
66. *Republic*, 509–11; *Phaedrus*, 250B.
67. Willms, op. cit., p. 22.
68. *Timaeus*, 28A–29C.
69. Ibid., 48E–49A.
70. Ibid., 92C.
71. So cautious a use of Jaeger's disputed thesis should be allowable. Werner
Jaeger, *Nemesios von Emesa*.

an image just because it is midway between being and nonbeing.

Hellenistic Platonism imagined many levels of spiritual reality, so that also spiritual realities could be seen as images; thus also 'image' acquired the sense of archetype as well as ectype. This move involved several developments: Under the influence of increasing religious concern it occurs that when Plato's Ideas are reintroduced into philosophy they are identified as the thoughts of God. These in turn come to be called, following the artisan metaphysic, the archtypical images that all lower reality is created to imitate.[72] From here it is a short step to calling the divine mind itself 'image,' especially in a myth-laden atmosphere.[73]

Thus the way is prepared for platonizing thinkers of many sorts to seize on this notion of an intrinsically mediating kind of being and to create a whole image ontology to serve later antiquity's overwhelming desire for bridges between God and us. 'Image' came to be the name for the whole principle of mediation between transcendent and given reality and for the intermediary metaphysical realities through which that mediation was to take place.[74] This is the point where Origen adopted the concept.

V.

We come finally to theological language. The starting point is that, for Origen, speaking about God is identical with exegeting the Bible. Origen was a radically biblicist theologian. For him, the

72. Albinos, *Epitome,* 8, 2 (cited from C. J. de Vogel, *Greek Philosophy: A Collection of Texts*): "With respect to God, an *idea* is his thought; with respect to us, a primary intelligible . . . ; with respect to the sensible cosmos, a pattern. . . ."

73. For this whole development in great detail, see Willms, op. cit., pp. 25 ff. Cf. also Jaeger and Crouzel, *Théologie de l'image de Dieu chez Origène,* pp. 25 ff.

74. Philo, *De specialibus legibus,* I, 81 (cited from de Vogel). "The Logos is an image of God [εἰκὼν θεοῦ], through whom the entire cosmos has been formed [ἐδημιουργεῖτο]." In *De opificiis mundi,* 6, 25, the world is in turn "an image of the image [εἰκὼν εἰκόνος]." To Philo's extensive use of the motif, see Willms, op. cit., pp. 75 ff. The archtypical Man of the *Corpus Hermeticum* is "very beautiful, having the image of the Father. . . ." I, 1, 12 (cited from de Vogel). So also "soul" is for Plotinus "a certain image of *Nous.*" *Enneads,* V, 1, 3. And "Nous" is the "primary image" of the One. V, 1, 6 (cited from de Vogel).

Bible is the sole source of the knowledge of God. "Those who believe . . . derive the knowledge that moves to a good and holy life
from no other source than from the words of Christ. Now the words
of Christ are not only those which He spoke in the days of His
flesh; before then the word of the divine Christ was in Moses and
the prophets." [75] This is so because Christ is the subject of the
whole Scripture,[76] and because it is only from Scripture that we can
learn of Him.[77]

If we then remember that it is the "deeds," the "works and motions"—that is, what we would call the history—of Christ, which is
the image by which we know God, we can go one more step: Theological language is narration of this history. The life of Jesus
Christ, in both its inwardness and outwardness and including His
pre-Incarnation history in Israel, is the image by which God is present to us so that we may speak of Him. "He is the image of the
unutterable and unnameable and unspeakable reality of the Father." [78] In that we recount this history we are speaking of God.[79]

Indeed, it does not appear that Origen is much concerned to distinguish between the events themselves (as we would put it) of
the history of Israel and Christ, and the witness to those events. He
is not much concerned about what happened back there in abstraction from its verbal and written presence now. Very little moderniz-
ing is needed to say that the "historical" with which he is concerned
is the event-as-witnessed in the text. It is the witnessed history that is
the image of God. Thus he can argue that some of the evangelical
stories could not in fact have taken place as recorded—and that they
do quite as well, or better, as stories that image God than if they
were literal records.[80] He constantly refers indiscriminately to
events and to records of events.[81] And as we will see, "historical

75. *First Principles,* preface, 1. Cf. R. P. C. Hanson, *Origen's Doctrine of
Tradition,* chapters iii, v, viii, ix, xi, esp. pp. 83 ff.
76. E.g. *Commentary on John,* VI, 2.
77. *First Principles,* I, 3, 1.
78. Ibid., IV, 4, 1.
79. "Prayerful penetration into the allegorical depths of the Bible is the
same thing as penetration into the depths of knowledge." Völker, op. cit., 97 f.
80. E.g., *Commentary on John,* XIII, 39 f.

events" [82] and the "letter of Scripture" [83] are interchangeable on the one hand, as are the "sense of history" [84] and the "meaning" [85] of "mere words" [86] on the other hand. It is, after all, precisely the history of the Word that we are dealing with, the history of His speaking.

As follows from what has already been said in this section, theological speaking is itself involved in the dialectic of prototype and ectype. The image-prototype relation between Christ's history and God as the meaning of this history is paralleled by an image-prototype relation between the words in which we tell of Christ's deeds, and the Word in the words, which they mean. "He who speaks about the Truth, even if he says many things . . . speaks only *one* Word. . . ." [87] The relation of Christ to God and of our words to the Word are simply two sides of the same reality.

There is, says Origen, a triple sense and use of Scripture. "One person is edified in simple fashion by the flesh of Scripture, for so we name the immediate text and teaching. Another rises above this and is edified by the . . . soul of Scripture. And another, the perfected one . . . , is edified by the 'spiritual law' which is a 'shadow of things to come'." [88] We may assimilate the second of these senses to the other two: This "soul" of Scripture is sometimes a distinct moral sense, sometimes only the personal application to us of the spiritual sense. When the moral sense is the "soul," the personal sense is included in the spiritual; when the personal sense is the "soul," the moral sense is included in the literal. Origen has, therefore, basically a twofold sense and meaning of Scripture; and from now on we will operate with it. [89]

81. E.g., the collocation "revealed through the prophetic writings and through the appearance of the Lord." *Commentary on John*, VIII, 17.

82. τὰ ἱστορικά.

83. γράμμα.

84. ὁ νοῦς τῶν ἱστορικῶν. *Commentary on John*, X, 5.

85. λόγος.

86. λέξις.

87. ὁ δὲ λέγων τὰ τῆς ἀληθείας, κἂν εἴπῃ τὰ πάντα . . . ἕνα ἀεὶ λέγει λόγον. . . . *Commentary on John*, V, 5.

88. *First Principles*, IV, 2, 4.

89. For documentation, cf. Henri de Lubac, *Histoire et Esprit*, pp. 141–48.

The *body* of Scripture is the account of the history and religion of Israel; its center is the history and teachings of Jesus Christ. This is what is said and written. But the *spirit* of what is said, itself unsayable, is nevertheless what is meant—and somehow uttered, hidden under the mere words. We must sharply distinguish [90] between the "mere words" [91] and what they point to.[92] In the uttered presence, the word reality, of the physical events of the evangelical history, the unspeakable prototypical meaning of those events—that is, God's reality for us—is posited. This is the "eternal gospel," [93] the final self-communicative presence of God which reveals "face to face" the "glory of God and the reasons and truth of things," [94] the "unutterable words which only God and his Only-Begotten can . . . speak. . . ." [95] It is this eternal gospel which is the true content, the imaged prototype, of our discourse concerning Christ, which is "the mysteries hidden under [Jesus'] words and the realities of which His deeds were mirrors." [96] The temporal witnessed-to events are the images of the last Word-who-is-God-for-us.

The observable historical events [97] of Scripture are images of spiritual realities open only to pure intellectual intuition.[98] The truth that the Evangelists wished to communicate is therefore to be found not in their narrative of observable events [99] but in the hidden object of their inward vision.[100] "The meaning of the historical events [101] has been abstracted from them by the [Evangelists] who wish to teach us, by telling of external characters, what their intellect has beheld. The Evangelists have used many narratives and sayings to express the marvelous and ungraspable divin-

90. *Commentary on John*, I, 8.
91. λέξις.
92. τὰ δαλούμενα.
93. Ibid., I, 7.
94. *First Principles*, II, 6, 7.
95. ἀρρητῶν ῥημάτων.
96. *Commentary on John*, I, 7.
97. τὰ ἱστορικὰ καὶ τὰ σωματικά.
98. τὰ πνευματικὰ καὶ τὰ νοητά. *Commentary on John*, X, 18.
99. ἐν τοῖς σωματικοῖς χαρακτήρσιν.
100. *Commentary on John*, X, 3.
101. ὁ νοῦς τῶν ἱστορικῶν.

ity [102] of Jesus. They have woven into the Scripture with words, as
if it were a visible thing, that which they have seen in a purely inward way. Thus the narrative is there only for the sake of their mystical vision." [103] Or, to take an example from the Old Testament,
Joshua's illumination by the Spirit meant that he could see "how
his own accomplishments were shadows of certain true realities." [104]

The whole prototype-image dialectic of the two natures of Christ,
of history and its divine fulfillment, of narrating words and their
transcendent meaning—and the subtle interplay of all these pairs—
comes to clear if drastic expression in the famous exposition of the
healing with spittle: "Was not the Lord's spittle a symbol of the
Word . . . ? But such a Word does not come to us bare of matter
and observable images. Therefore Jesus spat on the earth and made
mud. Cannot we interpret this so, that the whole Scripture . . .
consists, with respect to divine knowledge, of the spittle of Christ,
with respect to its telling in histories and human deeds, of the dust
of earth. . . . With this it is necessary to anoint the eyes of the
blind. But then they must go to Siloam. The way to Siloam is his
humanity, Siloam his divinity . . ." [105] Or again, the histories of
Scripture are the "flesh of the Lamb." [106]

The task of understanding Scripture is, therefore, that of penetrating through the written text and the audible word [107] to the Word
hidden in the "shuttered storehouse of the common words." [108] We
must distinguish between a "visible gospel"—that is, the Evangelists'
narratives of observable events and our recounting, investigation,
and proclaiming of those events—and the "intelligible and spiritual
gospel." The task of scriptural understanding is that of translating
the one into the other.[109] "Our whole struggle is to reach into the

102. "δύναμις." Cf. P. G. i, p. 390.
103. Commentary on John, X, 5.
104. Ibid., IV, 4.
105. Fragments to John, LXIII.
106. Commentary on John, X, 18.
107. γράμμα καὶ αἰσθητὸς διὰ φωνῆς λόγος.
108. Commentary on John, I, 4.
109. τὸ αἰσθητὸν εὐαγγέλιον μεταλαβεῖν εἰς πνευματικόν.

depths of the meaning of the Gospel and seek out its truth, bare of all types." [110]

VI.

That is to say, the trick in theological speaking is the Platonic trick of so speaking of and in this world that our speech is opened toward transcendence, that our words open the meaning that this world has in its imaging reference to what lies beyond it. In Plato this is done by the "dialectic," by the exchange of challenge and response in which two seekers mutually refine their language toward the unattainable but infinitely approachable goal and limit of "what we really mean." "What is justice?" "It is . . ." "But doesn't that commit you to saying that . . . ?" "Well, let me then say that justice is . . ." And so on, moving the word 'justice' ever closer to what both all earthly acts of justice and the word that names them "really mean."

In Origen the instrument by which our words open this world toward its final meaning and are themselves opened toward their final meaning is not dialectic, but allegorical exegesis of Scripture.[111] The opening to transcendence is affected by interpreting biblical history as the reflection of the final and transcendent goal of that history.

Here is the fundamentally Christian, un-Platonic, drive of Origen's understanding of theological utterance. Scripture is a shadow of eternal verities which are also "things to come," the *eschaton*. The Platonic superworld is identified with the biblical consummation,[112] and *this* is the mystery hidden in our symbolic language:

110. *Commentary on John,* I, 8.

111. Above all, *First Principles,* IV entire. "In accord with the platonic vision of the world, material things are symbolic, derived realities. . . . They serve . . . as the point of departure from which knowledge mounts to intelligible things. The means of this ascension was the dialectic for Plato. For Origen it has become the spiritual exegesis of the Bible." Crouzel, *Origène et la "Connaissance Mystique,"* p. 235.

112. The Fathers are customarily faulted for interpreting the Biblical eschatology in terms of the Platonic two-reality vision. But in their historical situation the interpretation was, of course, really just the other way around.

"The interpretation is spiritual when we are able to show of what heavenly realities the Jewish worship was an example and of what good things to come the law is a shadow." [113] The "spiritual realities open only to pure intellectual intuition," of which the observable historical events are images, are none other than the events of the last Exodus.[114] If it is the imperfection of empirical experience which the Platonic dialectic sought to overcome, it is the imperfection of historical experience which Origen's allegorizing sought to overcome. The justification for the method is found in the historical discrepancies in the biblical records, records taken seriously as historical records precisely in the type of analysis that can lead to discovering such.[115]

"If then the earthly law is a 'shadow' and our life on earth is a 'shadow' of Christ, is not the true reality which casts all these shadows [116] that revelation which will . . . [reveal] the glory of God and the reasons and truth of things 'face to face' and no longer 'through a glass darkly'?" [117] The "flesh" of the Lamb, the histories of Scripture, is only for the "night," for this life.[118] The true disciples know that their hope of grasping the Truth cannot be reached in this life. But they believe that it will be fulfilled when they have acquired the new mode of being.[119] Then they will have transcended the immediate meaning of the scriptural texts and our speech based on them, and will cognize God genuinely and no longer in types and shadows.[120] Then they will know God as He knows Himself, see Him with the "eyes of the Logos, with which those also see who participate in Him." [121] The apocalyptic host follow their leader, the Word, precisely in the purity of their knowledge. "All things are open before their intellectual intuition. . . .

113. *First Principles,* IV 2, 6.
114. *Commentary on John,* X, 4.
115. E.g., ibid., X, 1–6.
116. *Harum omnium veritas umbrarum.*
117. *First Principles,* II, 6, 7.
118. *Commentary on John,* X, 18.
119. Ibid., XIII, 40.
120. Ibid., XIII, 24.
121. Ibid., II, 7.

Obscurity and puzzlement are gone, and all . . . penetrate more and more into the mysteries of God's Wisdom [in Origen, = 'Word']."[122]

We said that theological speech is "symbolic." We may now add "eschatological." It is the eschatological vision of God that is the imaged content of our knowledge of the historical, fleshly gospel. It is the eschatological speaking in "unutterable" words (this, then, simply an alternative parable for the mystic vision) that is hiddenly present in our fleshly talk of the fleshly Christ. Our present verbalizing about the historical Christ is the anticipatory image of what we will then see. "Our stumbling preaching about Christ—this preaching of Christ born and crucified—is an authentic form of the Word. Beyond it is the second coming of Christ. . . ."[123]

Theological utterance is eschatological in the sense that its imageable but unutterable final meaning is the eschaton. But it is not only symbolically *about* the consummation of existence. It is eschatological also in a second sense, that when that effort of cognition which is our talk about God is successful, that achievement *is* the fulfillment of existence, is the consummation. Now we see the Father *in* the Son.[124] But when this seeing reaches its goal, then we see, as it were, *through* the Son. Then we see as He sees.[125] The one who reaches this is "like the Son an eyewitness of the . . . Father's reality; He no longer intuits Him from the Image. . . . And this, I believe, is our last goal."[126] This vision is the end of the history of salvation.[127]

Nor is this transformation wholly a matter for the next world. Already in this life the true children of God are those who strive toward the perfect knowledge of God, who "not only believe in the common way, but, more than ordinarily clear-sighted, already are coming to understand more and more of the reality of Godhead."[128]

122. *Commentary on John,* II, 8.
123. *Commentary on Matthew,* 32.
124. ἐν υἱῷ.
125. ὡς ὁ υἱός.
126. τοῦτο εἶναι τὸ τέλος. *Commentary on John,* XX, 7.
127. *Commentary on John,* I, 16.
128. Ibid., XX, 33.

For them the end of this world is already a present reality,[129] and they therefore "adore the Father in spirit and truth not only in the time to come but in the present time. Yet those who now adore in Spirit . . . adore in the foretaste [130] of the Spirit only. . . ." [131]

Thus, theological speaking (as the verbalizing corresponding to seeing God, in image or directly) is eschatological in the sense that doing it is transforming existence toward the final consummation. The goal is that we "become sons of God . . .[132] transformed by the act of knowing the Father." [133] "The ground of our existence [134] subsists in our being created after the image of our Creator." We, like all beings other than God, are real only as such images. If, then, we actualize this ground, "we will live as likenesses of God." [135]

The language game of scriptural exegesis—that is, of God-utterance—is not, therefore, purely descriptive. When we play it, we are not merely describing, at several removes of images, the final goal of our life; *we are, by playing this language game, moving through those images toward that goal.* The knowledge of God is knowledge-in-action, or it is not knowledge of God at all. "Even if one can recite the father's doctrine of God, having learned that He only is to be worshiped, but does not *live rightly,* [the Scripture] says that he has no knowledge of God." [136] The allegorical sense of Scripture is always double: Scripture points symbolically to the end of all things and in so doing to the end, and so to the direction and movement, of my life.[137] Indeed, whatever he may say in theory, Origen's actual allegorical exegesis constantly is accomplished by finding not so much a reference to last things as to concrete applications to our present life. The mystical meaning of Jesus' life is found in His

---

129. Ibid., X, 10.
130. ἐν ἀραβῶνι.
131. *Commentary on John,* XIII, 18.
132. Reading υἱείς following Gögler's emendation (Origenes, *Das Evangelium nach Johannes*), p. 113.
133. ἐν τῇ γνώσει τοῦ πατρὸς μορφωθέντες. *Commentary on John,* I, 16.
134. προηγουμένη ὑπόστασις.
135. *Commentary on John,* XX, 22.
136. Ibid., XIX, 3.
137. Cf. de Lubac, op. cit., pp. 143 ff.

work as risen Lord here and now among us.[138] It is after all a mystical cognition—that is, a transforming cognition—that we perform when we exegete Scripture spiritually.[139]

The words that the true followers of the Word have are thus foretastes and surrogates of the "unutterable" words of II Corinthians 12:4, of the thunder words which could not be written of Revelation 10:4. Only in such words can the mysteries of God be adequately expressed.[140] "I use these predicates not as if they could be used of God in their common senses, but because I lack the unutterable words with which only He, and his Only-Begotten with Him, are able without metaphor to speak and think about Him." Yet our words are not mere surrogates. In a remarkable passage which must, for the sake of flavor, be quoted in full, Origen identifies the white horses of the apocalyptic host (Revelation 19:14) as symbols of that host's knowledge of God, and then says: "Consider the white horses of those who follow the Word, how they are clothed in pure white linen.[141] Linen grows on earth. Are not, therefore, the linen garments types of the earthly language once worn by the voices that now speak more purely of ultimate reality?" [142] Our words are not only surrogates for the words that God and His blessed speak; they are the present clothing of those words—and are not wholly forgotten even when the consummation is come.

The life of the children is therefore a history of the refinement and enlargement of their language, with the eschatological speaking of God and the blessed as goal and limit. "There are many utterances of God, not only those which have been written but also the unutterable which man is not permitted to speak. . . . He who has

138. E.g., the commentary on the cleansing of the temple in the *Commentary on John*, X, 23–24. Cf. de Lubac, op. cit., pp. 260 ff.

139. Cf. Völker, op. cit., pp. 62–144.

140. *Commentary on John*, XII, 5–7.

141. Origen has taken ἐνδεδυμένοι to modify τοῖς ὕπποις. The text of Revelation is syntactically ambiguous; ἐνδεδυμένοι could modify either τοις ὕπποις or τὰ στρατεύματα. But the clear sense of the passage demands τὰ στρατεύματα as the modified substantive. So Gögler (p. 148) has corrected Origen's text, apparently unconsciously, to make it match the original intent of Revelation, thereby missing the equally clear sense of Origen's text.

142. *Commentary on John*, II, 8.

heard any word of God is thereby 'of God.' The more utterances of God he hears, the more fully does he become 'of God.' So that . . . if anyone hears all God's words . . . , he will be perfectly and irrevocably a child of God. . . . We advance, therefore in being 'of God' and in hearing the utterances of God—understanding ever more of them until we have grasped all God's words, or at least as many as those worthy of the Spirit of adoption are allowed to grasp, whether now or hereafter." [143]

Thus theological speech is eschatological also in a third sense. Every word of our witness to Christ is the clothing of an eschatological word and therefore carries within itself an eschatological dynamism. It is a seed, growing to burst the silence of the ages in the praise of the last day.[144] When we live in such words, we are on the way to that day. Indeed, these words are so fulfilled with the last victory that for the earthly Jesus to be crucified, it was necessary for Him to fall silent.[145] And when we live in and through His words, we are immortal.[146]

VII.

There is one problem that must be faced here. Does Origen believe that translation from the "physical gospel" to the "spiritual gospel" results in a language no longer symbolic, no longer a language of images? Does he, that is, see the language in which Scripture is exegeted allegorically as standing in a fundamentally different relation to its transcendent object from the spiritually uninterpreted text itself? Can we achieve an utterance that just *is* the spiritual utterance? Is there an earthly language to which what we have been saying does not apply? Sometimes it certainly seems so.[147] Very often Origen identifies the "spirit" of Scripture, the final sense imaged in the text, with the results of allegorical exegesis.

This conclusion is also suggested by Origen's contention that there

143. Ibid., XX, 34.
144. Ibid., XIII, 46.
145. Ibid., XIX, 10.
146. Ibid., XX, 34.
147. Cf. above pp. 41 f.

are in this life those who already are able to transcend the limitation
of physical images. He distinguishes sharply between mere faith and
knowledge, between the believer and the gnostic.[148] The gnostic is
precisely the one who lives "no longer in the letter that kills . . .
but in truth . . . without types and shadows." [149] Yet this cannot
be Origen's main opinion—however inconsistent he may sometimes
be.

Origen is quite clear, however drastically he sometimes expressed
himself, that the actual accomplishment of the gnostic striving, the
direct and imageless vision of God, is possible only in the final consummation. The rule is absolute that all our knowledge of God on
this side of the line, however spiritualized, is "through a glass
darkly." Other than so, "no one has seen the Father, neither apostle
nor prophet—and will not till they are one as the Son and the Father are one." [150] The mystic vision of the gnostic is but the "foretaste" of the new life, a foretaste present only in and through the
conditions of the old—that is, "in a glass, darkly." [151]

In any case, this final vision is essentially a wordless event. It is the
gift of "unspoken and mystical beholdings." [152] Whatever the "unutterable utterances" [153] of the last communication are, they can
hardly be a spoken language. The one who goes beyond talking in
types and symbols does not invent a new vocabulary and logic; he
transcends words altogether: ". . . it is better to be an eyewitness of
the Word and hear Him as He teaches without sense-organs, bringing the Ideas of Truth as images before the reason . . . without the
use of teachers, than to hear the word about Him through others'
service. . . ." [154] Insofar therefore as this vision is the hidden content of the knowledge of the gnostic, insofar as he already possesses
its "foretaste," he experiences a wordless reality. As soon as he seeks

148. *Fragments to John*, SCIII; *Commentary on John*, XX, 30. Cf. Crouzel,
Origène et la "Connaissance Mystique," pp. 474 ff.; Hanson, op. cit., pp.
73 ff.: Völker, op. cit., pp. 76 ff.
149. *Commentary on John*, XII, 24.
150. Ibid., I, 16.
151. Ibid., XIII, 18.
152. ἀπόρρατα καὶ μυστικὰ θεωρήματα. *Commentary on John*, I, 30.
153. ἀρρήτες ῥήματα.
154. *Commentary on John*, XIII, 42.

words for this experience, he finds exactly *words*: that is, the language of the flesh of Christ. A Christian knowing that in this life transcended the flesh of Christ would be purely inward.[155] But precisely this is not allowed in this life. For the sake of edification we must speak—and that means preaching the "bodily gospel," preaching the historical crucifixion.[156] Where public language (and what private language would be is hard to imagine) is needed, there is the realm of history and its merely symbolic reality.

". . . There are many utterances of God . . . , also the unutterable which man [that is, living man] is not permitted to speak. . . . if anyone hears all God's words . . . , he will be perfectly . . . a child of God. . . ."[157] We repeat this fundamental passage as the key to this whole problem. Our life in words is a history. The final pole of this history is the "unutterable utterances." But the history itself is nevertheless a history of utterances, all the way to that final pole—for that pole is eschatological. The progress of the gnostic is not, therefore, the invention of a nonsymbolic utterance, not yet, except inwardly, the abandonment of language. It is a deepening meaningfulness of words, a deepening identical with their increasing transparency toward that which is not words, the full attainment of which is eschatological.[158]

Is it, then, that the fleshly knowledge of the simple believer is no true knowledge at all, symbolic or otherwise? Neither can this be so, for we have the explicit affirmation of Origen that the grasp of the simple believer is limited to the "body" of Scripture, *and* that he is benefited thereby [159]—indeed that this is saving knowledge: "And the one who cannot eat all things, who cannot attain general understanding, nevertheless is saved by this simple confession of faith."[160]

We must, from both sides, remain by this: In the historical testimony the eschatological truth is imaged, is mirrored. The technique

155. ἐν κρυπτῷ χριστιανισμός μόνον.
156. *Commentary on John*, I, 7.
157. Ibid., XX, 34.
158. To the progression in mystical experience, c.f., Völker, op. cit., pp. 62–90; Crouzel, *Origène et la "Connaissance Mystique,"* pp. 443–95.
159. *First Principles*, IV, 2, 5, 6.
160. *Commentary on Romans*, IX, 38.

of theological utterance—that is, allegorical interpretation—neither transcends this situation nor creates it on the basis of some prior presymbolic language situation. It *polishes the mirror*. It is the way in which all theological utterance works (unconsciously in the simple believer?), for theological utterance works precisely in that each actual utterance annuls itself in favor of one closer to the eschaton, closer to wordless, face-to-face experience.

VIII.

A theological sentence works, according to Origen, by being in motion, in motion along the path from bare uninterpreted events to the transcendent meaning and fulfillment of those events. An acceptable utterance about or to God is one by uttering which we move toward direct confrontation with Him; an unacceptable utterance is one that stands still or moves backward. Here is Origen's rule of theological utterance.

But what do we mean when we say that a sentence is "in motion"? We mean that it has been derived as the successor to a previous, now no longer needed, form of words, and that it contains within itself reference to its own successor by which it will in turn be annulled. The fundamental supposition is a radical distinction between what a form of words says and what it means. (This is not the distinction between intension and extention or even the realist distinction between meanings and things. Both terms of these distinctions appear on each side of the one we are concerned with.) What we can say of God is never what we mean, but only its image. Thus we can speak of Him only by a never-ended succession of self-annulling utterances, each of which refers to God precisely by canceling itself—not in favor of God, for this, too, would make God its direct object—but in favor of another utterance, which in turn cancels itself, and so on in an infinite series, of which adequate speech about God is the limit.

The usage rules of such a language will be given by stipulating the path of this movement, by stipulating, for any utterance of a given sort, what it must succeed and what sort its successor must be.

The sentences that stand at the beginning of the path make up the literal report of the biblical history. The verification rules for these are the normal rules of textual and historical scholarship. Origen was a pioneer in this field. The direction to move from this beginning is fixed by the rules of allegorical exegesis, which are thus, in fact, the usage rules of theological language. And these in turn are set by the *plot* of biblical history, by the ordered movement of revelatory history toward its goal.

The next question therefore must be: What is that plot? What is the order of succession of images? What is the order of succession of theological utterances?

The order of ascension is that of the complex reality of Christ's person. We mount from His outer to His inner humanity, and then to His divinity, and then through the (for us) multiple facets of His divinity: ". . . our stairs are the Only-Begotten." [161] If Origen had been merely a platonizing gnostic, this vertical order would have been all. But for him, the simultaneous hierarchical order of images in Christ is also the temporal order of the evangelical history; and it is this latter order that actually provides the succession rules that we have seen to be the essential rules of theological language.

On the one hand, all the periods of biblical history are directly related to their transcendent fulfillment. The spiritual meaning is equally imaged in all of the events witnessed to. "The perfect of former generations know no less than the apostles of what Christ has revealed to the apostles. For the same One who taught the apostles revealed also to them the unutterable mysteries of deity. . . ." [162] In the passage already cited from *De Principiis* [163] the Old Testament law, our created existence, *and* the life of faith are all taken together as a "shadow" of the consummation. In principle: ". . . historical events are not types of other historical events . . . but of intelligible realities." [164]

161. *Commentary on John*, XIX, 6.
162. Ibid., IV, 4.
163. II, 6, 7.
164. *Commentary on John*, X, 18.

Yet Origen can also speak of the earthly coming of Christ as itself the reality imaged by the Old Testament. "Jesus is the husbandman who brings from his storehouse 'things new,' that is, the evangelical teaching, and 'things old,' that is, the . . . meaning of . . . the words of the Law and the Prophets, *of which the prototypes* [my italics] are to be found in the gospel." [165] It is also a principle that the deeds of Old Testament worthies are to be "figuratively referred to Christ, whether to his human or divine nature. . . .": [166] thus Solomon is a type of the Son, and Hiram, who provided tools and skills to Solomon, of the human nature assumed by the Son.[167] Origen can put it quite flatly: "The law transmitted the sacramental mysteries in images and shadow pictures, leading . . . to the teaching of Christ. . . . but when the Saviour came . . . , He brought the teaching to its goal and revealed the Truth in the images . . . , being Himself that Truth. . . ." [168]

This contradiction can be resolved if we remember that, despite all his platonizing, Origen is dealing with the steps in a history toward its goal. When it is the relation between revelatory history prior to the Incarnation and the Incarnation which is in view, then we must say that the Incarnation is the fulfillment of what went before. But when Christ's temporal appearance is in turn referred to the "eternal gospel," then it too is seen as image and shadow. Each step in the history is fulfilled in the next. Yet only by virtue of the final goal of that history does it make sense to speak of "steps" and "fulfillment" at all. Moreover, the goal of a history is not in the same series with the events of that history, and so in a sense is immediate to all. Thus note the very nice dialectic in this allegorical expansion of John 4:22. "The 'we,' literally, is the Jews. Allegorically, it is 'I, the Word, and those transformed to my image, who are saved by the Jewish words.' For the mystery which is now revealed has been revealed by the prophetic writings and the appearance of our Lord Jesus Christ." [169] On the one hand, the step from

165. *Commentary on Matthew,* II 15.
166. *First Principles,* I 3, 1.
167. *Commentary on John,* X, 41.
168. *Fragments to John,* IX, 19.
169. *Commentary on John,* XIII, 17.

the Jews to Christ is the step from letter to meaning, from image to prototype. Yet when we think of the revealed mystery itself, the Jewish Scripture and the coming of Christ are together the revelatory medium.

The Gospel mysteries are present already in the Old Testament. But they are veiled. Since the person of the Son *is* the content of the Gospel, the life of that man who is fully one with the Son is an "embodiment," a direct enactment, of the Gospel. Thus this life, enacted as one of the events in the history recorded in Scripture, reveals the true Gospel content of them all. It removes the veil. It is the key, the principle of understanding for all the rest. Moreover, it is the key because its presence as the last event of that history is the "cause and reason " [170] for that history having any transcendent gospel meaning.[171] The Son is known in the Old Testament but is not yet actual in His known form." [172] The fields of Scripture are "white unto harvest when the Word . . . is present, who makes clear and illumines all the fields of Scripture, full precisely of his presence." [173]

Origen thus sets up a three-step history of image and fulfillment: "We must understand that just as Law is a shadow of 'good things to come' when it is expounded truly, so also the gospel teaches a shadow of the true mysteries of Christ." [174] Those three steps give the plot of the path along which theological utterance must move. A theological utterance is historical narration at one of the first two of these steps. It is a correct utterance when it cancels itself in the direction of the next step.

IX.

Finally, within a language functioning in this way, what of the names and predicates in a theological saying? Such as 'loves' in "God loves me?" According to Origen, all our words denote things

170. ποιητικόν.
171. *Commentary on John,* I, 6.
172. Ibid., IV, 4.
173. Ibid., XIII, 42.
174. Ibid., I, 7.

of this world and as a consequence do not strictly apply to God at all. Replying to Celsus' assertion that "God is unnameable," Origen says, "The assertion . . . may be taken in two ways. If it means that none of our words and signs can represent the peculiar nature of God, it is correct. . . ." [175] We use our words of God only because we lack the right ones, the unutterable words which God and His Son speak in private between them. [176]

Yet, although "all things having to do with deity are unnameable," they are somehow "shown to us men through human speakings. . . ." [177] Our theologumena do give a partial knowledge of him. [178] As a consequence, Origen can continue in his reply to Celsus: "But if you take 'nameable' only in the sense that it is possible . . . to represent something about Him, so as to lead the hearer to such a knowledge of God as is suited to man's nature, then He may be called 'nameable.'" [179] Note the recurrence of the motif of "leading." Knowledge of God is a goal to which our words only lead. Yet they can do this only because they do themselves represent something of God. How?

Origen seems to distinguish between the way in which a predicate works within its proper language and its ability, all that apart, to point to something. [180] "Words used of [the eternal Son] are not to be taken with their co-reference to time." [181] There is something, the ultimately bespoken reality, which is present on both sides of the ontological divide, so that our words can function across the divide.

The Word of God is "not plural. He is not words. He is one. . . . All other words . . . even if they are words about Truth . . . are particular words. Uniqueness and harmony and oneness are missing. Because of separation and conflict oneness is lost from them. . . ." [182] Here the adequate Word and our words are sepa-

175. *Against Celsus*, VI, 65.
176. *Commentary on John*, XXXII, 28.
177. *Fragments to John*, XIV.
178. Ibid., XIII.
179. *Against Celsus*, VI, 65.
180. If anyone wishes to object that this is an untenable distinction, I agree. Cf. below pp. 91 f. But right now we are only expounding.
181. *Fragments to John*, I.
182. *Commentary on John*, V, 5.

rated by the ontological divide, on each side of which wholly different "languages" (on that side, the language of 'unutterable utterances,' the language of the Word) are appropriate. Yet somehow
the difference is bridged so that the ultimate object of speech is
named also by our language: "He who speaks about the Truth, even
if he says many things . . . , speaks only one Word. . . ." [183] Again,
how?

There is a fascinating passage in the Commentary on Matthew
which points the way here. "We can discover why it was appropriate for the Saviour to call . . . Himself 'Son of Man.' He showed
thereby that just as God when He deals in history with man [184] is
called parabolically 'man'—and indeed somehow becomes one [185]—
so also the Saviour, being already the Son of God, becomes according to the order of God's work in history [186] 'Son of man.' He thus
imitates, when He deals in history with men, the God who is
parabolically called, and somehow is, 'man.' " [187] Let me paraphrase
this: "When God deals in history with men, he makes himself the
subject of anthropomorphic predicates. These predicates are not
mere metaphors: God really has—somehow—become what these
words say He is. So also with the Son: If God is thus 'man,' his Son
is 'Son of Man.' " It is the act of God's grace by which He under-
takes a history with man which—somehow—bridges the ontological divide so that our words, despite their belonging to a wholly inappropriate language game, have an intrinsic referent in God.

Another set of passages, in the Commentary on John, deals explicitly with the problem of predicates and the difference of ontological
mode between God and creatures. "God is altogether and in every
sense one. But our Saviour, when God set Him to be the atonement
and ruler of all creation, became many for the sake of the
many. . . ." [188] " . . . Now with each of . . . [these many] names
[we must] draw out from the name the intellectible reality present

183. Ibid.
184. ἀνθρώπους οἰκονομῶν.
185. τάχα δέ πως καὶ γίνεται.
186. κατ' οἰκονομίαν.
187. Commentary on Matthew, XVII, 20.
188. Commentary on John, I, 20.

in the thing named and give grounds to show how the Son of God is to be called this name. . . ."[189] Here the gap between God and the sphere of our language is again the oneness of God and the manyness of our words, and here it is very directly the coming of Christ as God and man at once which bridges this gap.

If we next examine the context of these passages, we find that the *grounds* that legitimize applying the various names to the Son are in every case given by the general plot of the history of salvation.[190] Our words belong to a language game with inappropriate rules (they presuppose time and its plurality). But in His historical dealing with us, centered in the Incarnation, God so enters our plurality that our words, in defiance of the inappropriateness of their plurality, do find an actual object in Him.

Can we specify more exactly the nature of this reality in God which thus can be named by the same names as realities in us? Can we say *how* there can be in God a real object of anthropomorphic description? Origen, called on to explain how we can use certain words of God, relies constantly on the same pattern. Challenged with respect to "hand," "arm," and the like, he responds: ". . . we do not press the literal meaning [191] but puzzle out how such words may be taken so as to be sensibly and worthily used of God. Thus the 'heart' of God is to be taken of his power of theoretical and practical reason. . . ."[192] With regard to "fire": "He consumes evil thoughts. . . ."[193] Of "sight": ". . . whatever in bodily nature is called seeing is, between the Father and the Son . . . , knowing. . . ."[194] Most clearly of all: "God is named 'light' by transfer from bodily light to unseen and unbodily light, which is called 'light' because it is the power of illuminating the eyes of the intellect."[195]

In each case a similarity of function or effect allows the transfer of

189. *Commentary on John,* I, 24.
190. Ibid., I, 20 ff, 24 ff.
191. ψιλὴν καὶ λέξιν.
192. Ibid., I, 39.
193. Ibid., I, 1.
194. Ibid.
195. *Commentary on John,* XIII, 23.

a word across the barrier. And for that similarity Origen sometimes uses a fateful word: "analogy." [196]

Yet this determination of how our words can fit God does not really transcend the "somehow" of the passage with which we began; it only specifies it. It says that there is something in God which *somehow* has the same function for Him as 'light' or 'reason' or what will you for us. We therefore summarize this section as follows.

What we call, for example, 'love' in man is the image of an eschatological something, of an aspect of God-for-us-at-the-end. Since this is so, we can call this something love also, knowing that strictly the word 'love' names only the image and not the prototype. As referring to the prototype the word itself is an image. Yet this naming is not purely metaphorical, not an as-if naming. For somehow it fits. Somehow God is love. There is something in God that functionally resembles love in us. We cannot get beyond this "somehow" and see exactly *how* our words fit. But the event of God's activity in our history guarantees *that* they do. And we have rules for how to speak so as to, as it were, activate this "somehow": the rules of allegorical exegesis posited by the plot of that very historical intervention.

196. E.g., ibid., I, 26.

3. Thomas: Analogy

At the very beginning of the *Summa Theologica*[1] the problem posed is the apparent lack of anything specific for theology to do: "Whether it is necessary to have any other body of teaching[2] besides the secular disciplines." The difficulty is that ". . . man ought not strive for what is above reason. . . . But those things which are subject to reason are handled adequately in the secular disciplines."[3] We need paraphrase this only slightly to see that it is exactly the logical positivists' objection: "If it can be investigated [if it is 'subject to reason'[4]], it is the object of a science; if it cannot be investigated, there is nothing informative to say about it [no 'teaching' is needed]."

The reply Thomas makes to this is not in the first instance an appeal to the possibility of there being things not subject to investigation yet nevertheless proper objects of doctrine, of informative lan-

---

1. I,1,1. For an interpretation of this same section from a question very near to ours, cf. the essay by Gerhard Ebeling, "Der hermeneutische Ort der Gotteslehre bei Petrus Lombardus und Thomas von Aquin," *Zeitschrift für Theologie und Kirche,* 61, 3, pp. 283–326.
2. *Doctrina.*
3. I,1,1.
4. *Rationi subduntur.*

guage. This comes,[5] but in the second place. His first reply is that such a body of didactic language is "necessary for man's salvation." This is further explicated: ". . . man is directed [6] to God as to an end that surpasses his reason." That is, a didactic language other than that of the sciences and common sense is needed so that man can fulfill his directedness toward a goal that is transcendent and therefore not grasped in other language.

Later,[7] difficulties are again raised which are analogues to contemporary difficulties with religious language. The first is the problem of evil, in its formalized form, the problem of "infinite goodness," and the other "infinite-something" predicates which seem to be essential in speaking of God. How can we use a word controlled by such predicates in the same sentences with language about this evil and suffering world—without obvious falsehood? But if we avoid using the word in such contexts, then of what use is it? The second difficulty is the principle that was later known as "Occam's razor": "What can be explained by few principles should not be explained by many. But it seems that everything in the world can be explained on the supposition that God is not. . . ." This principle was the very heart of the reductive language analysis practiced by the positivists: If we can say what we want to say without using a certain word, then what independent meaning can that word have?

To the first of these objections Thomas makes a traditional, and rather unconvincing, reply. But to the second he again answers with the teleological character of existence. If we consider this, Thomas asserts, then there *are* things we want to say which can only be said by using 'God.'

It seems clear that, for Thomas, theological utterance is a language activity justified by a certain character of human life: its directedness to a goal beyond it. And we may, I think, go further. It seems plain that this language activity is not, for Thomas, merely descriptive of man's final goal. It is a language, a doctrine, that man

5. I,1,1.
6. *Ordinatur.*
7. I,2,3.

must have in order to attain this goal. It is a language by whose use man is given his transcendence, and not merely a description of it. There is at least a hint here of a language activity other than the describing activity—an activity which is a doing and accomplishing, and in which what is creatively posited by the utterances is the final meaning of the life of the speaker.[8]

II.

What are the criteria for the use of such a language? What rules decide whether a given sentence is acceptable or unacceptable? Thomas poses the question in this form: What sort of "argumentation," if any, is proper to theology?

Thomas answers that in large part the same sort of argumentation is proper as that used in any discipline: The majority of the sentences of theology are derived, following the laws of evidence and formal logic, from the axioms [9] of the body of knowledge. But in the case of theology the axioms of the science "are the articles of faith." [10] These are not verifiable by normal means. If the adversary admits none of the articles of faith, there is nothing more to be done.[11]

How, then, are the articles of faith verified? In his further development of the theme of man's intrinsic goal-directedness,[12] Thomas argues that "blessedness" is necessarily desired by every man, since in its general sense "blessedness" simply means "ultimate goal of will," so that 'He desires blessedness' is equivalent to 'He desires what he desires and the means to what he desires.' He then argues that "blessedness" in its more special sense of "the vision of God's essence" is "identical in the real order" [13] with the more generally

8. To this, cf. the extraordinary book by Thomas Bonhoeffer, *Die Gotteslehre Thomas von Aquins als Sprachproblem,* an imaginative and, alas, often inventive exegesis of this whole side of Thomas. I am at once indebted to this work and put off by it.

9. *Principia probanda.*

10. Cf. also I,1,2.

11. I,1,8.

12. I–II,5,8.

13. *Idem secundum rem.*

considered final object of the will, differing only in "the way it is known." [14] Thus Thomas can assert that "all things, in seeking the perfections proper to themselves"—which they of course cannot help; 'I seek what I seek' is analytic—"seek God himself. . . ." [15]

The theological language activity is the one in the doing of which we move from unconscious, inauthentic seeking of our goal—and this we all in fact *do*—to conscious, authentic seeking thereof. "The goal must be foreknown, in order that men may direct their intentions and actions to that goal." [16] This is the function of theological speech, which necessitates its existence beside science and philosophy. Therefore, its utterances justify themselves by the way in which they function in life, by the way in which they lead us to the goal we do in fact desire. Nor is this a private justification. The seeking of a good, and the seeking of the particular good—God— with which this language is concerned, is an activity in which all men are involved.[17]

We can arrive at the same point from Thomas' more direct answer. The articles of faith, as the axioms of the whole set of theological sentences, cannot be established within theology. How then? By derivation from a prior body of knowledge. There are, says Thomas, some bodies of knowledge whose axioms are "self-evident," [18] such as arithmetic and geometry. "But there are others which proceed from axioms known to be true in the light of a prior body of knowledge, as the axioms of perspective are established as theorems in geometry. . . ." Theology "is of the second sort, for it proceeds from axioms known by the light of a prior body of knowledge. . . ." And what is this? ". . . The knowledge which God has . . ." [19] The statements of theology are to be established by deriving them from the content of the mind of God. But surely this is

14. *Secundum rationis considerationem.*
15. I,1a,1.
16. I,1,1.
17. For the pointer down this line of thought, I am indebted to Bonhoeffer.
18. *Per se noti.*
19. *Ex principiis notis lumine superioris scientiae, quae scilicet est scientia Dei. . . .* I,1,2.

not a verification we can perform or a criterion we can use? And so this language not one we can speak?

Now this is indeed not a criterion we can manipulate on demand —which is just what we already said, that the truth of the articles of faith cannot be established by argumentation. But our citation of Thomas omitted one word. It reads in full: ". . . from axioms known by the light of a prior body of knowledge, the knowledge which God has *and the blessed.*" [20] The prior body of knowledge which justifies the sentences of theology is one that we do not now have, to be sure, but that we *will* have when we reach the goal to which those sentences seek to guide us. For the attainment of a share in God's knowledge of Himself is the end toward which man transcends himself.[21] Revelation is permission to anticipate that sharing in God's knowledge of Himself which is the final end of man.[22] When and if we attain the fulfillment of our existence, that event will justify or falsify the articles of faith, and so all theological utterances. We can, therefore, say of theological language, also as it is used by Thomas, that it is eschatological, and in a double sense, in this going beyond Origen: (1) it is a language by the speaking of which transcendence is posited; (2) its sentences are verified or falsified by the eschaton.

We must of course, remember that for Thomas theological language is not only a nondescriptive language activity of anticipation and promise: its sentences state present facts. On the one hand, the eschatological basis for this speech is God's present cognition of Himself,[23] and His communicating of this is a "teaching." [24] On the other hand, it is precisely information that man needs in order to carry out his self-transcendence: "Thus it was necessary for man's salvation that certain things be made known to him. . . ." [25] In a way quite foreign to Origen, correct theological speech is for

20. *Scientia Dei et beatorum.* I,1,2.
21. II–II, 1,2: I,12,1.
22. II–II,171–74.
23. Cf. Question 13.
24. II–II,171,4.
25. *Quod si nota fierunt quaedam.* I,1,1.

Thomas a matter of uttering true statements. Theology, when all is said, is a theoretical, descriptive science.[26]

III.

So we cannot avoid the question: How so descriptive? Thomas' explicit reply to this question is: Statements about God are analogously descriptive.[27] It is therefore Thomas' famous doctrine of analogy to which we must devote the remainder of this chapter. But before we turn back to the text, some qualifications must be made.

St. Thomas' *general* doctrine of analogy is, in the medieval sense, a logical doctrine and not a metaphysical one. The word 'analogy' figures in our reflections over how we name things, not in our naming of them.[28] This logical doctrine is stated very clearly by Thomas: "For those words used analogically there is neither one intension [29] . . . nor a mere diversity of intension. A word used variously, in this way, signifies diverse relations to some one thing: as 'healthy,' used of urine, signifies a symptom of the animal's health, used of medicine, the cause of the animal's health." [30] "When anything is predicated analogically of several things, it is found according to the proper intension of the word in only one of them, from which the others are named." [31] ". . . In all analogical predication to a plurality of subjects, all but one of the predications must be made with respect to that one. And the definition of the word as used in that one case must appear in the definition of the other uses of the word." [32] For Thomas what a word immediately names is a ratio, a reality *as known*. Our word "intension" will do as an equivalent. A word has thus a proper intension. But it may be used

26. I,1,4.
27. I,13,5.
28. This has been, contra Thomists old and new, proved by Ralph McInerny, *The Logic of Analogy.*
29. *Ratio.*
30. I,13,5.
31. I,16,6.
32. *Illud unum oportet quod ponitur in definitione omnium.* I,13,6.

for other intensions in such a way that its various intensions do not make a mere arbitrary collection but are unified by definite relations to the primary intension. So with 'healthy' of a healthy animal (primary intension), a healthy climate (necessary condition of animal's health), and a healthy coat (symptom of animal's health). When the word is defined in these secondary uses, its primary definition will appear as part of the new definitions.[33] Thus if 'healthy,' used of an animal, means 'proper balance of hormones,' 'healthy' of a place will mean 'conducive to proper balance of hormones.' Now where a word is so used that simultaneous reference to two or more such intensions is involved, it is used analogically. The definition of its analogical meaning (staying with 'health' as our example) is then '. . . to proper balance of hormones.'[34] It will be seen that this general logical doctrine is simply an analysis of a common way in which we in fact use words.

We are concerned with Thomas' doctrine of analogy only insofar as he uses it in that explanation of how our language can describe God which he gives in the *Summa Theologica*. This explanation is at once logical and metaphysical; the logical pattern called analogous predication is found to be the pattern of our speech about God, a pattern that we do and can properly use only because of certain alleged metaphysical facts.[35] These metaphysical facts can themselves be stated only by analogous language. It is this whole explanation with which we will be concerned.

We will, moreover, limit ourselves to interpreting the *Summa Theologica,* in those portions that deal specifically with the doctrine of God, with little reference to his other works. And we will ignore

33. I,13,10.
34. For precise detailing of this vague and sketchy account, cf. McInerny, op. cit.
35. For an attempt to interpret Thomas' doctrine of analogous predication of divine names as a purely logical doctrine—even in the *modern* sense—cf. J. F. Ross, "Analogy as a Rule of Meaning for Religious Language," *International Philosophical Quarterly,* I, pp. 468–502. But at the crucial point it is apparent that these "language rules" will work only if a metaphysical situation, an "analogy of being," is presupposed. Cf. E. L. Mascall, *Existence and Analogy.* As an interpretation of Thomas, moreover, this attempt is vitiated by adherence to the traditional Cajetanian statement of the problem.

the traditional Thomistic interpretations. We are allowed and required to restrict ourselves in this way by the collapse of the Thomistic attempt to construct from all Thomas' various uses and mentions of analogy one metaphysical doctrine of analogy.[36] There is no such doctrine.[37] There is only a general pattern of predication which Thomas puts to a vast variety of concrete uses and the name for which he uses as part of the explanation of a great variety of matters. We are concerned with one of those uses—to speak of God—and with one of those explanations—his answer to the question of how we can speak of God at all.

IV.

Thomas' stipulation of words used of God as analogously predicated is explicitly an attempt to overcome the oscillation from using words with certain meaning rules, to withdrawing those meaning rules, to returning to those same rules when attempting to regain the content of the words—an oscillation that threatens to make nonsense of theological language, and the very difficulty to which recent philosophers have called attention. He would call the one pole of this swing the attempt to use words "univocally" of God and creatures; the other pole, an "equivocal" use.

To repeat our example: "God loves me." "What do you mean by 'love'?" "How my father behaves to me when I am ill; he does all he can to help, etc." If we could stick to this—that is, stick to the rule for 'love' we have given—'love' would be "univocally" predi-

---

36. In particular, the whole motion of an "analogy of proportionality" as distinguished from an "analogy of attribution" is irrelevant to Thomas' discussion. Besides McInerny, cf. Hampus Lyttkins, *The Analogy between God and the World,* and G. Klubertanz, *St. Thomas on Analogy.* Let me here acknowledge my general dependence on these two works.

For a clear presentation and stout defense of the classic Cajetanist interpretation, cf. M. T.-L. Penido, *Le Rôle de l'Analogie en Théologie Dogmatique,* pp. 12–53.

37. The Thomists' doctrine is of course an option in itself; but since it is not that of Thomas, it is not the doctrine I have chosen to investigate. Indeed, I am inclined to agree with the Thomists' position on the necessity of analogy for metaphysics, etc.; cf. Penido, pp. 53 ff.

cated of God and father—that is, with the same intension in both
uses. But precisely the attempt to speak accurately of God will not
allow this. As Thomas puts it: ". . . all perfections which exist in
created things separately and as a collection, pre-exist as *one* reality
in God. . . . Whence nothing can be univocally predicated of God
and creatures." [38] The problem is exactly Origen's.

Therefore we start withdrawing the rules. "Do you mean He *always* does all He could?" "Not exactly." "But doesn't your father?"
"Well, God's love is not quite like Father's." Et cetera. If we continue on this path to the end, we have none of the original usage
rules left, in Thomas' framework: 'love' as applied to God no longer
has at all the same intension as when applied to father; its use of the
two is equivocal. But this is intolerable; it leaves 'love' as applied to
God without *any* rules—that is, cognitively vacuous. For the peculiarity of this particular equivocation is that as the old rules evaporate,
no new and wholly different intension is set up. But that 'God is
love' is vacuous is, says Thomas, contrary to fact: ". . . according to
this nothing could be known or demonstrated of God. . . . But this
is against the philosopher, who demonstrates many things of God,
and against the apostle in Romans 1:20. . . ." We would say: This
is a reductive analysis, which says that what people suppose to be
the function of their theological utterances is not. It is therefore a
last resort.

If theology would settle on one pole or the other, it would have
no logical problems. If it would use words univocally of God and
creatures, all would be well—except that it would not be talking of
God. If it would settle for equivocity and, in this case, cognitive
vacuity, it could very well justify itself as some nondescriptive language act—but this act Thomas has no interest in performing. But
theology seems to switch from one to the other, and so to be in logical chaos. Apparently the solution would be to find some stable
place in the middle. It is exactly this that Thomas seeks to stipulate.
Analogy "is a mode of community [of meanings] which is a me-
dian between pure equivocation and simple univocation. For in analogical predications neither is there one intension, as in univocal

38. I,13,5.

predications, nor a total diversity of intensions, as in equivocal predications. . . ."[39]

V.

In I, 13, 5, which is the *Summa's locus classicus* on this issue, the possibility of speaking about God and the analogous character of this speaking are traced to there being a specific relation of the creatures of God: "Thus whatever is said of God and creatures is said insofar as there is a specific relation of the creatures to God, as to the cause and reason of their being and intelligibility. . . ."[40] It is a fundamental ontological fact that makes possible speech about God, in one breath with speech about creatures, and determines the logic of such speech.

This fundamental God-creature relation is analyzed in Question 2, in which the proofs for the existence of God are developed. As proofs these are, of course, dubious. But it is not as proofs that we are interested in them. And it is not as proofs that they are important within the structure of the *Summa*. It is as ontological analyses of the fundamental difference and relation of God and creatures that they set the basis for the following questions of the *Summa*, and that we are concerned with them.

The common feature of all the proofs is the discovery that the entire sphere of what is and can be known and described (whether this description is physical or metaphysical makes no difference) contains within itself no reason *that* it is or that it as a whole is *what* it is and not something else. The experience hidden in these proofs is the impact of the questions: "Why is there anything? Why not rather nothing?"[41] and "Why *this* world and not some other?" Such questions will be experienced only by a being who wants *reasons*—that is, by man in his search for the point of his own exis-

39. I,13,5.
40. *Principium et causum.* The four-membered phrase I have used brings out, I think, the highly compressed content of this two-membered technical locution.
41. *Warum gibt es überhaupt Seiendes-und nicht viel mehr nichts?* Heidegger, *Einführung in die Metaphysik.*

tence. They will be experienced by the eschatological being, by that being who is what he is only as he becomes it—and that in the radical sense that he receives his reality from a future not in his own hands.[42]

If being is not to be sheer unintelligible darkness, there must be, says Thomas, a being who is the explanation of all beings. (Note that this being that is the Reason of beings cannot itself be one of those beings—so that 'being' is here used analogically.) That being is *not* sheer unintelligibility is an unstated axiom for Thomas—as for all classical Western philosophy.[43] There is, therefore, such an Explanation of beings. Moreover, this being, in order to escape the obvious regress to infinity—"But why is there this being?"—must be ontologically determined as its own explanation: ". . . and this all understand to be God." [44] We have here Thomas' exposition of the fundamental Western ontology as created by Augustine, the ontology of God as absolute Being and of creatures as dependent beings.

Or—which is the same thing—we can say that in Question 2 the meaning of the word 'God' is set, the meaning which this word can have in a language that is also about creatures, and which it is to have in the *Summa*. 'God' means (to express Question 2 in one phrase): 'the first cause and reason of all that reality which we find as we look about.' [45] 'God' means 'the eschatological Reason without which existence is absurd.' [46]

How then can we obtain sentences that have 'God' as their subject? From His activity as a cause—that is, from examining His effects. Sentences with 'God' as their subject must be derived in this way because 'first cause' is all that the word 'God' means—at least to begin with. And since God can be known only from His

42. For a remarkable exegesis of Thomas as the one in whom there breaks through the modern understanding of being as self-transcendent, as *geschichtlich,* see J. B. Metz, *Christliche Anthropozentrik: Uber die Denkform des Thomas von Aquin.*

43. Parmenides.

44. I,2,3.

45. "Cause and reason" translates *causa efficiens et finalis.* The shrinkage of "cause" to what the medievals called "efficient cause" makes circumlocutions constantly necessary.

46. Cf. Metz, pp. 73 ff.

effects, He can be "named"—that is, words can be found suitable for talk about Him—only from His effects.[47] All speech about God is, therefore, in language drawn from our speech about creatures.

Now God is the cause of *all* things—and this introduces the difficulty. If He is cause of all things, there is no class of objects of which He is a member. Much causation is "univocal": that is, the cause belongs to the same class as its effects and so can be univocally named together with them. Thus man begets man, and billiard ball moves billiard ball.[48] Given a man, we can say: There is a cause of this, and it is a man. But the cause of the existence of a class as a class, the cause of a class of objects' possessing that character by which they are constituted a class, cannot itself possess that character and be a member of that class; otherwise it would be its own cause. "A univocal agent is never the universal cause of a whole class, for then it would be in respect of that class its own cause. . . . Therefore a universal cause of a whole class is not a *univocal* cause."[49] God is the cause of all things: that is, He is their cause simply insofar as they are things at all. He is the cause of the defining character of the class of all entities. As a consequence, He belongs to no class at all. He is in *no* respect a univocal cause. "If there is any cause which is contained in no class, its effects . . . will not resemble their cause by being jointly definable by species or genus. . . .[50] And such is the relation of God's creatures to God. . . ."[51]

Our knowledge of God from His effects can never, therefore, amount to a knowledge of what God is.[52] We can never say: "God is . . . ," for the word that would appear in the blank would be a generic word, and no such word can be univocally used of God. He belongs to no class. "In this life, God cannot be seen in His essence."[53] If God did belong to any class, it would be the class of "beings." For there is, so to speak, a closer approach to univocal

47. I,13,1.
48. I,4,3.
49. I,13,5.
50. *Secundum eandum rationem speciei aut generi.*
51. I,4,3.
52. I,3,prol.
53. I,13,1.

causal activity of God on His effects in this, which is the defining
character of the whole class of His effects, than in any other character. But this does not help us, for "being" is not a class, there being
nothing outside it and so no differentia by which it could be defined.[54] By this line, too, we end with the impossibility of knowing
what God is.

Moreover, since we cannot know what God is, the words that we
use to speak of Him, the "names" we use as the predicates of sentences with God as subject, can never name His essence. Since our
knowledge of creatures cannot give us knowledge of God's essence,
our creature-language cannot name it. (We would now, of course,
argue just the other way around.) "In this way . . . we can name
Him from creatures: but not so that the name . . . points out His
essence. . . ."[55]

From His effects we cannot, therefore, know or say what God is.
But this does not condemn us to total ignorance: ". . . because they
are his effects, dependent on him as their cause, we can learn from
[creatures] to know of God that He is, and to know those things
about him which must necessarily pertain to him if He is to be the
cause of all things, transcending all his effects. Whence we learn of
him: his relation to creatures, that He is cause of them all; and the
creatures' differentia from him, that He has none of those characters
which He causes [in creatures] and that those characters are not absent from him because He lacks them but because He exceeds
them."[56] Here is the fundamental pattern which Thomas uses
throughout questions 3 through 26 in deriving the "attributes" of
God. The development is analytic; Thomas argues to those things
that God must be in order to be first cause—and 'first cause' is what
'God' means.

That is, we cannot know what God is, but we can unpack the
statement *that* He is. Given the statement 'God exists,' we can go on
to 'A first cause exists,' since 'God' is equivalent to 'first cause' by
definition. And if there is any character 'F' such that 'A first cause

54. I,3,5.
55. I,13,1.
56. I,12,12.

exists,' together with statements true of creatures—such as 'Creatures are complex entities' implies 'An entity possessed of "F" exists,'—we can move to that sentence and perhaps to a series of such sentences. Thus we can go to 'A perfectly simple entity exists,' of which 'God is perfectly simple'[57] is to be viewed as a mere grammatical variant.[58] And so for each of the 'God is . . .' sentences of questions 3 through 26.

The whole doctrine of God is therefore an analytic development of the assertion with which it begins: 'God is'; that is, it is an analytic development of the original answer to the question: "Why is there anything? And why this?" It is an analytical development of the original posit of a meaning of existence, of the original "There *must* be a reason." It is remarkable how faithful Thomas' analyses are to his original statements of the purpose of theological language, which we summarized in calling it eschatological.

Thus knowledge of God's essence is denied us in this life. All our present knowledge is essentially negative; as we have just seen, it marks off God's reality without defining it. Its sentences are fundamentally denials of some likeness of God to what we know—however affirmative they may be in grammatical form: ". . . of God we cannot know what He is, but rather what He is not. . . ."[59] Knowledge of God's essence will be a gift of the last day: "The principle of supernatural cognition . . . is God Himself, who is not seen in His essence even by the prophets. He is seen by the saints in the Father's house. . . ."[60] It is the goal of our present knowledge.[61] And insofar as God now reveals Himself to us, our knowledge is an anticipation under the conditions of present existence[62] of the vision

57. I,3.
58. I wish to point out that this really very simple analysis also demonstrates the identity of Thomas' two assertions that we cannot know more of God than that He is, and that we can know a great deal of Him analogically —two assertions often assumed to be contradictory or at least "varying emphases." E.g., by R. L. Patterson, *The Conception of God in the Philosophy of Aquinas*, pp. 254 ff.
59. I,3,prol.
60. II–II,171,2.
61. I,12,1–10; II–II,174,2.
62. II–II,171,224; 173,1.

of the blessed. There is therefore hidden in all our talkative knowledge
of God, as its heart and meaning, an essentially wordless experience.[63] Yet this experience is given precisely in order to be communicated to others, and that means in order to come to words.[64]

VI.

Before we can continue on this line, there is one other matter we
must note. *All* our present knowledge of God is as described above.
Among other important things, this means that there is no logical
difference between natural and revealed knowledge of God.

Whether it be the phenomenon of the persistence of change in nature, or the Resurrection, we have before us effects of God's causal
power, from which we argue to truth about Him. Thus, although
some of these effects are natural and others supernatural, the logical
structure of the statements about God to which they lead us is the
same: ". . . in this life we do not even by the revelation of grace,
come to know of God *what* He is . . . ; nevertheless we do come to
know him more fully insofar as more and more excellent of his
effects are made visible to us. . . ."[65]

The process by which revelation thus makes God's effects more
visible to us is conceived by Thomas in perfect structural parallel to
the process of natural knowledge.[66] We know by abstracting concepts from sense images as these are unified and worked up for in-
tellection by the imagination.[67] Revelation is the strengthening of
the abstractive powers of the intellect and (sometimes) the provision of additional content to this power.[68] This latter can take place
at any level. God may provide supernatural sense images by causing
supernatural external events to take place and to be seen. Or He
may intervene directly to infuse sense images into the soul. Or He

63. II–II,175,1–3.
64. II–II,176 f.
65. I,12,13.
66. See on this entire matter Per Persson, *Sacra Doctrina: En studie till
förhällandet mellen ratio och revelatio i Thomas av Aquino teologi.*
67. II–II,173,2.
68. I,12,13.

may infuse concepts directly.[69] At no point is the structure of knowledge altered: "Prophetic vision is not vision of the divine essence itself. . . . It is a vision in various similitudes, as these are illuminated by divine light." [70] The entire process has come to its essential completion with Christ and the apostles, so that the revealed truths are now given as the teaching contained in Scripture.[71]

To be sure, revelation does lead to knowledge of God and so to the use of names for Him and the asserting of propositions about Him, which would not otherwise be given: ". . . from divine revelation we attribute to him things to which natural reason does not attain, as that God is three and one." [72] But the division between natural and supernatural truths concerning God is not a division in logic.[73]

69. II–II,173,2, and 174,2.
70. II–II,173,1.
71. For proof, see Persson, op. cit., pp. 46 ff.
72. I,12,13.
73. We can show this by pointing out that no division in logic is reflected in the division of that part of the *Summa* that treats the doctrine of God (Part I). Thus the example given of a revealed truth is the doctrine of the Trinity. But in Part I this doctrine is itself the principle of division: questions 2–26 deal with the oneness of essence; questions 27–43, with distinction of persons (I,2,prol.). And in *each* of these divisions *both* natural and revealed truths are treated. Thus the section on God's essence is subdivided into three parts (I,2,prol.): "Whether God is" (Question 2); "What God is" (quentions 3–13); "What God does" (questions 14–26). The first of these contains the eminently natural proofs of God's existence; the third deals with predestination, among other things. Since the *Summa's* division of the doctrine of God is made precisely according to the logic of the doctrine, it can be seen that the division between natural and revealed knowledge is not a division in logic.
   A closer approximation to a division of Part I corresponding to the division of nature and revelation can be found by examining Thomas' summary of the content of natural knowledge of God: We can know that God is; that He is first cause; that He is (analogically) all that He must be to be first cause; that as such He is none of these things which creatures are; and that this last is so because He is in excess all that creatures are (I,12,12). This seems quite clearly to correspond to the first two parts of the first main division (questions 2–26) of Part I: "Whether God is" and "What God is"; which would make revealed knowledge correspond to the third part: "What God does." And it does seem that Thomas thinks of the notion of 'God' as

Thus revealed knowledge is not a special kind of knowledge. A consequence of this is that it is the literal meaning of the text of Scripture that communicates the truth revealed to the prophets and apostles. Thomas teaches the usual fourfold sense, but the "spiritual" senses have no basic theological significance for him: ". . . all the senses are based on one, the literal. Only from this can theological argument proceed. . . ." [74] As a consequence there are no theologically significant *special* rules of Scriptural exegesis. Nor do the rules of Scriptural exegesis, as a further consequence, figure as special rules of theological language—contra Origen.

This does not mean that Thomas reduces the *content* of all knowledge of God to natural sources. It sometimes seems so in Part I of the *Summa*. Without exception the various predicates proved of God are proved by deriving them from the notion of that being whose existence is proved from reason alone in Question 2. But this only shows how intimately natural and revealed knowledge of God interplay in Thomas' doctrine. For if we go back to Question 2, article 3, and ask: *"Whose* existence is being proved by reason alone? Whose mode of being is being analyzed?" we will find as the reiterated answer: that first efficient and final cause of all things "whom everyone calls 'God.'" [75] But who is "everyone"? Obviously, all those whose language has been formed by the Old Testament, the at least culturally Christian, Jewish, or Mohammedan who were the "everyone" for Thomas. A Hindu would *not* use 'God' in this way. It is the Creator whose mode of being is analyzed in Question 2 and whose attributes are there drawn out from that analysis. We must remember that all our theological utterances, including those we can know by nature, are in their *use* a function of our yearning for the fulfillment of the biblical promises.

---

given by nature, and of most of our information about what this being has in fact done as given by revelation. But that this is still not a division of logic is shown by the fact that the whole second half of Part I (questions 27–43) stands outside it, and, more important, by the fact that, as we will see (cf. pp. 85–87), the logical criterion of the predicates proposed for God in questions 14–26 is their reducibility to those established in questions 2–13.

74. I,1,10. Cf. Persson, op. cit., pp. 56 ff.
75. *Quam omnes Deum nominant.* I,2,3.

VII.

We pick up the argument from the fifth section of this chapter. Statements about God are therefore neither univocal nor equivocal: they are analogical. It is time to go into this in greater detail. We ask first: Why can they not be univocal?

They cannot because God is the Creator and therefore not a univocal cause. Thomas asserts that all causes produce effects in some way resembling themselves. "Every cause causes effects similar to itself in that respect in which it is a cause." [76] This is a metaphysical law to which there are no exceptions. Even a nonunivocal cause must therefore resemble its effects in some way, so that the cause can be in some way named from the effects. Yet the unlikeness of a nonunivocal cause to its effects is far more obtrusive.[77] It is the unlikeness we wish now to specify, leaving the likeness to the next section.

In the passage to which we constantly recur, the matter is put by saying that the cause-effect likeness of God and creatures is imperfect: "Every effect that does not fully utilize the causal power of its cause resembles its agent . . . imperfectly. . . ." This inadequacy of God's effects fully to represent His creative power and so fully to represent Him—as a son represents his father in both ways—is then identified with the ontological difference between God and creatures, with the different ways in which they are what they are: ". . . all perfections which exist in created things separately and as a collection, pre-exist as one reality in God . . . ." [78] Or, specifying the ontological difference in another way: "If there is a cause that is contained in no class, its effects will attain only a remote resemblance to the form of the cause. . . ." [79]

If God and His effects resemble each other at all—which they must—then there must be attributes somehow possessed by both.

76. *Omne agens agat sibi simile inquantum est agens.* I,4,3.
77. I,13,5.
78. I,13,5.
79. I,4,3.

But God is ontologically different from creatures; He is what He is in a different way. Which is to say, He possesses his "attributes" in a different way. "Any perfection in an effect must be found in its effective cause, either according to the same intension if the cause is univocal (thus man begets man), or in a *more eminent mode* if the cause is equivocal. . . ." [80] Exactly corresponding to this difference in ontological mode between God and creatures is an inappropriateness of "mode" in our creaturely language—to which we now turn.

The following distinction is fundamental to Thomas' whole theology: "Considered as to *that which they signify,* names [drawn from creatures] properly pertain to God. . . . Considered as to their *mode of signifying,* they are not properly used of God, for they have the mode of signifying appropriate to creatures." [81] The unlikeness between God and creatures is that names drawn from creatures are unsuited to God in their "mode of signifying." What does this mean?

Literally, the phrase *modum significandi* would mean "way of going about signifying." This leads to the suspicion that the "mode of signifying" of a word is the set of rules for how and when to use that word. And closer examination bears this out.

We can, we said, distinguish two kinds of usage rule: those that stipulate where and how a word is to be used with respect to other words, and those that stipulate the nonlinguistic circumstances in which a word is to be used. We called the first sort syntactical rules; the second, semantic rules. " 'Chair' is a substantive" is a syntactical rule; " 'chair' means something to sit in" is a sematic rule. The first specifies linguistic signals for using the word; the second, nonlinguistic.

It is immediately apparent that a word's mode of signifying includes the syntactical rules for the use of the word. It is exactly the

80. I,4,3.
81. *Quantum igitur ad id quod significant huismodi nomina, proprie competunt Deo. . . . Quantum vero ad modum significandi, non proprie dicuntur de Deo; habent enim modum significandi qui creaturis competit.* I,13,3.

normal stipulation of the kind of word a term is that must be left behind when it is transferred to God: for example, ". . . whenever a name drawn from a created perfection is attributed to God there must be excluded from its signification everything that pertains to the imperfect mode proper to the creature. Thus knowledge is not a quality in God . . . but substance. . . ." [82] In individual cases it is invariably the rules stating whether a word names an attribute, or a substance possessing attributes, or the like, that we are instructed to disregard in using those words of God. [83]

It is not so immediately apparent that the mode of signifying includes also the semantic rules. But it does. Two lines of reasoning show this. First, given a word like "justice," its Thomistic definition is "a quality leading to just acts." Thomas interprets this as a definition by genus and differentia: "quality" is the genus; the remainder, the differentia. [84] Thus if we eliminate "quality" from the intension of the word as applied to God, we have eliminated the rule specifying the general class of cases to which the word applies. We no longer have a specification of the nonlinguistic cases in which to use this word.

Second, Thomas teaches that there is a difference between *what* a word names and the set of signals by which we are led to know when and where to predicate it. The one he calls "that for the signifying of which" [85] a word is used; the other he calls "that from which a word is imposed to signify something." [86] His favorite example is that a stone is recognized as a stone by causing a pain in one's foot when kicked, but that the name does not therefore signify "pain-in-foot-causer." The "that from which" of our words is always a set of signals: "heat, cold, whiteness, and the like. . . ." [87] If the dropping of a word's inappropriate mode of signifying means, in the case of transfer to God, dropping its reference to creatures, this

82. I,14,1.
83. E.g., I,3,6 obj. 1 and reply; I,4,1 obj. 1 and reply.
84. Cf. McInerny, op. cit., pp. 157 f.
85. *Id ad quod significandum.*
86. *[Id] a quo imponitur nomen ad significandum.* I,13,2.
87. I,13,8.

means dropping its "that from which a word is imposed," the whole set of rules by which we are told in which nonlinguistic circumstances to use it and when not to use it.

It is, then, the rules for how to use a word that are meant by its "mode of signifying." "Our intellect apprehends [characters] as they are in creatures, and as it apprehends them it signifies them by names. . . . Considered as to their mode of signifying, [such names] are not properly used of God, for they have the mode of signifying appropriate to creatures." And therewith our final point is also made. It is the fact that, when our words are used of God, their usage rules do not apply, that is their nonunivocity in this use.

These two stipulations—of the difference of ontological mode between God and creatures, and of the inappropriateness to God of our language's mode of signifying—are for Thomas simply two ways of saying the same thing. Our language works by rules that assume a certain mode of being, especially the distinction between a thing and what it is, which is reflected in our linguistic distinction of subject and predicate. God does not exist in this way. Thus the linguistic mode of our language falls short precisely of the ontological mode of God.[88]

It is exactly this difference between God and creatures that is worked out in the section [89] of Part I devoted to "What God is."[90] This section has the interesting alternative title, "In what way God is."[91] And negative formulation of both titles are said to be more accurate: ". . . we are to inquire in what way He is, that we might know of Him what He is. But since we cannot know of God what He is but rather what He is not, we cannot discuss in what way God is but rather in what way He is not."[92] In this section Thomas discusses God's simplicity, perfection, goodness, infinity, immutability, unity, deity, and entity. In what way are these names of what God is not? Clearly "God is one," for example, is not a materially negative

88. I,13,1.
89. (Questions 2–13).
90. I,3,prol..
91. *Quomode sit.* I,2,prol.
92. I,3,prol.

statement like "God is not mean." I suggest that it is rather a statement of how the mode of signifying of our language does not apply, and that the attributions to God of simplicity, perfection, etc., are all of this character.

Yet "God is one," "God is perfect," etc., appear to be statements about God, not only about our language about God. Indeed they are. The point is that exactly *as* stipulations of the inappropriateness of our language's mode of signifying, they are also stipulations of God's mode of being. The difference between two realities with respect to the mode of signifying of what can be said about them *is* their mutual ontological relation. And vice versa.

What, finally, are these logical-ontological determinants of the difference between God and creatures? Each of the predicates of questions 3 through 13 represents one such determinant. But they can all be reduced to one: "Therefore, any being whose being is distinct from its essence must be caused to be by something else. This cannot be said of God, for we call God the first efficient cause. It is for this reason that in God being and essence are not distinct." [93] Thomas distinguishes between *what* a thing is and *that* it is, and asserts that in all others but God these are distinct: that is, if we could exhaustively answer the question *what* a creature is, we would still have an open question *whether* it is. If this is so, then there is no explanation of a creature's existence in what that creature itself is: it is a dependent, "caused" being. God is the cause uncaused, *the* explanation. With Him, therefore, being and essence are the same: *what* He is is the reason that He is, and *that* He is is the content of what He is. And therefore, for example, "the divine goodness, which in itself is one and simple, is necessarily represented multifariously in creatures. . . ." [94]

VIII.

Yet the language whose mode of signifying is appropriate to creatures (and we have no other descriptive language) is not there-

93. I,3,4.
94. I,23,5.

fore condemned to total equivocity when used of God. Why not?

Let us, for a change, take as our text a passage from the *Summa contra gentiles:* "All created things are kinds of images of the first cause, that is, of God. For a cause causes what is like itself. Now the fulfillment of an image's existence is that it represents its exemplar by a likeness to it. For it is for this that an image is made." [95]

"A cause causes what is like itself." This is a neo-Platonic principle which Thomas often simply uses as a rule. But for Thomas the rule carries heavy theological freight. God is not just any cause of creatures; He is "the primary exemplary, effective and final principle." [96] He is *exemplar* cause of all creatures—that is, their model and perfection. He is *effective* cause—that is, what we now call "cause." He is *final* cause—that is, the good and purpose of creatures. He is, in short, the Creator. He is at the beginning and at the end. He is the ground of our being here and the transcendent goal to which we go and from which we have meaning. It is in this complex causal relation, in which God is in all temporal modes the ground of His creatures, that a "likeness" between them is posited.

For this whole causal and explanatory relation and for the likeness posited in it, Thomas uses a great variety of terms: "proportion," "likeness," "representation," "assimilation," "participation," "imitation"—of which the last two are the most significant.[97] But the best way to get the Thomistic meaning of them all will be to turn to his explication of this "effective, final, and exemplaristic" causality—that is, to his doctrine of creation.[98]

God is the effective cause of the being of creatures: He makes them happen. He has a purpose in creating them, and they therefore have a goal, an end. But this end can only be God Himself, for otherwise He would have, at one remove, a goal other than Himself—

95. *Summa contra gentiles,* III,19.
96. *Summa Theologica,* I,6,4.
97. To all these, see Klubertanz, op. cit.
98. I,44 f. For the radical difference between Thomas' doctrine of participation-imitation and the doctrine of medieval Platonism in general, see the fundamental work of R. J. Henle, *Saint Thomas and Platonism,* especially pp. 374 ff.

which is contradictory to the meaning of 'God.' God is, therefore, the end of creatures. He is their final cause.[99] This purpose of God can only be to communicate His own perfection, for otherwise there would be a subsisting value other than God. Thus He is exemplar cause.[100]

In less abbreviated expression, now bringing in the key doctrine of ideas: "God is the primary exemplar cause of all things. To show this, we must consider that in producing anything there must be an exemplar in order for the effect to follow a determinate form. Thus an artisan produces a determinate form in his material because of the exemplar to which he looks—whether this is an externally viewed exemplar or an interior exemplar conceived by the mind. Now it is plain that natural entities do follow determinate forms. This determination of forms must be traced back to its first principle, the divine wisdom, which thinks out the order of the universe. This order consists precisely in the distinctions of things. Therefore it must be held that the known realities [101] of all things subsist in the divine mind. These we have called 'ideas,' that is, exemplar forms subsistent in the divine mind. Although these are pluralized in respect of their relation to things, nevertheless they are not really distinct from the divine essence [we remember, in God there is no plurality]. . . . And therefore God himself is the primary exemplar of all things." [102] Here we must pause to note that this operative center of Thomas' whole explanation of how we can speak of God is exactly a version of that artisan-prototype-image ontology of which we found a version in Origen.[103] Thomas makes this quite explicit.[104]

All creatures are, therefore, imitations of God. "God knows how

99. I,45,4.
100. I,19,2.
101. *Rationes.*
102. I,44,3.

103. I must limit myself to speaking of a "version" of this ontology because of the difference between Platonic direct "participation" and the Thomistic "participation" as a name for the multiple involvement of the creature with its Creator. Henle, op. cit., has moved me to this caution.

104. I,14,8; I,15,1.

his essence . . . can be imitated," and the knowledge of each way in
which this can be done is an "Idea." [105] "There can exist nothing
which does not proceed from the divine wisdom by some imitation,
as from its primary effective and formal principle. . . ." [106]

God is the primary cause—that is, the cause of all being whatso-
ever. First of all, therefore, the very fact of existence is an imitating (or "participating" or "likeness") by the creature of its cause.
"God is being by His own essence, and all others by participation."
"[God's] effects will attain to Him . . . according to some sort of
analogy, in the way in which being itself is common to all. And in
this way all things which are from God are likened to Him insofar
as they are beings, since He is the primary and universal principle of
all being." [107] So also the fundamental "perfections"—the ways in
which existence is fulfilled and brought to its goal by achieving
"unity" or "goodness" or the like—are imitations of God. "Every
creature seeks to attain its own perfections, and this is a likeness of
the divine perfection and goodness. . . ." [108] "Insofar as any creature
has any perfection, insofar it represents and is similar to God—not
indeed so as to represent Him as it would something of the same
species or genus, but as a principle excelling His effects. These
effects fall short of His form, yet do attain some similarity to
it. . . ." [109] The whole true and proper nature of a being consists
precisely in imitating in some special way the divine perfection.[110]

When, therefore, creatures are called "beings" or "good" or "one"
or the like, it is their character as mirrors of God that is being
named. "A thing can be called 'good' and 'a being' from the one
who is primarily and essentially 'being' and 'good,' insofar as it participates in Him by some sort of likeness, however remote and defi-
cient. . . ." [111]

This whole situation, finally, can be handled by language in two

105. I,15,2.
106. I,9,1.
107. I,4,3.
108. I,44,4.
109. I,13,2.
110. I,14,6.
111. I,6,4.

ways: (1) The inherent perfection of a creature, which is in fact an imitation of God, may be named from what it is in itself. Then 'good' means simply 'quality of doing justice,' etc.; and there is no problem with the language. The fact that this goodness is imitative of divine goodness is then covered by a material metaphysical assertion to that effect. (This assertion will, of course, use 'good' analogously.) (2) We may call a creature 'good' by reference to the transcendent divine reality of which something in the creature is an imitation. Then 'good' means 'that created character which causally imitates God's goodness.' The word is then used analogously.[112]

This whole affair may be taken the other way around—and it is this that interests us. For if creatures are in their being and perfections imitations of God, then God is the exemplar of creatures. To be sure, we cannot say that God resembles His creatures: "Although we must agree that in some way creatures are similar to God, we can in no way admit that God is similar to creatures." [113] But if we keep always in mind this specification of the one-way nature of the relation, we can say: "Whatever goodness we attribute to creatures pre-exists in God, and that according to a higher mode of being." [114] More generally: "Any perfection present in an effect must be found in its effective cause . . . in a more eminent mode if the cause is equivocal. . . . Since God is the primary effective cause of things, it follows that the perfections of all things pre-exist in God according to a more eminent mode. . . ." [115]

In these passages Thomas claims an identity of character, between God as prototype and creatures as ectypes, which is spanned over the difference of ontological mode discussed in the previous section. This likeness in unlikeness of God and His creatures enables us to speak of God in creature-language. Since our words are about creatures, they can be meaningfully used of God in that He is the exemplar of creatures.

The word that names this likeness is used *analogously*. It seeks to

112. *Quae est formaliter sua bonitas.* I,6,4.
113. I,4,3.
114. I,13,1.
115. I,4,2. Cf. also I,6,2.

point to something across the difference of ontological mode. Or—
what we have seen to be exactly the same—it seeks to signify its
"that which is signified," a perfection found (in varying "modes")
in both God and creatures, in defiance of its own "mode of signifying," which is appropriate only to creatures' mode of being. For we
can get into this relation between God and creatures from one end
only, the creature end. Therefore the first of the two alternatives
open to us in speaking of creatures is not open to us in speaking of
God. We cannot directly speak of God's characters as they inhere in
Him. For God is not available for inspection. He can be known
only from His effects. Only the second alternative is open—the analogous use of words.

We must therefore distinguish between priority in reality and priority in knowledge. In reality the primary intension of an analogous
name is God's nature. If we could know God directly, then our
speech would be analogous only when we extended it to creatures
(as in the second alternative above). But we cannot. Therefore, although in reality God's nature is the primary intension of, let us say,
'good,' in our speaking we must treat as the primary intension
'good' taken as the name of a created inherent reality, and include it
in the definition of the analogous sense which applies to God.
'Good,' used of God, means, for *us* 'the divine creative and fulfilling
prototype of the creaturely quality of doing justice, etc.'

One common misunderstanding must, finally, be prevented. A
word used analogously of God does *not* name an overarching concept under which God and creatures are subsumed. For, as is now
plain, the perfections that such words seek to grasp are not shared by
God and creatures. They are aspects of God—distinguished from
each other as "aspects" only in His condescension to us—shared by
His creatures. This must be reflected in our usage as well. There are,
Thomas says, two patterns of analogy. A word may be used analogously of several realities "either because several entities are all related to some other, as medicine and urine are called 'healthy' insofar as they . . . are related to the health of an animal, of which
one is cause and the other the symptom; or because one entity is
related to another, as medicine and an animal are called 'healthy' in-

sofar as medicine is the cause of the animal's health. And in this latter way only are things predicated analogously of God and creatures. . . ." [116]

IX.

What words, then, can be used analogously of God? We return to the structure of Part I. The section on "What God is" [117] works out, we said, the ontological difference of God and creatures. Certain notions are the operative keys throughout this discussion: "being," "unity," "goodness." Throughout, the arguments turn on decisions about how God *is* what He is, and the decisions are made by using as a criterion the demand for absolute unity and perfection. For the most part, these notions do not themselves become subjects of discussion. But when one, "goodness," does come up, somewhat incidentally, for direct discussion,[118] immediately the discussion of "analogy" is initiated. And at the end Thomas turns to explicit discussion of "Being" as *the* name of God [119]; whereupon the classic treatment of "analogy" occurs.

A word used analogously, we have seen, is one that is somehow meaningful on both sides of the division between God and creatures. Those fundamental terms of ontology which we use in positing the difference are necessarily meaningful on both sides, since we use them precisely to talk about what differentiates both sides. As the key words of ontological discussion they are therefore intrinsically multimodal—that is, analogous. They are words that in order to fulfill their function, in order that we may do what we want with them, must be used analogously: for what we want to do with them is precisely to talk on both sides of the ontological difference, to open ourselves and our language into eschatological fulfillment. This is the only reason we have such words; and if we are to do this with them, we must use them analogously. With "being" we posit our self-transcendence; and with "good" and "one," its goal. There-

116. I,13,5.
117. I,3–13.
118. I,4–6.
119. I,13.

fore "Being" is *the* analogous name of God.[120] And at the next level are "good" and "one."

We can get at the same result from another way. As the primary cause God is the cause of things being at all—so that when we name Him from His effects, "Being" is the name we must use. The concepts of "goodness," "unity" (and "truth": this occupies a middle position between this level and the level next to be described) are "equivalent" with "being." [121] That is, if a thing is, it is in some way good,[122] and it is in some sense a unity [123] (and it is *truly* a being).[124] Thus if it is legitimate to say "God is being," we can go on to say "He is good" and "He is one"—which gives us the same first two levels as above.

Both these lines of thought come together in one passage: "Whence if God is subsistent Being, no perfection can be lacking in Him. For all perfections pertain to the perfection of being: anything is perfect in the way and extent in which it has being." [125]

At the third level are those predicates, which, when we abstract from their mode of signifying, reduce to one of the above, to one of the "transcendent" concepts. These are the names of God's *actions:* [126] "knowledge," "will," "power," "life." In each case the appropriateness of these categories for talking about God is demonstrated by showing how, if their mode of signifying is ignored, they follow from what has already been established about God in the section on "What God is." Thus, for example, that God *knows* is shown by argument that immaterial and knowing entities are the same, and that God's immateriality has been established as part of His simplicity.[127]

Finally, there are those things that can be said of God only metaphorically and not, strictly, analogously. These are those words whose creaturely mode of signifying is part of "that which is signi-

120. I,13,11.
121. *Convertitur cum ente.* Cf. I,16.3.
122. I,5,3.
123. I,11,1.
124. I,16,3.
125. I,4,2.
126. I,14–26.
127. I,14,2.

fied," so that we cannot abstract from it. "Certain names signify perfections . . . in such a way that the imperfect mode in which the creature participates in the divine perfection is itself included in the very signification of the word—thus 'stone' means 'material entity of such and such sort.' Such names cannot be attributed to God except metaphorically." [128] An example suggested by this passage is "God is the Rock of my salvation." Note that Thomas does not say that this statement is false. On the contrary, he would assert that rocks also participate in divine perfections, so that He is exemplar of something in the rock. It is only that our *word* "rock" cannot be reshaped into an (analogous) name for that perfection. Or, what is for Thomas the same, this participation is cognitively opaque to us.

At one extreme, therefore, we have words that, if they are to be used at all, will be used in ontological language and therefore analogously. These are the fundamentally appropriate words for use with 'God.' At the other extreme we have words debarred by the way in which their usage rules are set up: the mode of signifying is not separable from the object spoken about, from being used with 'God' in sentences claiming other than poetic truth. And in between are words whose logic is such that, if for some nonlinguistic reason we want to do so, an extension of meaning can be effected to give them an analogous intension in which they may properly be conjoined to 'God.' [129]

X.

Let us summarize Thomas' specifications of the logic of theological language. He conceives of theological utterances as having the function of positing for us the transcendent goal of existence. In that we speak theologically we secure such a goal. We may say, therefore, that the criterion of theological utterance is whether a given such utterance does in fact open speaker and hearer toward the eschaton, toward the fulfillment of their lives.

128. I,13,3.
129. I confess that I am not as sure of this sentence as I try to be.

But it is clear that such a criterion will work only if we know what the goal of life is—unless, of course, we are willing to have each man create his own goal by his particular language. Such would not be Thomas' game. He is not interested in self-transcendence in some direction or other. He is interested in our self-transcendence toward the Creator and Redeemer of the Bible. Therefore our theological utterances must be descriptive; they must identify and cognitively secure the transcendence to which they point. It is this aspect of theological language that Thomas tries to stipulate in the doctrine of analogy. How does this work?

It is clear that the doctrine of analogy does not provide rules for a special theological language. It directs us to use the ordinary language which we use to make statements about objects, and to make certain special stipulations. Thus 'good' as applied to God means 'the divine creative and fulfilling prototype of what is called "good" in creatures.' In this definition we have the word in its primary intension plus a stipulation of the ontological difference between that which it now names and that which it named in its primary intension—that is, a stipulation of the nonapplicability of its mode of signifying.

Thus, analogous language about God is language operating under directions to use the ordinary object-language, including in one's statements stipulations that the misleading ontological presuppositions of the meaning-rules of that language are to be ignored in some specified way. (It is worth noting that logical statements *about* theological utterance are thus made an essential *part of* theological utterance itself. God cannot be spoken of at all apart from logical-ontological reflections—apart, that is, from our strivings to find meaning. Which brings us back to the first paragraph of this section: the perfect mutual necessity of the parts of Thomas' analysis is amazing.)

We are also provided a criterion for distinguishing predicates logically suitable for use with 'God' from those logically unsuitable. If its mode of signifying is not included in the intension, a word is logically suitable; otherwise it is not. Note that this is a criterion of *logical* appropriateness, not of *material* appropriateness; it is not a rule to the effect that 'God is not such-and-such.' 'God is not a stone' is just as much a use of 'stone' with 'God' as is 'God is a stone.' It is a criterion of what words belong in the series of potential God-predicates at all. Thus it rules out 'God is not a stone' just as much as 'God is a stone.' 'God is good' and 'God is not good' are both left open.

Between options such as this last, the criterion is given by the original situation in which we come to use 'God,' the fundamental posit of a meaning for the things and events of this life which is made by calling them "effects of God." Whether we say 'God is good' or 'God is not good' will depend on what "effects of God" are in fact forthcoming—including both those in nature and history at large and, most especially, those recorded in the Bible. These last must be included and, indeed, preferred, because the 'God' in "effects of God" is exactly the one about whom the Bible speaks. If we wish to speak of some other God, we are playing a different language game from the one Thomas is concerned to understand.

Finally, the verification or falsification of such statements will occur on the day when the transcendent meaning of life is reached (or perhaps not reached). It is this verifiability that makes theological utterance, in Thomas' terms, "argumentative"—that is, continuous with our other descriptive speech.

4. The Continuing Problem

A certain common understanding of language can be found in Origen and Thomas. In both, the ontological difference between God and man makes the ordinary conventions of language inapplicable when we talk of God. Both, in spite of this, posit some sort of likeness of the creatures to God which makes it possible to talk of Him if we use language in a way appropriate to the mode of likeness. In both, belief in this likeness results from the retention of the ancient artisan-prototype-image scheme as the fundamental ontological scheme. Both, therefore, see theological language as able to point to *something* in God that is the prototype of a created perfection, but as not able to specify the relation between the prototype and the image, because our ordinary usage rules do not operate. Both hold that theological language is cognitive. Both are so oriented that we called their language "eschatological."

It is also evident that Origen and Thomas diverge at at least two points: First, for Origen the image that makes speech about God possible is the history of Jesus Christ. Origen may be said to have a "christological logic." This emphasis is wholly absent from Thomas, for whom the image is all created reality. Second, Origen speaks theologically about Christ by moving to a "higher" level of speech, by developing a language, defined by rules of its own, *other* than the normal object-language by which we deal with the things of this world. His language is "spiritual." Thomas does not set out on this path.

Let us first attend to the common pattern and ask whether Origen and Thomas have succeeded in stipulating consistent, explicable, and appropriate rules of theological language.

II.

We must, I believe, conclude that a language operating as Origen and Thomas believed their language operated could not do what they intended it to do. Some of the difficulties are philosophical; others, theological. We will sketch each set in turn.

If, as we have argued, "mode of signifying" is a Thomistic name for the usage rules of an expression, and if, as Thomas asserts, the mode of signifying of our ordinary language is inoperative when this language is used of God, and if, as Thomas further says, the mode of signifying which *would* be appropriate is not available to us, does this not simply mean that there are no rules at all for this use of language? But how then is theological language meaningful? The same question can equally well be asked of Origen.

Both give assurance that what is meant by such language is something really given in God. For Origen this assurance is provided by God's self-involvement in our history; Thomas provides it by defining: 'God' = 'causal prototype of all being.'

But these assurances are helpful only on the assumption that we can *mean* more than we can say. This appears a most dubious assumption. There is indeed a sense in which when I grope for the right utterances, there is something I as a person mean that I cannot yet say (though such cases are fewer than careless use of "Oh, you know what I mean" would imply). But here the question is whether my *utterance* can mean more than it says. Thomas states explicitly that the inapplicability of the mode of signifying does indeed involve just this dubious assumption: "But when we use this name ["wisdom"] of God, we do not intend to signify anything distinct from his essence. . . . Thus when 'wisdom' is predicated of man, it in a certain way describes and comprehends the signified reality—but not so when it is predicated of God. Then it leaves the signified reality as something uncomprehended and beyond the meaning of the word." [1]

Indeed, the whole image-analogy explanation of the meaningfulness of theological utterance seems to be of the same sort as saying that the cause of a fever is "a feverish humor." "Analogy" is hardly the name of a set of usage rules. It is rather simply a name for the difficulty. It hardly establishes a stable position between univocity and equivocity. Rather it simply says, "Theological language must not be either." Thus it points rather to the problem than to a solution.

This does not mean there is anything the matter with 'analogy'; the word is most useful. And there can be no objection to speaking metalinguistically of an expression, or even of a whole language activity, functioning analogously to some other. (Indeed, 'language activity' and even 'expression' are analogues quite in Thomas' sense.) But 'analogy' does *not describe* that function.

III.

The theological objections appear decisive. The image ontology central to the position of both Origen and Thomas arose as the fundamental *myth* in Platonism. Plato achieves a high degree of secularization both in his analyses of the perfection that is the fulfillment and the origin of all reality, and in his analysis of the contingent, unideal character of reality as we first encounter it. It is exactly the *relation* of the two which he did not succeed in demythologizing—if he ever wanted to. Here he remained bound to —or supported by—his religious heritage.

The intermediate realm, in which the two sides of being are united, was for Plato the *demonic* realm. Moreover, this demon is

1. *Summa Theologica*, I, 13, 5. For a thorough and devastating critique of the whole notion of saying more than you say, cf. C. B. Martin, *Religious Belief*, pp. 136–45.

Eros, the dynamism of human life which strives always to overcome all separation.[2] This uniting dynamism "in the center of being" is "a miracle that reason cannot explain, but that preserves the universe. . . ."[3] It can, therefore, be described only by *myth,* only in the language of religion.[4] "Image" was, as a description of a kind of language, Plato's word for myth and, as an ontological category, his name for that reality which only myth can evoke.[5]

"Image" marks, therefore, the precise point of Plato's adherence to the religion of Zeus and Eros, the religion of perfection and of our inborn dynamic striving toward it. It marks, that is, exactly that side of Greek religion which is in flat contradiction to Christian faith: this inborn dynamism is exactly what Paul called "works-righteousness."

Arguments from the historical background of a conception are, of course, always tricky. But this very pattern is actually present in both Thomas and Origen. Thomas' technical precision makes it convenient to begin with him. The gap of mode (of being and so of being signified) between God and creatures is bridged by "being." But is not 'being' an empty word? Does it not make all our "analogous" statements about God vacuous? As the predicate that applies to *everything,* does it, applied to some specific entity, tell us anything about that entity? Clearly not, unless we share certain others of Thomas' fundamental positions. For Thomas 'being' was not an empty word, because he held that 'good,' 'one,' 'true'—and perhaps 'beautiful'—were "convertible" with 'being.' That is, he held the metaphysical doctrine that if a thing *is,* it is *good, one, true,* and *beautiful* (in the mode appropriate to its mode of being); he made the fundamental mythic presupposition that what is and what ought to be are metaphysically one—which is exactly what the Gospel denies. Thomas' image-analogy logic works only on the presup-

2. Cf. especially and obviously, *Symposium.* Friedländer, *Plato,* pp. 41-44, 179 f.

3. Friedländer, op. cit., p. 179.

4. Ibid., pp. 190-207. Cf. in Plato especially the myth of Atlantis and that great myth, the *Timaeus.*

5. Willms, *EIKWN: Eine begriffsgeschichtliche Untersuchung zum Platonismus,* pp. 9-12, 22 f.

position of a position that can only be labeled "epistemological works-righteousness." [6]

For Origen theological speech is telling of Jesus in such a way as to pierce the eschatological barrier and to make explicit the transcendent conclusion of His existence. In terms more directly Origenistic, it is painting a word picture of Him in which His divinity, the transcendent reality in which He is founded, is visible. Theological speech is, therefore, a variety of the Greek artisan's attempt to realize in a concrete existent thing the ideal and transcendent fulfillment of that thing—that is, to transcend in his own act of creativity the division of what is and what ought to be. A claim to portray God in the power of such an act is the same claim to epistemological self-justification we found in Thomas. The terminus of these endeavors is, alas, what Origen said: "The purified intellect, having transcended all that is material in order to perfect the vision of God, is deified by what it beholds." [7] A noble goal—but not the goal of the believer.

Indeed, it must be admitted that the interpretation of Origen in the last chapter is in the best possible light. There is, after all, a constant tendency in Origen to do exactly what we argued he could not consistently do: try to transcend the historical incarnation altogether. Origen's talk about God is perhaps not tied nearly so securely to his historical revelation in Christ as I make it out to be. [8]

6. One of the most effective contemporary defenders of analogy is E. L. Mascall in *Words and Images.* He holds that it is the very virtue of analogy to be the cognitive mode of "unsecularized man," the primitive direct grasp of God and creature in one image prior to any differentiation of immanence and transcendence in the image (pp. 106 ff). Precisely! That is why it is *not* the logic of *faith's* utterance. And what, moreover, if we were, despite all Anglo-Catholic romanticizing, irreversibly secularized men? The same position as Mascall's is developed by H. D. Lewis, *Our Experience of God.*

7. John XXX, 27.

8. I would, in short, *like* to believe Henri de Lubac correct: "If we wish to summarize in one word the spirit of this exegesis, we may say that it is an effort to grasp the spirit in the history, or to assume the movement from history to spirit. This is a double effort . . . for in transcending history it founds it by giving it meaning." *Histoire et Esprit,* p. 278.

The sense of the evangelical histories [9] is not really seen *in* the observable events, but rather by a "mystical vision," "by pure intellectual intuition." [10] The evangelical narratives are mere means of adaptation to those of inferior intuition: "the evangelists wove into the Scripture by means of mere words, as if it were a visible thing, that which in reality was shown to them in a purely intellectual way." Thus the link of meaning and history is so tenuous that Origen can say, "I do not complain when [the Evangelists] change the historical fact . . . for the sake of their mystical purpose. . . . For their task was to be physically and spiritually true at once; when the two will not coincide [!] they prefer the spiritual to the physical. . . ." [11]

I suggest that the root of this painful tension is Origen's identification of "history" with the "physical" side of the Platonic "physical"/"spiritual" dichotomy. Because of this identification his thoroughly evangelical attention to history as the locus of speech about God, and to narrative of history as theologically meaningful by reference to the end and fulfillment of history, constantly slips away into fruitless and arbitrary allegorizing. This identification is closely connected with his use of the Platonic image ontology.

If we turn to the *differences* between Origen and Thomas, we note immediately that they cancel each other out. Origen's christological concentration, whereby we speak of God precisely by speaking of Christ, is undone by Thomas. And Thomas' sober self-restriction to language continuous with our other language is ignored in Origen's flight to ecstatic speech. Moreover, these two circumstances seem connected: Origen can be christocentric precisely because he does not limit his christocentric language to language continuous with our other cognitive language. And Thomas can do this later only by, in all questions of logic, ignoring the basic Christian claim that it is in Christ that we know God. I suggest that this situation amounts to an internal contradiction in the image-

9. ὁ νοῦς τῶν ἱστωρικῶν.
10. τὰ ὑπὸ τοῦ νοῦ . . . τεθεωρημένα.
11. *Commentary on John*, X, 5.

analogy logic, which arises where the attempt is made to speak of
the *Christian* God on its terms.

IV.

But how does it happen that we are so easily able to perceive philosophical and theological pitfalls that remained invisible to Origen
and Thomas? I believe that it is, quite simply, because something
has happened in the meantime to reveal structures of human existence not previously revealed—and, quite probably, to close other
possibilities previously open. More precisely, I believe two closely related things have happened: the triumph of scientific method and
the discovery of the historicity of man's being. In its own way, each
destroyed faith in the metaphysical presuppositions of the image-
analogy analysis.

A scientific hypothesis is by definition held loosely and temporarily, pending further confirmation or disconfirmation. Its truth,
moreover, must be independent of all hopes and commands, of all
evaluations. The enormous success of the cognitive enterprises devoted to the finding and testing of such hypotheses has awakened in
us a salutary suspicion of all eternal verities, and most especially of
those verities whose unchangeableness depends on the supposition
that at the level of eternity the valuable and the factual coincide.

That man is a historic being means that his creativity is not defined
ahead of time, that what ought to be is not determined by what is.
That man is a being of history means that he exists precisely in that
he projects his future, in that in free positing of what must and shall
be, in free positing of the good, he transcends what he is and has
been. It means that he is freed from the shackles of an eternally defined "nature of man": that the coincidence of "being" and "good"
which underlies the entire image-analogy language is revealed as a
prison from which we are called to escape.

We no longer live in a mythically structured reality (whatever
other, perhaps more sinister, delusions we may be prey to); we do
not, and are not allowed to, apprehend images or think in analogies.
The presuppositions of such apprehension have been discovered,

and thereby discredited. Origen and Thomas were spared this discovery—they had problems enough of their own.

V.

Must we then cease theological prattle altogether and either abandon faith or turn it into pure mystical or ethical inwardness? The
course of our discussion certainly seems to lead to this conclusion.
The possibility cannot be easily dismissed. The history of the modern world is a progressive actualization of the first option. And
there is a sense in which all modern theology and, even more, piety
grasp at the second.

Yet another way of looking at the divergence of Origen and
Thomas suggests a different conclusion. We may note that the particular emphases of Origen and Thomas, the emphases we noted as
most particularly Christian yet as mutually incompatible within the
prototype-image scheme, point precisely to the discoveries that have
made the traditional language useless to us. Thomas jealously
guarded the continuity of theological language with ordinary fact-
stating language; he insisted on its reality as an earthly witness to
earthly events. It is precisely this twist in the believer's approach to
existence which is one necessary presupposition of the scientific enterprise—and which functioned historically in just that role. Origen,
for all his platonizing, insisted that *Jesus Christ* was the image of
God, thereby directing man's pursuit of the meaning of life toward
history. Again, there is no doubt that that exclusively Western apprehension of reality we call historical is culturally connected to this
need in Christian speaking.

We shall take, therefore, Thomas' insistence on the informative
character of theological utterances, and Origen's insistence that only
the history of Jesus Christ makes such utterance meaningful, as our
permission to go on with our search and as hints of the directions in
which to look. Their joint understanding of the eschatological function of theological utterances gives a starting point for our search.
We have also an outline for our work: Chapter 5 will deal with
theological language as a putative fact-stating enterprise compared

with the fact-stating enterprise of science; that is, it will follow the track of Anglo-Saxon logical analysis. Chapter 6 will deal with theological language as speech about history and as itself historical event; that is, it will take up the continental concern for hermeneutics. The outcome of our involvement with Origen and Thomas is not, therefore, primarily negative—as will become apparent in detail in the course of the study.

5. Analysis: Verifiability

The positivist fathers of logical analysis dismissed religious discourse out of hand as meaningless, since its utterances are conclusively testable neither by observation nor by deduction. This dismissal remains the hidden background of our worries about the logical status of utterances about God; their dynamic is comparison of theological discourse with scientific discourse. But the form in which the positivists pressed the comparison advanced discussion very little. The verification criterion, applied to theological discourse, is clearly a metaphysical dogma. Why, after all, must all informative utterances be either empirically testable or analytic? As a dogma the criterion leaves us, on the one hand, with nothing to say, yet on the other hand is all too easy to dismiss. For while believers, of all people, cannot object simply because the verification principle is a dogma, we can justly point out that it is only a rival dogma to our own, and that, moreover, a dogma that says all dogmas are meaningless is an oddity.

We may say, therefore, that serious analysis of religious discourse began only in 1944 with John Wisdom's paper entitled "Gods."[1] He

1. Now available in Antony Flew, ed., *Logic and Language,* First Series, Basil Blackwell, Oxford, 1951, pp. 194–214, from which I will cite.

accepted from the positivists that God can no longer be seen as "an experimental issue." That is, a believer does not *necessarily* expect any occurrences in the world not expected by unbelievers; his statements are not hypotheses verifiable by future experience. Wisdom tells a fateful parable to make this point. "Two people return to their long neglected garden and find among the weeds a few of the old plants surprisingly vigorous. One says to the other 'It must be that a gardener has been coming and doing something about these plants.' Upon inquiry they find that no neighbor has ever seen anyone at work in their garden. The first man says to the other 'He must have worked while people slept.' The other says 'No, someone would have heard him and besides, anybody who cared about the plants would have kept down these weeds.' The first man says 'Look at the way these are arranged. There is purpose and a feeling for beauty here. I believe that someone comes, someone invisible to mortal eyes. I believe that the more carefully we look the more we shall find confirmation of this.' They examine the garden ever so carefully and sometimes they come on new things suggesting that a gardener comes and sometimes they come on new things suggesting the contrary and even that a malicious person has been at work. Besides examining the garden carefully they also study what happens to gardens left without attention. Each learns all the other learns about this and about the garden. Consequently, when after all this, one says 'I still believe a gardener comes' while the other says 'I don't' their different words now reflect no difference as to what they have found in the garden, no difference as to what they would find in the garden if they looked further and no difference about how fast untended gardens fall into disorder. At this stage, in this context, the gardener hypothesis has ceased to be experimental, the difference between one who accepts and one who rejects it is now not a matter of the one expecting something the other does not expect." [2]

Suppose we accept this parable. What will come of accepting it depends on how disabled we think an utterance is by not being experimentally adjudicable. If we are very impressed by scientific dis-

2. Flew, *Logic and Language*, pp. 194–96, 200 f.

course as a paradigm of knowledge—as in my view we ought to be
—we may be tempted to take the point of the parable so: Since the
one who says something like "There is a good God" does not
thereby predict any occurrences in the world other than those expected also by one who says, "There is no God," or even by one
who says, "There is a malicious God," he does not by his utterance
communicate to me any information about what is in fact so. Such
utterances are informationally empty; and since they pretend to
communicate information, are to be rejected as pseudo-propositions.
Anthony Flew will adapt the parable to just this point and so press
home—in salutary fashion—the dominance of the scientific paradigm.[3]

But Wisdom does not use the parable in this way. He does not
conclude that there is *no* issue between the believer and the unbeliever, so that the believer asserts nothing about what is so. Instead, he asks whether there may be a *nonexperimental* issue between them.

The one *applies the name* 'God' in his description of the pattern
found in the garden; the other does not: ". . . and with this difference in what they say about the gardener goes a difference in how
they feel about the garden, in spite of the fact that neither expects
anything of it which the other does not expect."[4] Moreover, such an
application of a name to manifest an attitude, though it cannot be
experimentally tested, can very well concern what is so. There are
many disputes that cannot be settled by new experience, yet in them
one assertion is right and another is wrong, and, moreover, about
the facts. Wisdom cites, as chief paradigm of such an issue, disputes
in courts of law about whether Jones, of whose conduct there is an
agreed-upon record, was or was not "negligent" in so behaving. The
issue will be argued by tracing and retracing the *pattern* of the facts,
by comparing other records of behavior to bring out missed connections of the facts or to debunk unduly stressed connections. The
matter will be settled by a ruling of the judge, a ruling that is neither direct deduction nor precipitated by new observations, yet is not

arbitrary. For it has been arrived at by rational procedures and settles the issue of "what happened." [5] Just so "The world has a benevolent Gardener" can be argued by rational procedures, which lead to our taking a position much as a judge gives a verdict.

Along the way Wisdom has rejected a possible suggestion, which later, when it was actually made, he denied explicitly.[6] This suggestion will arise if someone uses the parable to argue that believers fail to make any genuine assertions, and someone replies by admitting this but claiming that "really" they are not trying to do that but are rather doing something else: expressing an attitude and stating a commitment to a certain way of living. Antony Flew did the first in the opening essay of a group of short essays, which have since, under the title "The University Discussion," become with only partial justice the center of discussion of these issues.[7] A whole parade of writers have done the second.

Flew stretches the parable out, to display the way in which the believer retreats step by step from an original robustly factual assertion. The two watch to detect the gardener. Nothing is seen. The believer suggests the gardener may be invisible. So fences, bloodhounds, etc., are used, with no results. The believer then says the gardener is inaudible and intangible as well. At last the skeptic despairs: "But what remains of your original assertion? Just how does what you call an invisible, intangible, eternally elusive gardener differ from an imaginary gardener . . . ?" The fine bold propositions of theology are doomed to the "death of a thousand qualifications" by our refusal to allow anything to count against them. If all possible states of affairs are consistent with an utterance—and those about God seem to be held by believers in just this way—then how does that utterance assert anything? [8]

Flew is really pointing to two difficulties, though he does not

5. Wisdom, op. cit., pp. 202 f.; and Wisdom, "Religious Belief," *Paradox and Discovery*, pp. 43-56, p. 54.
6. "Religious Belief," pp. 50-54.
7. Now in Antony Flew and Alasdair MacIntyre, ed., *New Essays in Philosophical Theology*, pp. 96-130.
8. Antony Flew, "Theology and Falsification—A," *New Essays . . .* , pp. 96-99.

clearly say so. We may imagine a conversation: "God is loving." "What do you mean?" "He behaves to me as my father used to." "What did your father do?" "He cared for me—and just so I have been cared for all my life." "Well, that's true enough. But it seems to me that it's your wife and friends and Social Security, that care for you. I don't see God cooking in the kitchen." "God works invisibly through people, through my wife and the others." "They are his tools?" "Not quite, more like partners." "I will go and ask if God has told them to care for you, or if they are doing it of themselves." "Fine, but remember that God's promptings are voiceless and that by them He gives true freedom, so you mustn't contrast 'God told them' with 'of themselves.'" "But then why drag God in at all?"

The difficulty here is with identifying God, with securing the admission into discourse of 'God' as a word with a referent of its own. Perhaps 'God' is but a certain *way* of referring to the same reality to which 'the world,' or perhaps 'the order of the world,' refers—or 'people' or 'I-Thou relationships.' But then it certainly is tempting to say that 'God is good' differs from 'It is good that the world is orderly' or from 'It is good to know others deeply' only in providing a special vehicle for expressions of this approving attitude, and says nothing more about what is so.

Now suppose the conversation had continued so: ". . . I have been cared for all my life." "It doesn't seem so to me. Here you are —sick. Now if your father were alive, would he cure you if he could?" "Of course." "Then why doesn't God if He is so father-like?" "Well, God's love is different from merely human love. It isn't incompatible with his allowing suffering." "What *is* it incompatible with?"

The difficulty here is the uncontrollability that seems to afflict the things we say *about* God, as soon as it is about God that we say them. If the first difficulty could be overcome and God identified, this difficulty *might* persist, depending on what means had been used to introduce 'God'—we will come to this last point later. How does 'God loves us' differ from 'God hates us' if all states of affairs in our lives and world are compatible with both? And if the two utterances do not differ, how does either assert anything about what is so? Are they not perhaps merely expressions of varying *responses* to what is so?

Of those who answer Flew's challenge by accepting the possibility I have just posed, we will mention only a selection. R. M. Hare replied in the same series of articles [9] that it seemed to him if theological sentences were to be taken as factual hypotheses, they would be empty. But, said Hare, this is not their true function at all. Rather, religious utterances express a "blik." To indicate what he meant by this coinage, Hare told several more or less helpful parables, the point of all of which is that two people may agree entirely on the facts yet be in genuine opposition. If I may put Hare's point rather less ambiguously than he does, and take a more current example: the anticommunist sees the same Russian moves that the liberal interprets as signs of Russian relaxation, as so many evidences of their diabolical cleverness. Neither position can be moved by evidence, since all possible eventualities can be favorably interpreted by either side. Yet we should scarcely call the utterances expressing these positions meaningless. They are not factually meaningful, but they are not thereby discredited. They are meaningful as expressions of a blik, which is a deeper level of meaning than factual assertion. For a blik is a policy toward the world prior to and presupposed by all knowledge about the world. And the utterances that express such a policy necessarily will be unverifiable and unfalsifiable: for included in the policy they express will be a decision about what is to count as verification in the first place. The main example of a blik is the normal man's insistence on correlating the items of his experience, expressed in the blik expression that every event has a cause. Religious utterance is of this sort: unfalsifiable but of fundamental import.[10]

Paul Schmidt puts the matter with admirable flatness: ". . . the

9. R. M. Hare, "Theology and Falsification—B," *New Essays . . .* , pp. 99–103.

10. It is plain that this position is essentially the same as that of R. B. Braithwaite in *An Empiricist's View of the Nature of Religion,* possibly the most famous statement of this general view. A summary of this line of analysis is provided by W. T. Blackstone, *The Problem of Religious Knowledge,* pp. 73–107.

primary purpose of religious language is to produce certain attitudes in oneself and in others."[11] Religious language *evokes* and *invokes* attitudes.[12] Assertions enter into religious language only because opinions are a principle means of forming attitudes. Schmidt distinguishes between "beliefs-in" and "beliefs-that." One "believes in" Jones and "believes that" he is, for example, honest. *Faith* is then a religiously significant set of beliefs-in: that is, a set determinative of basic attitudes. It is plain that beliefs-in involve beliefs-that; belief *in* Jones involves at least belief *that* he is trustworthy. The beliefs-that associated with a set of beliefs-in and so with a particular faith may be more or less well verified, or perhaps unverifiable. It is at this point, several steps removed from the center, that we may speak of religious *knowledge* and of the greater or lesser rational justification possessed by a given body of religious language.[13]

Finally we should mention Hepburn's comparisons of religious language to poetry.[14] Poetic imagination and, possibly, religious imagination dissolve the familiar pattern we make of experience, and make new ones. In both cases the creation of new patterns of experience has the object of greater integration. Poetry and religious language are symbol-structures through which experience can be grasped as not miscellaneous but integrated: ". . . the ideal aim is the total transformation of a life's 'happenings' from a 'meaningless' succession of events into a purposive, coherent movement. . . ."[15] Now poetry's absurdity-overcoming provision of symbols is free creation; that of religious language claims to be *response* to characters of the situation. Thus the slant on reality embodied in a religious language is not an autonomous blik; it must somehow *fit* reality to be appropriate. Which is not to say that it must be a *reflection* of reality: perhaps there are alternative realities, and religious utterance in the making of the choice. Hepburn himself, it should be said, is skeptical of ever coming to utterances about *God* by this route and commends a religious language that is the telling of a

11. Schmidt, *Religious Knowledge*, p. 77.
12. Ibid., pp. 81 ff.
13. Ibid., pp. 78 ff.
14. Ronald Hepburn, *Christianity and Paradox*, pp. 138–48.
15. Ibid., p. 140.

parable of a way of life. The religious quest is then the ceaseless refinement of the parable, converging on an "imaginary ideal focus"
which stands where "God" does in "dogmatic" religion.[16]

There is clearly an element of truth in these analyses. It is surely
right that theological utterances are not *hypotheses* about something. He who prays or hymns or proclaims is engaged in a different language project from that of describing facts in an experimentally testable way. It may seem that this point is so obvious that it
was no great service to make it. Yet it is constantly forgotten by
church-goers who sit in the pews exactly as if attending a lecture,
and even more by the preachers who in fact deliver lectures instead
of preaching and officiate instead of leading in worship.

As to what this other project or projects might be, all these suggestions are excessively vague. This is, I suggest, because they have
no actual body of theological utterances clearly in mind as the object
of their analysis. They are, of course, thinking primarily of Christianity. Yet to make their view plausible they must abstract from the
actual things that believers in Christ say. For the entire starting
point of this analysis—that theological utterances are not "really" intended as assertions—cannot by any means be made plausible of
specifically Christian utterances.

No analysis of religious language exclusively in terms of blik-
evocations or the like, no analysis that says that religious utterances
are not "really" assertions, is even remotely satisfactory as an analysis of the language of Christian faith. The first and simplest reason
is that it is descriptively inaccurate to say: "No assertions are being
made here. Something else is being done." Believers constantly
make assertions, genuine or pseudo. None of the proposals we have
just outlined is really an analysis of what is in fact said by believers.
They are proposals that we stop saying that kind of thing on the
grounds that we cannot thereby accomplish what we intend, and
that we devote our speaking energies to some other language enterprise. And this *other* language enterprise is then analyzed.

16. Peter Munz, *Problems of Religious Knowledge,* gives another view of
this type. Religious knowledge is, he says, perfectly straightforward rational
knowledge about the "symbol-picture" of the world, which is the picture
where we do not abstract from the existential.

It may well be that these proposals have merit. But they are not at all analyses of the actual language of what people call faith. Stead has put it very neatly: "Whereas the theologian professes to use symbolic statements, making obscure but would-be informative references to heavenly mysteries, and having ethical overtones, the skeptical philosopher regards the mythological elements as logically non-significant; so that the ethical element is the only element he can recognize. This is rather as if one should say of a machine whose function one does not appreciate, that all it does is to generate a little heat by friction. This is understandable, but may be misleading. It will not do to say that a roulette-wheel is really a kind of stove." [17] What ought to be said is: "This is for gambling—and that is to be disapproved of."

The general argument of all these proposals is clearly circular in the vicious way: "The logic of religious language is in order—if we strip it to its essential content." "And what is this essential content?" "The part whose logic is in order." Or, as C. B. Martin has remarked, this kind of theism could make theists of us all—and so what? [18] The root of the confusion is in the very method employed. "I have . . . to show how the different types of religious statements . . . refer to attitudes rather than to the heterogeneous things they seem to refer to," said Schmidt.[19] But what can the distinction of "seeming to . . . " and "really . . ." mean applied to *referring?*

In any case, it is plain that the blik analysis misses the use of *Christian, theological* utterances entirely—whatever may be true of "religious language." Schmidt's "To pray for peace is to invoke attitudes on our part that will lead to peace" [20] is for a believer in Christ the reduction to absurdity of the whole approach. Religious language, functioning as reductionist analysts describe it, is a perfectly justifiable and internally meaningful language game; the believer will simply not choose to play it. For within Christian theological language the fundamental utterances, evocative or expressive as they are, are all historical *narratives.* Thus: ". . . and in Jesus

17. Stead, p. 113.
18. C. B. Martin, *Religious Belief,* p. 16.
19. Schmidt, op. cit., p. 89.
20. Ibid., p. 87.

Christ . . . who was conceived, born . . . , suffered. . . ." "Our
Lord Jesus Christ, in the night in which He was betrayed . . ."
Even apparently non-narrative hymns, prayers, and blessings turn
narrative in the "who . . ." clauses, as "Oh Lord, who hast given
thine only Son that . . . , " and will conclude with that compressed
narrative of the whole Christian story: ". . . in the name of the Father and of the Son and of the Holy Ghost." And the sole Christian
reality for which uniqueness is claimed is the "Gospel," which is
simply the story of Jesus told as the story of things done by God.
Thus it is only *as* historical narrative that Christian God-language
evokes or expresses whatever it evokes or expresses. The same point
can be made by the simple observation that in the "Gospel"—that is,
the central type of Christian theological utterances—God is spoken
of always in the third person.

Christian utterances about God operate to posit an attitude to life
exactly *as* narrative language. As a consequence the question of their
truth or falsity cannot be declared irrelevant—whatever may be their
evocative efficiency. For here the speaking that posits the ends of life
does so not by free choice or invention but by a narration that is
either justified as cognition of the course of events or not at all.
Hepburn had pointed out that talk of speech which "posits a final
unity to life" is ambiguous.[21] For the power of words to overcome
the antinomies of life is sometimes autonomous in respect to the
actual situation, sometimes *not*. Poetry is autonomous: it need not
be correct in order to fulfill its transforming function for us. But if
theological language is simply poetry, it is nonsense poetry.[22] A
creatively fictional narrative and a narrative that pretends to be factual but is not are not the same sort of thing. The first is a game we
may, and sometimes ought to, play; the second is a fixed game, a
game for suckers.

If, with Wisdom, we reject the suggestion that religious utterances are not really assertions, we are back with his position: religious utterances, unless they are nonsense, express an attitude and
precisely *so* say something that can be right or wrong about what

21. "Poetry and Religious Belief," pp. 138–48.
22. Ibid., pp. 81–103.

the case is. Wisdom develops this in later essays. With parables and oblique remarks, he hints at the variety of ways there are for words to reveal the truth: as when a woman is trying on a hat, there is a pause, "and then a friend says in tones too clear, 'My dear, it's the Taj Mahal.' Instantly the look of indecision leaves the face in the mirror." [23] Some of these ways, like "It's the Taj Mahal," hardly are utterances that could be verified by collecting new data or by some definite deductive procedure—indeed, it is humorous to suggest seeking either—and yet they are statements about what is so. ". . . It is submitted that questions which neither further observation . . . nor yet further thought will settle may yet present real problems and even problems as to matters of fact. It is submitted that questions 'which have no answers' may yet present problems which have solutions. . . ." [24]

It is clear that there are questions that cannot be settled by new observations, yet that are questions of fact. The accountant who has before him all the facts he needs, can still face a real question whether the firm is solvent. He has to find the statement that grasps the situation—in a fashion somewhat analogous to "It's the Taj Mahal." Yet the accountant can usually settle his issue by a definite deductive procedure.[25] Statements about God cannot be settled in this way. Are there cases analogous to the case of God, where neither observation nor deduction can settle the issue, yet where we can see how a matter of fact is at issue?

Here Wisdom returns repeatedly to his favorite paradigm of the law court: ". . . when lawyers argue before a court such a question as 'Was there negligence or not?' 'Was there consent to risk or was there not?', then those lawyers and that court . . . aim at the truth. Such questions . . . may be argued when 'we all know what happened.' . . . On such occasions no further observation . . . will settle the matter." And a step-by-step procedure, such as that of the accountant, is not always available to the court. Yet its question *can be*

23. Wisdom, "The Logic of God", *Paradox and Discovery*, pp. 1–22, pp. 2–6.

24. *Paradox and Discovery*, introduction.

25. "The Logic of God," p. 6; "Religious Belief," pp. 43–56, p. 54.

argued and is "directed towards a firmer, fairer apprehension of what it was that happened." [26]

Thus 'What is the meaning of all things?' is a real question despite the logical absurdity of pointing to something and saying "The meaning is this." When a play eludes us by its complex or allusive plot, we ask "What does it mean?" And there are ways of going about finding the solution—as a child who has grasped a simple play and is stumped by a more complex one, can ask "What does it mean?" as a request for help in performing in this case the "sort of movement of the mind" successfully achieved earlier. "In the same way when we ask 'What is the meaning of all things?' we are not asking a senseless question. In this case, of course, we have not witnessed the whole play. . . . But with the words 'What is the meaning of it all?' we are trying to find the order in the drama of Time. The question may be beyond us . . ." but is not therefore meaningless, any more than when asked by the child about a play that is too complex for him.[27]

Does evil and unloving power only determine human destiny? "Or is there also at work a good and loving power?" To this question, the claim that God Himself has dwelt in history, "in the body of Jesus," is a kind of answer. The claim may be obscure, but it can be investigated.[28] "Was there such a person as Jesus is alleged to have been?" Who did what He is supposed to have done? And then: "How far does the rest of experience show that what this man said is true? Did what Jesus said reveal what we hadn't known or what we had known but hadn't recognized?" Besides this kind of investigation, the question calls for reflection. "He made himself the Son of God. 'Preposterous presumption' the priest said, but was it the truth? The facts agreed upon, still a question is before the bar of reason, as when, the facts agreed upon, still a question comes before a court." The question "calls for very careful consideration and not the less when what's relevant is conflicting and not the less when

26. "Religious Belief," op. cit., p. 54.
27. "The Meanings of the Questions of Life," *Paradox and Discovery*, pp. 38–42, pp. 40 f.
28. "The Logic of God," pp. 19 f.

what's relevant is not enumerable because there is not a separate name for every relevant feature. . . ."[29] "Was Jesus God incarnate? . . . The question is . . . slippery. . . . But it is not true that nothing is more relevant to it than another, so that nothing supports one answer more than it supports the other. On the contrary, every incident in the life of Christ is relevant . . . ," as is, above all, their pattern.[30]

Moreover, an affirmative answer to this question implies the existence of God. "And to this question every incident in the history of the world is relevant. . . ."[31]

It cannot be said that Wisdom has done much more for his claim that religious utterances at once express an attitude and tell the truth about reality than to set it off with comparisons. Yet perhaps this is the main thing that can be done. And his comparisons are very illuminating. Indeed, they seem to me already to suggest most of the notions we will find to be keys in this chapter: the *verdictive* character of theological utterances; the idea that what the verdict is about is something like the meaning of a *play;* and locating the relevant considerations for or against a particular verdict by way of the claims the Gospel makes about Jesus.

Let me at this point begin a further development of one of these notions. Grasping the meaning of a *drama* is the paradigm case in which we know something that is so by a movement of the mind that can also be described as the expression of an attitude. When we speak of grasping the meaning of a play, there are doubtless many factors involved, not all of them necessarily present in any one act we would so name. But surely one thing we very often mean is that we grasp the *unity* of the play, that seeing or reading it is, or has become, perhaps in memory, what we call "an experience."[32] We see how its parts fit together, or rather, we experience them as parts.

29. Ibid., pp. 20 f.
30. Ibid., pp. 21 f.
31. Ibid., p. 21.
32. I take over this expression for this purpose from John Dewey, *Art as Experience.* In general my thinking here is influenced strongly by this work.

How do the parts of a play fit together? Again, presumably, in many ways. But one fundamental pattern is surely the pattern of *expectations* raised and satisfied. An incident or speech or inflection leads us to hope for something, or fear something, from the future— or perhaps to be puzzled by our inability to hope or fear—and this expectation is then satisfied or disappointed in a particular way by later incidents. Finally the expectations aroused have all come to rest, no further projection of the future takes place, and we say we are at the conclusion of the piece. Just so it presents itself as an experience.

Surely it is just such a particular pattern of expectations and satisfactions or disappointments, making certain events an experience, that is what we mean by *an emotion*. If our act of experiencing the pattern is itself partly a language act, it is of such an utterance that we will say it is "expressive." In a case where the object of the experience is itself an utterance—a play is one case—the emotion will be the appropriate act of knowing the object, and our expressive utterance will at once express our attitude to the object and say something so or not so about it. Talk of dramatic unity or dramatic appropriateness is the paradigm for talk that is indivisibly both informative and expressive of attitudes.

To say that a theological utterance is a verdict upon the meaning of "the drama of Time" is to connect two suggestions that Wisdom himself does not explicitly connect. Let us make the connection and return to Wisdom to ask what sorts of consideration might tell for or against a particular verdict, such as that there is a good and loving Gardener. Wisdom's reflections on this point are found in a dialogue—the form is no doubt chosen to avoid final commitment to the suggestions advanced. I will schematize drastically.

That the world shows some order—we may say, that it can be compared to a play—is prerequisite to the meaningfulness of talk about God. But to say there is a God is not merely to say that nature is orderly. To say there is God, and a God who is thus-and-so, is to say that the world's order has a certain character. "The order of nature might have been of a character which would make it fair to say, 'It is all in the hands of someone who made it and then fell asleep' or, 'It's all in the hands of someone who arranges these little ironies of fate.' " [33] When we say instead, "There is a good and loving Gardener," we assert quite a different sort of order of events.

But is there any "agreement as to what to look for . . . , as to what the character of the order of events must be to count in favour of . . ." such an utterance as 'There is a good God' ? "If there were no agreement, that would make the question meaningless. But it is not true that there is no agreement. One could describe a future for the world which were it to come would prove the triumph of the Devil. . . . Descriptions of heaven are apt to be . . . extremely hazy. . . . But it's not true that we haven't a clue about the kingdom of heaven. . . . We don't know what would be heaven and this shows itself in . . . our feeble grasp of what . . . we want to do with the words, 'Will the kingdom of heaven come?' 'Does God exist?' But this doesn't prove that there isn't anything we want to do with them." [34]

It is impossible to avoid seeing it: Wisdom views the verification of theological utterances as eschatological. It is when Time is complete, when all events are presented to us as one great drama, that the issue of God will be settled: ". . . as the scroll of nature unrolls, the proof of an eternal God prevails—or fails—until on the day of judgement doctrine, like theory, must become a verdict and all be lost or won." [35]

Wisdom's understanding of the eschatological character of Christian theological utterance is, perhaps, a little surprising. It reflects both the extent to which Christian theological utterances are— perhaps partly unintended—the exclusive object of his analyses, and the sensitivity of his view of them. To be sure, rather more questions remain open than is acceptable even granting Wisdom's aversion to definition. Our descriptions of heaven are perhaps even hazier than he supposes, hazy enough to make reapplying Flew's kind of criticism salutary also here—and when a more developed notion of "eschatological verification" has been introduced, I will do

33. "The Logic of God," op. cit., pp. 13–24.
34. Ibid., p. 16.
35. Ibid.

just that.[36] Here let me merely pose some issues that will occupy us throughout the remainder of this chapter and the next, by baldly asserting: Only by a far more precise and radical stipulation of the relation between the two dramas to which Wisdom refers, the story of Jesus Christ and the whole drama of Time, will we in fact do anything useful with our "descriptions of heaven." But to get to the point where we can discuss this efficiently, there are other vital matters to clear up, and we turn to these.

II.

It is evident that the logic of all this is so far very vague indeed. How does an utterance go about "doing" two things at once? Does it do them in the same sense of 'do'? What senses of 'do' apply to utterances? What does 'expresses an attitude' mean?

Fortunately the means are at hand for making some progress toward clarity, in the work of J. L. Austin: his doctrine of the *locutionary, illocutionary,* and *perlocutionary* acts distinguishable in any uttering; and his careful investigations of the kinds of illocutionary acts.[37] Moreover, the task of applying these classifications to the analysis of theological utterance has been tentatively undertaken, not by Austin himself, but by Donald Evans, in *The Logic of Self-Involvement.*[38] Most of our direct discussion will be with Evans, though where he departs from Austin's own terminology, we will always substitute it.

In Austin's classification the "locutionary" meaning of an utterance is what it says. Its "illocutionary" force is the particular character of the *act* that is the *saying* of it; the illocutionary act is what one does in saying something. An utterance's "perlocutionary" effect is what is, or perhaps is not, *caused* by the saying of it.[39] In particular, Austin's great contributions are the isolation, with some preci-

36. See below, pp. 146–150.

37. See, above all, J. L. Austin, *How To Do Things with Words.*

38. I will select drastically from the matter of Evans' wide-ranging, not to say scattered, reflections.

39. *How To Do Things with Words,* especially pp. 94–107.

sion, of the illocutionary act as one facet of the act of speaking, and the classification of various illocutions.

He began with his famous discussions of what he called "performatives." [40] These are utterances where what is spoken about is performed in the act of speaking. Thus before the dignitary says at a launching, "I name this ship U.S.S. *Himalaya*," the ship has no name; afterward it has this name exactly; and the ship's acquisition of this name is the same event as the dignitary's act of uttering.

The relevance of this discussion to the logic of theological utterances is immediately apparent, and we will interrupt our report of Austin to point to it. A confession of faith, for example, is not a neutral factual report about the state of my beliefs; it is the believing. When the liturgical recitation of the Creed begins, I do not stop, examine my stock of opinions, and, in the unlikely event that these coincide exactly with those stated in the text of the Apostles' or Nicene creeds, adopt this text for making a report to God and the assembly. Why should such a report be wanted anyway? Rather, the act of recitation is the act of faith itself. So also a benediction is not only the priest's attempt to describe God's attitude toward those present; it is the *exercise* of that attitude. "I baptize you in the name of the Father, Son and Holy Spirit" is not a sort of radio commentary on what the priest is doing—self-delivered! It is the very doing. [41]

Deeper analysis led Austin to the insight that *all* utterances have some force of this sort, for which he coined the term "illocutionary force." This cleared the way for a detailed classification of illocutions. [42]

Constative utterances, such as 'I state that the cat is on the mat' or, with the constative force not explicit, 'The cat is on the mat,' have a content that is properly evaluated solely as true or false, accurate or inaccurate. The chief insight here is that making such an utterance is also but one sort of illocutionary act: I estimate, guess, warn, state, etc.

40. Austin, "Performative Utterances," *Philosophical Papers,* pp. 220–39.
41. Cf., oddly enough, Martin, op. cit., pp. 128 ff.
42. Austin, *How To Do Things with Words,* pp. 147–63; Evans, *The Logic of Self-Involvement,* pp. 30–40. The following is a mixture of Austin's, Evans', and my own classifications.

A *commissive* utterance commits me to a specified future behavior: for example, 'I pledge you my loyalty' or, with the commissive force stipulated by context, 'I will be loyal.' Such an utterance has an abstractable content: here 'The speaker will be loyal.' But within the commissive utterance itself this content is not appropriately judged as true or false, correct or incorrect. If I pledge my loyalty, then I do, and so do in saying so. I may be insincere but can be held to the pledge nevertheless. The commissive utterance can only be judged, later, as fulfilled or unfulfilled.

Such an utterance as 'I christen this ship U.S.S. *Himalaya*' is *exercitive*. Within some conventional or institutional structure I exercise authority and so bring about a conventional or an institutional state of affairs exactly in that I say what I say. It is not appropriate to ask whether the utterance is true, whether the ship really has this name. Supposing the requisite structures of authority are present and duly followed, what I say exercitively is so simply because I say it.

Behabitive force is especially important to theological utterance, according to Evans. In uttering behabitively I take up an attitude toward the person addressed or to what is talked about: for example, 'I love you.' Theological examples flock to mind: 'We glorify thee, O Lord,' or, with the behabitive force stipulated by context, 'The Lord is glorious.' Some, though not all, behabitives have an abstractable content which is properly judged as true or false: for example, 'I commend you for your self-restraint,' where 'You are self-restrained' is true or false. Yet even if this content is false, an attitude is still adopted toward the supposed state of affairs, which distinguishes such a behabitive from a constative.[43]

Verdictive utterances are such as 'I rate Jones above Smith' or 'I find you guilty.' Like an exercitive, such an utterance is, in part, true because the utterer says so, authoritatively. A convict is guilty partly because the judge and the jury have found him so. Yet while an exercitive utterance cannot be challenged by appeal to the kind of facts that obtain independently of the utterance in question and could be stated by a pure constative, a verdictive utterance can. For if the prisoner was in fact at home in bed at the time of the murder, he is

43. This account is partly my own—not Austin's or Evans'!

innocent no matter what the judge says. And if this is ascertained, the verdict will be overturned. "In a verdictive utterance, I say what *is* so; in an exercitive utterance, I authoritively say what is to *be* so. . . ." [44] Yet verdictives differ from constatives in that a constative can be accepted or rejected by some agreed procedure, whereas the issue raised by verdictives can only be settled by a method that depends on the conventional authority of the speaker.

We have repeatedly referred to context as determining the illocutionary force of an utterance. Some utterances stipulate their own illocutionary force by their form of words: for example, 'I pledge you my loyalty.' Here the context that determines the illocutionary force is the language itself with all its conventions. Most utterances, perhaps, depend on a narrower context. 'Smith will be loyal' may be a commissive or may be a constative prediction made by a third party or even, in a moment of reflection, by Smith—depending on the circumstances of the utterance. Evans rightly points out that such a context may be an *occasion* or a linguistic *tradition*. Thus 'Jones is guilty' is exercitive when said by the jury foreman on the occasion of reporting, and is constative when said by the same man at home to his wife. 'God is good' is behabitive and commissive said by someone brought up in the Christian tradition, but may not be said by an animist of his high god. [45]

It is important to note that a particular utterance may have more than one illocutionary force, as 'You are the most beautiful woman in the world' might be in context behabitive, commissive, and verdictive at once. We must also note the variety and complexity of the relations that obtain between the illocutionary meanings of our utterances and the facts. We must look at these.

Some behabitives have no abstractable content. Other behabitives and all verdictives have a factual content that is true or false independently of the behabitive or verdictive utterance. What part of the content of a verdictive can be taken independently of the making of the verdict varies from case to case. The factual content of an exerci-

44. *The Logic of Self-Involvement,* p. 36.
45. Ibid., pp. 50–55. It must be said that Evans' presentation of these matters is rather confused.

tive is a state of affairs that is, within the operative conventional or institutional structure of authority, objectively the case, yet depends solely on the exercitive utterance of which it is the content. The abstractable content of a commissive will on some other occasion be testable as true or false, but not as an element of the commissive utterance.

Moreover, utterances of all illocutionary sorts also have factual presuppositions. 'I apologize' presupposes that an addressee exists and that I have behaved boorishly to him. 'We praise thee, O Lord' presupposes that there is a being appropriately addressed as 'Lord.'[46]

I think we can at this point connect these observations to some earlier reflections. Plainly, every particular actual utterance, in its particular context, is determined within a web of illocutionary forces and factual contents and presuppositions which is unique. Every utterance is also in one connection or another one event in a network of events of the sort we called "an experience." I suggest that its location in some segment of its whole pattern of illocutionary forces and factual contents and presuppositions will be the same as its location in the pattern of expectations and fulfillments which are the unity of that experience. A complete analysis of an utterance's illocutionary forces would also be a description of the unity of the experience to which it belongs, and so of the emotion it expresses.

Evans develops two other notions which will be fundamental to his use of Austin for the analysis of theological utterances; and we must sketch these next. "If I were to ask 'What is your attitude to death . . . ?' your replies would not naturally be preceded by the phrase, 'In my opinion.' Rather you would say something like: 'I look on death as the mockery of human hopes (or as the gateway to a higher form of life). . . ."[47] An utterance translatable into this 'I look on . . . as . . .' form Evans calls an "onlook." An onlook has a commissive force; in such an utterance I declare a policy: for example, 'I look on Egypt's needs as the key to the situation.' It evidently has behabitive force and is the kind of behabitive with an

46. *The Logic of Self-Involvement*, pp. 34–36.
47. Ibid., p. 125.

abstractable content: for example, 'Egypt's needs are the key to the situation.' Moreover, the abstractable content of this behabitive force is in turn of the sort whose truth or falsity is declarable only as a verdict, a finding of the appropriateness of the commissive statement of policy to the object of the onlook. Thus an onlook has verdictive force also. This particular mutual dependence of several illocutionary forces defines an onlook.[48]

Some onlooks are "literal": I refrain from a simple constative utterance only because I do not *know* that x is y, or because x is not *yet* y; but 'x is y' is, either now or when the time comes, straightforwardly verifiable. Such are 'I look on Jones as a friend' or 'I look on Jones as our next president.' But some onlooks presuppose that 'x is y' would, if taken in its straightforwardly verifiable sense, not be true: for example, 'I look on Jones as a son.' Nevertheless such an utterance is not a mere metaphor, for it is a verdict that the policy of fatherlike behavior is appropriate to the object Jones. "When we use the formula 'look on x as y,' we assume that there is an appropriate way of thinking and behaving in relation to y, judge that it is appropriate also to x, and declare our intention so to proceed."[49]

There are several sorts of nonliteral onlooks. One such as 'I look on all Tories as vermin' says that the attitude appropriate to vermin is also appropriate to Tories, but suggests no independently evaluable reasons why this should be so. Evans calls such onlooks "parabolic." 'I look on students as parasites,' on the other hand, suggests "an independent similarity as the basis" of the appropriateness of the attitude: "as parasites feed on useful, self-sustaining organisms, so students. . . ." Evans calls such onlooks "analogic." Finally, there are two sorts of parabolic onlook. With some, although no independent basis for the comparison is suggested in the utterance itself, one could be found. With others, not only is no basis given, but none *could* be given. Such onlooks Evans calls "metaphysical."[50]

The other notion that Evans will use in analyzing theological ut-

48. Ibid., pp. 126–29. This is neater than Evans' presentation, probably too neat for *his* intention.
49. Ibid., pp. 129–31.
50. Ibid., pp. 131–41.

terances is that of the *correlative* behabitive or commissive. To 'I appoint you governor,' 'I accept the office' is correlative. The illocutionary force of the first utterance is precisely to create the situation in which the second is appropriate as a response.[51]

God, says Evans, is a "metaphysical" entity, that is, a being "that can only be described in terms of human attitudes" toward him "which are believed to be appropriate." Statements about God ought to be interpreted as parabolic onlooks or, more simply, as "parables." To say, for example, 'God is faithful' is to say that if we trust Him, we will be following a policy appropriate to Him. In some such onlooks the comparison is with characters of persons, as 'I look on God as a loving father.' But statements of His transcendence are also onlooks; when I say 'God is omnipresent,' what I say about God is specifiable only in terms of attitudes; I say that if I behave as if God were "a hidden man" whom I cannot evade, I will be behaving appropriately to Him.[52] It is important to Evans' analysis that to say, as a parabolic onlook, 'I look on God as a father' is "not a matter of acting *as if* I believed that God is like a father. Rather, I actually do believe that God is like a father, but what I mean by this is to be explained in terms of human attitudes." [53] Thus the verdictive force of a parabolic onlook is the discovery, rather than the imposition, of meaning.

But how can this be if the abstractable content of a parabolic onlook specifies my attitudes only? The claim that my onlook is a discovery and not an invention of meaning is the claim that it is correlative to a divine onlook, which as divine has exercitive force.[54] To judge that God is loving is to respond to His onlook and so to be true to the reality that is posited in the exercitive force of His onlook. Finally, if we are asked how we know what parables correspond to the divine onlook, we can only point to the authority of a religious teacher. "If there is a divine onlook, I am not in a position

51. *The Logic of Self-Involvement,* pp. 76 f.
52. Ibid., pp. 223–26.
53. Ibid., p. 133.
54. Ibid., pp. 139 f. This is again much neater than anywhere in Evans.

to claim knowledge of it myself"; otherwise my onlook would not be parabolic only, "but someone else may be." [55]

With this last point we clearly are in very deep water. Evidently the divine onlook requires communication in human speech, if we are to respond to it. But is not looking on, perhaps, Jesus as a reliable religious teacher itself an onlook that needs justifying? Let us, however, turn back momentarily from the labyrinth to attend more fully to the immediately previous point, that our theological onlooks are *correlative* behabitive-commissives.

In the formula 'I look on God as . . . ,' what follows 'as' will always be something known (instead of "known," Evans implicitly follows the lead of the positivists and says "observable"). Otherwise no specification of *appropriate* attitude would result from the comparison. Therefore an onlook on God can be reversed. We can say, "I look on the hidden, metaphysical God as such-and-such, in relation to these observables"; or we can say, "I look on these observables as such-and-such, in relation to the hidden, metaphysical God." An onlook in the second form—for example, 'I look on fatherly behavior as expressive of God's nature,' makes the verdictive force of theological utterances very plain. [56]

Exactly as in Thomas' analysis of "analogical" language, we can immediately see that the relation between the two forms of a theological onlook is not symmetrical, for God Himself is not observable; He is knowable only *by way of* the onlook. Looking on God as such-and-such is thus dependent on looking on the observable as such-and-such. Moreover, it is clear that the logic of Evans' position suggests that our ability to speak about God at all depends upon one fundamental onlook: that we regard all or some observables as utterances of God, with exercitive and other illocutionary forces. And indeed he makes just this point about both the created world as a whole and the life of Jesus, [57]—which covers the relevant ground.

This must be right. If—as I will agree—a fundamental onlook on

55. Ibid., pp. 233, 227.
56. Ibid., pp. 226 f.
57. Ibid., pp. 145–67.

the world is basic to speaking of God, then that onlook must be that we regard the world as an utterance. For it is exactly when we ask after the *meaning* of the world that language about God arises; and to direct the question of meaning at something is surely to regard it as an utterance. We go rather beyond Evans if we pick up earlier thoughts and suggest that the divine utterance which we hear in the world and to which our theological utterances are correlative, is that complex kind of utterance we call a drama. And we part with him altogether if we point out that a drama must have dialogue, that even a pantomime is dependent on the program.

For Evans seems to suggest that the utterance to which we respond is not verbal, that creation and God's act in Christ are non-verbal performances which have illocutionary forces that merely *can* be made verbally explicit.[58] It is hard to think what this might mean. If it means only that gestures are part of language, it is trivial. If it means that to begin with we have a world independent of language, a thing to be seen only, and that we then somehow come to take it as an utterance, surely this is incredible. We can hardly distinguish between looking on the world as an utterance and looking on it as an utterance saying some particular thing. And this later we can do, also according to Evans, only by following the authority of a religious *teacher,* for only so do we know what onlook-utterance the world is.

Once again the very difficult problem of the relation between reality-as-a-whole and Jesus, as utterances of God, appears. Again we will bypass the problem, to point to one thing that is sure: from the very beginning the world that we may come to look on as an utterance of God is a world that includes the phenomenon of literal utterances that call us to question the meaning of the world and suggest to us what that meaning might be. It is the in the literal sense talkative world in which we actually live all or part of which we may come to interpret as God's utterance.

Who speaks the words that thus belong to God's illocutionary actions? God directly, in dreams or inspirations? Some religions have

58. *The Logic of Self-Involvement,* pp. 158, 167.

thought this. But the answer of the Christian faith has been that men speak them. The "Word of God" of which Christian theology speaks is the human word of the prophets, apostles, preachers, and perhaps of any persons at all who call us to consider the future of our actions. Here again the matter of the next chapter opens. For our immediate purposes, the point is that theological speech is therefore inherently *conversational, antiphonal.* Our utterances to and about God are correlative to authoritative divine onlook-utterances —which are themselves spoken by our partners, or by us to other partners, in a dialogue between human speakers. Theological utterances function only in and as a back-and-forth of exercitive and verdictive utterances. Priest: "Do you believe in . . . ?" Catechumen: "I do." Priest: "I baptize you in the name of the Father, Son and Holy Spirit." Congregation: "Praise God, from whom all blessings flow." This is the pattern.

The drama of Time, which we may come to regard as God's address to us, is, after all, not a drama of which we are the *audience:* it is the drama of our lives. We are ourselves actors. Theological utterance is indeed not merely informative, but not because it is *un*informative. It is *formative,* creative.

III.

There is a sense, therefore, in which theological utterance is a self-sustaining activity. We might well be tempted to say that the reality to which the verdictive and behabitive forces of our theological utterances must be true is posited solely in the exercitive force of others of our theological utterances. And such an interpretation would not necessarily make theological utterance a trivial game of self-assurances. For it is not a game one person can play by himself. It is intrinsically a conversation. Only the exercitive force of an address to me by someone other than myself posits the situation within which my confession and praise is appropriate, and my utterance therefore retains the character of response to *news.* And we could argue that the factual presuppositions of our utterances are provided by the existence of the community in which the conversation occurs, by its history, and perhaps also by exercitively posited realities.[59] Such an analysis need not even imply that man creates his own god, in any crude sense. For God would here be the reality of *what happens between* men when communication about the meaning of life succeeds, and it might even be possible to argue that this reality antecedes human life as something *we* do.

Of such discourse Wittgenstein's remark would be true: "If someone said: 'Wittgenstein, do you believe in this?' I'd say: 'No.' 'Do you contradict the man?' I'd say 'No.' . . . the religious man never believes what I describe. . . . I can't contradict that person. In one sense I understand all he says. . . . I could say: 'I don't believe in this,' and this would be true. . . . But not that I could contradict the thing." [60] The situation between religious and other discourse would be a sort of *discontinuity of adjudicability*, where no religious utterance could ever be supported or falsified *on grounds statable* in nonreligious language. This is the real matter at issue in the problem of verifiability. Of course religious utterances are testable in *some* way: there is necessarily a method by which members of religious communities decide what is to be said and what is not to be said about, for example, God or the soul. If there were no such method, religious language could not occur at all; and manifestly it does. The question is whether there is any continuity of adjudicability between theological utterances and our other factual claims, whether the unbeliever in his language can object to the things believers say, in any other way than by pure logical critique, as "It doesn't mean anything."

None of the considerations by which we could excuse fleeing the whole problem and taking religious utterance as a wholly separate and self-sustaining language activity is false. Yet we cannot get off so easily, for reasons that have controlled our discussion from the beginning. Such a theological game would be a sort of communal

59. An example of such an analysis is William Hordern, *Speaking of God.*
60. Ludwig Wittgenstein, *Lectures and Conversations on Aesthetics, Psychology and Religious Belief,* pp. 53, 55.

speaking in tongues, meaningful only within the community of believers, about a god real only within the community. I suspect,
though I will not argue it, that this tempting analysis is in fact adequate as an analysis of the language of *religion*. Even the suggestion that God is in some subtle sense our creation would evidently
not be unacceptable to the devotees of the highest forms of religion,
such as Hinduism or Buddhism. And religionists have often remarked with satisfaction the discontinuity of adjudicability between
religious and other utterances. We are prevented from accepting this
suggestion as an accurate analysis of Christian *faith* by the circum-
stance, already remarked, that it contradicts the content of those
fundamental Christian utterances which are commands that we
should talk to those outside the circle of faith of our God as of a
god who is already theirs. The Christian God is essentially the justi-
fier of the ungodly. Therefore also even the subtlest suggestion that
He is the creation of His worshipers must be unacceptable.

Yet surely Wittgenstein's remark does point to something characteristic also of Christian theological talk. Even if Christianity is, as it
is now fashionable to say, *not only* a religion, it surely is also a religion. So let us push our present line of thought just a bit further,
before acting on its admitted inadequacy. This will also give opportunity for some discussion of Wittgenstein's cryptic—even for him—
sayings on the subject.

The issue between belief and unbelief is, Wittgenstein once said,
between different *ways* of thinking, "which needn't be expressed by
one person saying one thing, another person another thing." Indeed,
what the one says cannot be contradicted by the other; the statement
of one, not being possible in the other's language, cannot be denied
by him. Thus evidence is irrelevant. The issue between believers and
unbelievers is exactly about what is to count as reliable and depend-
able evidence. The particular way in which assertions are based on
evidence that holds in the one way of thinking, must appear pre-
posterously flimsy within the other. Neither can call the other reasonable or unreasonable, for the difference is about 'reasonable.' Not
even an explanation of 'what I mean' will necessarily pinpoint the

difference, for the explanation will itself be a piece of the one way of thinking.[61]

As a possible characterization of the difference between "ways of thinking," Wittgenstein suggests having "different pictures." [62] The "Last Judgment" is such a picture—and, if we are to take seriously Wittgenstein's saying that the difference between himself and a believer is that they have different pictures, we may suppose that one who lacks this picture and so has the "ordinary view of death" does not thereby think *without* a picture but has his elsewhere. Such a picture will "show . . . by regulating for all in . . . life." One has such a picture in "appealing" to it, in both one's thinking and one's action.[63] Here, clearly, is something like Evans' "onlook": "I look on death as overcome by life." Yet the scope is wider: if I have "the picture" of Judgment, this controls my decision not only about death but about all issues.

Is such a picture perhaps only an expression of a certain attitude? Wittgenstein gives the Wittgensteinian—and definitive—answer: "No. . . . It says what it says. . . . 'He could just as well have said so and so'—this remark is foreshadowed by the word 'attitude.' He couldn't just as well have said something else. . . . Isn't it as important as anything else, what picture he does use? The whole weight may be in the picture." [64]

It is rather, though Wittgenstein never says this explicitly in this connection, my whole language that such a picture determines. It determines, not what is true, but what is reasonable. In opposition to someone's picture, all one can say is: " 'I would discourage this kind of reasoning,' " to which he can reply, " 'I wouldn't discourage it.' That is, one would do something. We would take sides, and that goes so far that there would really be a great difference between us which might come out in [the believer's] saying 'Wittgenstein is trying to undermine reason,' and this wouldn't be false." [65] It is my "form of life" which "culminates in an utterance of belief in," for

61. Wittgenstein, op. cit., pp. 53–57.
62. Ibid., p. 55.
63. Ibid., pp. 53–56, 71.
64. Ibid., pp. 70 f. Cf. also p. 34.
65. Ibid., pp. 63 f.

example, the "Last Judgment." [66] And where such pictures are radically different, one no longer can be sure even *whether* or not he understands the other.[67]

Let us now skip back to a period of Wittgenstein's thinking much earlier than the suggestions we have so far picked up. In the last pages of the *Tractatus Logico-Philosphicus* we hear of "the mystical." This is "the feeling of the world as a bounded whole," the apprehension *"that* the world is"—as against knowledge, which is of *"how* the world is." [68] Only the mystical could be a revelation of God. The mystical "cannot be uttered. It only shows itself. . . ." [69] Therefore, given the last line of the *Tractatus,* "Of that of which one cannot speak, one must keep silence," [70] it would seem there can be no religious *language* at all.

But we hear also that ". . . ethics cannot be uttered," [71] in that the *value* of things in the world "must lie outside the world," [72] that is, must depend on what cannot be uttered, the boundaries of the world. Surely Wittgenstein does not mean that ethical discourse is somehow illegitimate. Evidently not, for just as "Ethics is transcendental," [73] so "Logic is transcendental,"; [74] and Wittgenstein's own book is logic. He says, to be sure, "My sentences are explanatory in that one who understands me finally recognizes that they are meaningless, when he has used them to climb—on them—over them." [75] But his logical sentences do have *this* use as a ladder, and so we may also ask what use ethical utterances and even theological utterances might have.

The "experience" needed to understand logic is exactly the experience of the mystical, *"that* there is something." [76] Logical sentences

66. Ibid., p. 58.
67. Ibid., p. 55.
68. Wittgenstein, *Tractatus Logico-Philosophicus,* 6.432, 6.44, 6.45.
69. Ibid., 6.522.
70. Ibid., 7.
71. Ibid., 6.421.
72. Ibid., 6.41, 6.42, 6.421.
73. Ibid., 6.421.
74. Ibid., 6.13.
75. Ibid., 6.54.
76. Ibid., 5.552.

show—*not* describe—what can be said and what cannot, not in the sense of what is or is not so, but in the sense of what might be so, given that anything is so. Thus they trace the boundaries of the world: [77] "The boundaries of my language mean the boundaries of my world." [78] The boundaries of my language, the boundaries of my world, are the boundaries of what I can experience, know, and will: "The world and life are one. I am my world." [79] So we have the function of one "transcendental" language activity—logic.

What about the function of the other transcendental language activity—ethics? There is a hint: "If good or ill will changes the world, it can only change the boundaries of the world, not the facts within it. . . . The world must become altogether a different world. It must, as it were, wax and wane as a whole. The world of the happy person is a different world from that of the unhappy." [80] We have to combine to make sense here: the boundaries of my world are the boundaries of my language. Ethical utterances function, then, not to trace the boundaries of language and the world, as does logic, but to *change* the boundaries of language and so of the world. How, he does not say—but we can suppose that it is by altering the very purpose for which we speak, by making what we do when we speak, when we "lay our language to the world," [81] a different thing.

Our interests shape our language. Consider a man poring over a map of England. "He sees a way of dividing the country different from the one used on the ordinary map. He feels tempted, say, to use the name 'Devonshire' not for the county with the conventional boundary, but for a region differently bounded. . . . What he says is: 'The real Devonshire is this.' We could answer: 'What you want is only a new notation, and by a new notation no facts of geography are changed.' It is true, however, that we may be irresistibly attracted or repelled by a notation. (We easily forget how much a . . . form of expression may mean to us, and that changing it isn't

77. Wittgenstein, *Tractatus* . . . , 5.6–6.3951.
78. Ibid., 5.6.
79. Ibid., 5,621, 5.63.
80. Ibid., 6.43.
81. E.g., *Philosophische Bemerkungen,* pp. 84 f.

always as easy as it often is in mathematics or in the sciences. A change of clothes or of names may mean very little and it may mean a great deal)." [82]

If we try to move on to theological utterance, the hints become even more tenuous. As a subnumber to the aphorism about the good or ill will, Wittgenstein says, "As also the world does not change in death, but rather ceases," [83] and then continues in a parallel subnumber to the only more than rhetorical mention of God in the *Tractatus*.[84] Perhaps whether we have a "world" at all is in question here, the courage to speak up at all, the willingness to "lay our language to the world," and so take the risk of being wrong, the courage to submit to reality. The foreword of the *Philosophische Bemerkungen* says, "I would like to say 'This book is written to the glory of God,' but that today would be a piece of knavery, that is, it would not be rightly understood. It means: the book is written with good will, and insofar as it is not written with good will, out of vanity and the like, the author would gladly see it condemned. He can not purify his book of such ingredients more than he himself is pure of them." Perhaps theological utterance is that which commands or permits us to speak up.

Perhaps, too, Wittgenstein would not separate ethics, which is deciding *what* we seek in having a world, from this courage to have a world at all. "Ethics and aesthetics are one," [85] and both perhaps also one with the revelation of God. Then theological utterance is that in making which we come to *value* the world and just so to "lay language on it," to speak of it.

It is dubitable that Wittgenstein intended as much as we have just suggested. It is certain that we violate his intentions if we combine the two sets of remarks we have discussed—but let us do so anyway. This will give the suggestion that theological discourse is that in which we on the one hand impose and on the other hand acknowledge a picture in terms of which we value the world and so come to

82. *Blue Book*, p. 57. Reprinted by permission of Harper & Row, New York, 1958.
83. *Tractatus Logico-Philosophicus*, 6.431.
84. Ibid., 6.432.
85. Ibid., 6.421.

speak of it. There is no such thing as valuing in the abstract: such a picture will always suggest *specific* values to be pursued in the world; that is, it will impose the interests that shape our particular language. A language, with its particular ways of dividing the world and relating the resultant parts, is a "whole culture," [86] a world. It is this the believer's picture gives him.

"The nature of language is a picture [here quite a different sense of 'picture'] of the nature of the world. And philosophy as the keeper of grammar can indeed grasp the nature of the world—not in sentences *of* language, but in rules *for* that language which exclude those combinations of signs that are to be meaningless." [87] But it is exactly what is meaningless and what is not that is in dispute between those who "use different pictures." It is the nature of my world which is set by a picture imposed on me.

Here, I think, is the explanation of the tendency of an utterance like 'God is good' to collapse on analysis to an uninformative tautology where God is good because that is how we define 'good'—and yet retain a feeling of importance unlike, say, 'All pink flowers are pink.' Such utterances are to be seen as those by which we *create* or acknowledge the fundamental reference points of our language and so the boundaries of our world as we live in it. 'God is good' is a proposed definition in which 'God' and 'good' define each other. Thus it is, in a sense, informationally vacuous—and yet taken from either end, it is a signpost to a proposed key word of language. It proposes the rule: Use 'God' to mark the direction of the series good, better, better yet . . . ; and use 'good' as a criterion of when 'God' is appropriate.[88]

When I pray or confess or preach, it is the *point* of life that I am positing. Reaching back to earlier discussions, we can interpret Wittgenstein's "the world" as the "drama of Time." This will also make clear why it is a "picture" of the sort of the "Last Judgment" in which the point of life is grasped. When we speak religious lan-

86. *Lectures and Conversations* . . . , p. 8.
87. *Philosophische Bemerkungen*, p. 85.
88. See Ian Ramsey, *Religious Language.*

guage, we are engaged in projecting the resolution and denoue-ment of life's story—which first gives our story a plot so that it is a story at all and not a mere collection of incidents, so that it has "a world."

Here is, perhaps, the explanation of the peculiarity of 'God' as a subject word: that when we use it, we always seem to attach qualifi-cations that logically prevent acquaintance with the supposed person named by 'God.' Thus we say 'God is good,' and hasten to add 'God is perfectly good,' thereby removing the whole matter from the realm of the observable. Ian Ramsey [89] says that qualifiers like 'per-fectly' are to be taken as instructions to develop a model in a certain direction. Thus to say that God is 'perfectly good' is to give instruc-tions to use the *model* of human goodness and develop it in this way: "As good as Jones?" "Better." "As good as Smith, who is bet-ter than Jones?" "Better." And so on. We speak of God, says Ram-sey, precisely in that we continue *indefinitely* with the series gener-ated by developing the model of goodness—or love, or power, or what you will—in this way. This analysis seems helpful. Only something more can and must be said about the direction in which the "odd qualifiers" like 'perfectly' instruct us to project what is said about God. To say that God is *'perfectly* good' is to project His goodness *forward to the end of our story.* It is to cry out for a certain kind of goal, and so of plot and meaning, for life. Since the goodness of God is thus an eschatological reality, it cannot be simply found in the present; and the good God is not an object of direct acquaint-ance.[90]

89. Ibid., pp. 65 f.

90. My position *so far* is, I suppose, related to Zuurdeeg's in his unfor-tunately loosely argued and formulated book, *An Analytical Philosophy of Religion.* There he calls religious language a particular, fundamental, sort of "convictional" language, the language by which man, defined as "man-who-speaks," establishes his existence.

Zuurdeeg argues that it is improper to speak of rules governing "convic-tional uses," since man does not "use" convictional language at all. Man *is* his convictions, so that convictional language *is* man existing (pp. 56-59). Only indicative language has logical structure. For the truth-functional un-derstanding of sentences clearly presupposes an understanding of language

There is of course another reason why Wittgenstein speaks of a "picture." He has in mind something like Evans' "parabolic on-look." The utterances by which the believer rules his language and world are supposed to be about reality. Yet they cannot be *about* anything in the way a straightforward hypothesis is about something. They are something *like* a "figure" of speech. And this brings us right back to our old problem.

Our discussion of Wittgenstein has, we may hope, given us some insight into *why* theological assertions are not experimentally adjudicable. The reasons are in themselves the glory, not the shame, of theological discourse. Our theological utterances are those in which

---

as indicative rather than convictional. Thus religious language is full of "illogical" paradox. Logic cannot serve as the metalanguage of religious language, and logical analysis of religious language in the Oxford style is impossible (pp. 62–68).

The business about not "using" convictional language surely is no more than a bad pun. Moreover, Zuurdeeg evidently thinks of "logic" as some particular fixed set of canons, in a way not conceived by even the logicians of the Middle Ages. Otherwise, the notion of a nonlogical *structure* of *language* is simply absurd.

But my most serious critique is that rejecting the applicability of logical analysis to convictional language denies it all cognitive use—more definitely even than does asserting its nonindicative character. It leaves religious language as blik-positing only. Thus Zuurdeeg, too, falls after all under our negative critique. And the alternative to a "convictional" language which maintains, by whatever sufferings, its continuity with "indicative" language, is not a return to primitive wholism. (Even if this *were* an option, I cannot imagine why Zuurdeeg wants it.) The alternative is nihilism. Thus we also cannot accept C. B. Martin's advice, in *Religious Belief*. The ceremonial language spoken *in* faith possesses, he says, its own logic and is secure in itself. The wise religious man will avoid any language *outside* the faith about the faith and will accept the consequent intellectual isolation (pp. 128 ff.). At the end of this whole train of thought, I cannot refrain from noting that the philosophical theology that would come of it is in fact nothing more than a skeletal version of that of Fichte and Schleiermacher. Indeed, there *is* only one possible Western philosophical theology, and it has already been created in almost inhuman perfection by these two thinkers. For Fichte in handy form, see Emanuel Hirsch, *Geschichte der neuern evangelischen Theologie,* Vol. IV, pp. 351–75. For Schleiermacher, his own *Dialektik*. The theology developed by Van Buren in *The Secular Meaning of the Gospel* is, at one remove, a bowdlerized version of this fine old tradition.

we *create* the reality of our lives—and therefore they do not need to be tested experimentally.

Yet if theological utterances have *no* continuity of adjudicability with the rest of our factual claims, this glory is vain. At least, so the Christian must judge. Should we be convinced that our utterances about God are true or false merely of a reality given only in the community of those who already make these utterances, we would thereby be constrained to give up the whole enterprise. Moreover, the paradigm of verifiability in all other areas of utterance is now, for better or worse, the image of the positive sciences. Thus the question of continuity of adjudicability is inherently a demand for comparison—no more—with the verifiability of hypotheses. We cannot forever evade Flew.

IV.

How utterances containing 'God' fit into the rest of our utterances, whether indeed they fit in at all or belong to a self-sustaining language activity with its own discontinuous kind of adjudication, depends, one may say, on "how you define 'God.'" Of course, undertaking to define 'God' or any other word, as a way to philosophical understanding, is a perilous project. For when we do this, we act as though 'God' were not already in discourse and had to be introduced in terms of words that are—which is contrary to fact. Nevertheless, if we are aware of what we are doing, it can be helpful, with matters where we have already lost our linguistic innocence,[91] to make the experiment of asking: if we were not already using this word, how would we introduce it into discourse?

With terms for particulars, like God, the question is how the term *identifies* some particular.[92] If I say, 'Jones is good,' and you do not understand 'Jones,' your problem is that you are unable to pick out *which* of the possible particulars that might be Jones is

91. Cf. Wisdom, *Paradox and Discovery,* pp. 47 ff.
92. The best account of all this is in P. F. Strawson, *Individuals,* especially pp. 5–19, 183–90.

meant, and your request for elucidation will be a request for further help in making the identification. Where I can say, '*He* is good,' and point, there is no further difficulty. But if I cannot, then I have to use a set of descriptions. I will say something like, 'Jones is the one who married Nancy Smith and works for Hinshaw's.' The phrases of the form 'who . . .' now affect the identification. How many will be required in a particular case depends entirely on the circumstances; but if no set affects the identification, the attempt to speak of a particular fails. We can identify only by names or descriptions; and "it is no good using a name for a particular unless one knows who or what is referred to by the use of the name. A name is worthless without a backing of descriptions which can be produced on demand. . . ." [93]

The use of such a 'who . . .' clause is implicitly a claim about what is so. 'The one who married Nancy Smith' fails to identify unless the person I am trying to identify did in fact marry Nancy Smith. The question about the logic of 'God' is thus the question about what sort of claims about what is so must be made in order to introduce 'God' into discourse. This is what will determine how God-utterances will be adjudicated. The needed truth claims will be the same as the abstractable contents of the reversed form of Evans' basic onlooks: 'I look on such-and-such observables as such-and-such in relation to God.'

What such onlooks are needed? Is the content of a parabolic onlook, 'I look on the world as a performative action,' a sufficient claim? A main point of the previous section has been that it is not, and Evans admits as much when, to prevent the verdict involved from being wholly arbitrary, he says we depend here on the authority of a religious teacher—for us, Jesus. Thus we argued that the world on which we may look as God's utterance is always one that already includes literal utterances instructing us to take it so. But to accept the authority of Jesus is surely itself a verdictive onlook. What is to guarantee that *this* verdict is not arbitrary? Indeed, it is plain that this onlook is already a theological assertion, for the one who knows God's onlook, as we cannot, is surely himself divine.

93. Strawson, op. cit., p. 7.

One might say that this onlook about Jesus needs no adjudicability in terms other than those of the language it makes possible. But this would be the position we envisaged and rejected in the previous section. And is "religious authority" even the right expression? Theological utterance, we may agree, has its home in the dialectic between the *world* as an utterance directed at us and a certain *specific* utterance, the story about Jesus. But is this a relation between what is taken on authority and the authority? Will *any* parabolic onlook suffice as the claim that introduces 'God'?

The relation between the world in general and Jesus in particular as the objects of our religious language has been sympathetically investigated by I. M. Crombie; and we turn to him.[94] According to Crombie, the "logical mother" of theological language is "undifferentiated theism." This arises from the experience, inseparable from human life, of the *incomplete* and *obligated* character of our life. In attempting to deal with this experience, we are driven to twist and distort language: we want to speak of ourselves as "contingent" (the variety of synonyms here is great), even though only statements can be contingent. Even more oddly, we cry out for that-which-is-not-"contingent" in this sense. And to make this cry we acquire the word 'God.' We do not and could not acquire knowledge of any entity by that name, for we have no idea what it would mean for there to be a noncontingent being. But we do acquire the word, and the word has a function in our lives: that is, it is meaningful.

Notice how the comparison with a drama emerges once again, though not as clearly as it might. If we may expand the comparison: we experience our lives as incomplete *stories,* as dramas missing their climax and denouement. For that we are mortal means that the possibilities raised by our past, by the part of the drama we have experienced, can never *all* be brought to rest, even by disappointment, except by an event that we apparently cannot experience. I therefore can never experience the whole play.

I can never, that is, experience my life as a meaningful whole—

94. I. M. Crombie, "Arising from the *University* Discussion," *New Essays in Philosophical Theology,* pp. 109–30.

and yet I must. What Crombie calls our speaking of ourselves as contingent and our call for what is not contingent, is our lament at being mortal, and our refusal to accept it.[95] 'God' is our cry for someone to finish our essentially unfinished stories, and so to make sense of them. In our God-utterances we posit what is to complete and fulfill our mortality. Thus Crombie is right in pointing to the *negativity* of our experience as the source of our talk about God. And we can also see why the language about "boundaries" always seems so appropriate to religion. It is exactly where we end, that we have begun to talk of God. If Crombie is right, we can also understand why we persist in so arbitrary a project as we have seen religious discourse to be. Arbitrariness is of its essence, for it is our demand that what is not, the completed drama of our lives, must be.

If Christian faith is in some sense something other than religion, it is just at this point. For it is exactly this undertaking of creating the fulfillment of our lives ourselves, in the power of *our* exercitive utterance, that the New Testament calls "works-righteousness."

It is therefore no surprise to believers that 'God' has that hollow ring to which our century has become so sensitive. If 'God is love' is equivalent to 'I need love,' this may be so, but it indeed tells nothing about the conclusion of life but only of *my* demand that it have a conclusion. The tendency of religious assertions to collapse into cognitive vacuity, a vacuity from which we cannot desist and which we embrace as the reality of our lives, is the horror of religious chatter. This horror has been seen and condemned by believers: "For what can be known about God is plain to them . . . but they became futile in their thinking." [96]

The "logical mother" of theological language, the language of religion-as-such, is a whore. It is our vain and self-defeating attempt to evade mortality. It is self-defeating because if we could in the power of our exercitive utterances create an eternity in which to evade death—perhaps "an eternity within us"—also then our lives would have no *conclusion,* and we could not live them as meaning-

95. See Robert Jenson, *A Religion Against Itself,* pp. 16 ff.
96. Romans 2: 19–21.

ful stories. *We* cannot utter that beyond ourselves *for* which we may live.

Back to Crombie. The "logical father" of theological language, he says, is the interpretation of some concrete reality in experience as divine. It is because we find something about which we are compelled to say what cannot be said without using 'God' that we come to speak theologically. For Christian faith, this reality is the complex of events named by 'Jesus Christ.'

Again I have perhaps tightened things up a bit more than Crombie would like. So interpreted, I agree. Let me put the matter even more my way: The "logical father" of theological language is an event that occurs *as* that over against which we thus experience our incompleteness. For believers, the career of Jesus is that event. Believers use that most dubious of words, 'God,' to say something vital they must say about Jesus of Nazareth, to say: 'What happens with him is the conclusion happening.' Were it not for what we must say about Christ, precisely the believer would have every reason to eschew 'God' altogether—its very use is a mark of idolatry. The early Christians were, after all, prosecuted as *atheists*.

In working out the particular logic of the language we use for this purpose, Crombie continues to be so close to what seems to me the right track that I will continue to work out my own view in conversation with his. Crombie says that religious utterance is the telling of "parables"—Jesus' own way of talking about God is the paradigm. In the parables all the words, like 'love,' 'justice,' etc., are used in their ordinary ways, and there is no trouble in knowing what would factually verify or falsify the statements of which the parable is composed, should we choose—in many cases, foolishly—to seek verification; some parables, those drawn directly from current incident, would turn out true; others would not. Thus 'love' in the parable of the "waiting Father" is not used in any transferred or attenuated sense: it means exactly what 'love' means in 'Father loves me.' So also in the very short parable told by the '. . . is love' in 'God is love.' We do not therefore know *how* what is said in the parable applies to *God,* since we have eschewed the "Like your fa-

ther?" "Well, not quite . . ." series of attempts to make our lan-
gauge fit God. But we use parables nevertheless—*on the authority
of Jesus Christ*, who authorizes us to speak of God and, in so doing,
to use certain particular parabolic statements.[97]

It is, however, "only the predicates" of theological language which
are parables; 'God' has the usual function with which the word is
given to us in "undifferentiated theism." With it, we apply the
pseudo-category [98] of divinity to our parables, thereby stipulating to
what these parables refer. Only, 'God' stipulates less a *what* than a
direction—the direction of our search for the noncontingent. "We
do not, that is, know to what to refer our parables; we know merely
that we are to refer them *out of experience* [my italics], and . . . in
which direction." [99]

At this point it will be helpful to compare the in some ways similar position of T. R. Miles.[100] The appropriate religious policy is, he
says, one of "silence qualified by parables." [101] A parable is a story
told to convey a message. Such parables are for the most part composed of utterances that are, in their form, straightforward empirical assertions: we know which situations would verify and which
would falsify these assertions, so that there is no problem with their
meaningfulness. These assertions may very well also be false, which
is irrelevant to their message. The message, finally, is the commenda-
tion of a way of life, of a slant on historical existence; and accep-
tance of a parable is the adoption of that way of life.[102] Thus: "Instead of 'Do you believe in the existence of God?' we should ask,
'Do you accept the theistic parable?' This rids us of the temptation

97. MacIntyre's view in "The Logical Status of Religious Beliefs," *Metaphysical Beliefs,* pp. 167–211, is very similar. The assertions of religion form
a total narrative, a "myth." We understand myths in much the same way
as we do novels. We construe 'Waverly loves' by considering what it would
be for anyone to love; so also with 'God loves' *in* the total myth. A myth is
accepted or rejected as a whole. See pp. 186–94.
98. Cf. Crombie, "The Possibility of Theological Statements," *Faith and
Logic,* ed. Mitchell, pp. 30–85; see p. 60.
99. Crombie, "Arising from the University Discussions," p. 124.
100. T. R. Miles, *Religion and the Scientific Outlook.*
101. Ibid., p. 179.
102. Ibid., pp. 36–46, 137–79.

to think of God as an 'extra entity. . . .' The questions whether there is such an entity and whether the theistic parable is objectively true can be met only by the way of silence." [103]

The difference between Miles and Crombie is that Crombie says we use the pseudo-category 'God' to refer our parables to the transcendent focus of our lives, whereas Miles refuses to use pseudo-categories and proposes silence for the same purpose. This silence is not merely not speaking, it is itself a directed action; in silence we turn our lives, shaped by the parable we accept, beyond themselves.

This proposal is subtle and persuasive. In practice it would be a sort of commonsense mysticism, equally attractive, perhaps, to the mystical tradition in Christianity and to some of those who call for a secular faith. Yet it would be the cessation of theological *speech*—though not of speech altogether—and if we remember how Christianity locates our transcendence exactly in our *communication* with those who do not yet share our parable, we will be compelled to refuse the comfort Miles offers. We will have to assume with Crombie the burden of this vacuous concept 'God'; that is, we will have to assume the burden of religion, in full awareness of its vacuity.

On a less dramatic level, some amendments also to Crombie's position seem required. It will not do to take the parables in question as those commended *by* Jesus. This would land us back with Evans' inadequate position. Surely the claim of the church has rather been that the stories in question are *Jesus' own story* "commended" by the fact that His life occurs as the event of God for us. Surely also this is most consistent with Crombie's general analysis. But then we must say: *Theological utterance is narration of the story about Jesus, qualified by and qualifying 'God,'* or any other of the 'perfect . . .' phrases of which 'God' is the logical product. Theological utterance is narration of the story about Jesus as the story about God.

Note that a second amendment to Crombie's position is contained in this formulation: "qualified by and qualifying." The relation between Jesus' own story and 'God' is more two-sided than Crombie makes evident. Let us finally go into this point in some detail.

103. Ibid., p. 179.

'God,' says Crombie, qualifies Jesus' story by referring it in "a certain direction." He says this is "out." But by this Crombie simply repristinates the worst features of the traditional position—and will entangle himself in the hopeless thesis that a sentence can say more than it says. 'God' refers Jesus' story not *out* but *forward*. What believers want to say of Jesus with this precarious language is: The absolutely last thing has happened, in the events of Jesus' existence. His story tells of the conclusion of our lives. We have Him to live *for*. The will of love-out-of-hate, and the destiny of life-out-of-death, which He enacted, is the content of our dramas—just *in* their essential incompleteness and mortality. Death and resurrection is the plot. To tell Jesus' story as the story about God is to tell it as narrative of the climax and denouement of my story and your story.

Vice versa, Jesus' story qualifies 'God' by giving it content. 'Godly' means 'appropriate to the career of Jesus of Nazareth.' The attributes of God—that is, the rules specifying under which circumstances to use 'God' (Speak of 'God' if there is . . .)—are set by the stages in the history of Jesus Christ. When, for example, we say 'God is just' and are asked what we mean, we point to Jesus' friendship with sinners.

Thus, all theological utterance can be compressed in the convertible sentence 'God is Jesus' or 'Jesus is God'—that is, in the doctrine of the Trinity. This formula is at once a two-way rule for language about God—in particular it sets the meaning of 'God'—and a material summary of all the assertions (if there are any) of theological talk.[104]

104. Hepburn has directed a vigorous polemic against any such "christological" solution of the logic of religious language in *Christianity and Paradox*, pp. 60–90. He defines a "christological" interpretation as one that holds that for any proposition about 'God' equivalent propositions about 'Jesus' can be stated. His argument is a thorough mix-up of three claims: (1) the certainly legitimate challenge to produce the rules of such an equivalence; (2) the assertion that this is impossible, since 'God' will have to be used in the definition, carrying meaning slipped in from elsewhere; (3) the demand that theologians "justify" the definition of 'God' in terms of 'Jesus.' The second claim is probably correct, though not in the way Hepburn asserts, since he confuses (2) with (3). The third is terribly con-

Some further questions are raised by the preceding. We may note first the circularity of the procedure by which 'God' defines 'Jesus' and 'Jesus' defines 'God.' This need not alarm us. The situation is common in many contexts. Thus we abstract a definition of, perhaps, 'tragedy' from characteristics of a group of plays—a group of plays selected precisely because they are "tragedies." The circularity is not vicious; at each turn the concept becomes richer and the reference group more precisely bounded. The situation is analogous here.[105]

More serious is the question: What *is* the "story of Jesus"? We have treated this phrase as if it denoted a known quantity. Even if we rush over a host of theological and philosophical problems, and simply say that the history of Israel is included in the story of Jesus, we still have to ask about both Jesus and Israel: Is the story we mean that told by faith, by believing witnesses such as the authors of the New Testament? Or is it the story the historian may, if he is lucky, come to tell after he has gone behind the believing witnesses? After he has put the historian's question: This is what the tradition and witnesses say. *Now*—what really happened? Is it the "biblical Christ" or the "historical Jesus" whose story is the content of theological utterance? The same question can be put another way: Is the "story of Jesus" separable from "told as the story of the meaning of my life?" Do we start with the story of Jesus as given and *then* tell it in this special way?

This nest of questions bears on the central problem of this chapter. The story of the "historical Jesus" is verifiable or falsifiable by empirical historical research in the ordinary way. The story of the "biblical Christ," the story of Jesus *as* the story about God and me, is not.[106] Is an empirical historical verifiability of "Jesus' story" part of

---

fused. Hepburn mixes up verifiability-as-such and verifiability by the kind of "evidence" old-style apologists used to produce. He just will not believe that radical Christians mean what they say, when they reject such apologetics.

105. I owe this example to Mitchell.

106. This latter has, to be sure, been disputed of late by W. Pannenberg. See next chapter, pp. 218–30.

the logic of theological utterances? This question cannot be answered within our present discussion. Here a door opens into the next chapter.

Finally, it is plain that everything Crombie and we have said so far may be true, and our theological statements still make a world of their own floating above the rest of life. The reference to the concrete person of Jesus Christ does *not,* as so far developed, indicate evidence relevant to the truth or falsity of theological utterances, other than that given in the illocutionary force of the utterances themselves. Jesus' behavior, past or present, is relevant to the truth or falsity of 'Jesus is loving.' But it is not relevant to 'God is loving' unless 'God is Jesus-like' is true. Now our analysis so far has indicated how believers *come to use* language in accordance with this latter sentence taken as a rule. But it has not indicated any way in which evidence relative to the truth or falsity of the sentence as a *statement* might be discovered. The question posed by Flew at the very beginning remains as open as ever.

Is 'God is Jesus,' besides being a rule of theological usage, an assertion? *Within* the language game played by this rule it is irrefutable, because any sentence contradicting it is within the theological language game disqualified as violating the basic rule of the game. The same holds in general of all the apparent assertions made by Christian faith.

But is this whole language activity cognitive in any sense that is continuous with our other knowledge claims? Is it in any specifiable way continuous with our other descriptive uses of language? This depends on whether there is extralinguistic evidence relative to the truth or falsity of 'God is Jesus' or 'Jesus is God,' so that these are, as well as being rules of theological usage, *assertions*. (The notion of this double function poses no difficulty in itself. The sciences are full of statements that function both as rules of derivation and as testable hypotheses.) If the theological language game is not cognitive in some sense analogous to our other cognitive activities, then it is, for all its consistency, an elaborate illusion. For the Christian faith's language activity is the telling of a story about a historical figure— and we may and must demand of it that it be *correct*. If it is a purely illustrative or mythical or parabolic story, it is also false.

Is there any point where the closed circle of our religious discourse breaks open to us? An obvious suggestion, and one often made, is that it is "religious experience" that verifies our claim that the world—or Jesus, or the world and the story of Jesus in the peculiar dialectic we have just traced—is an utterance of God. This is supposed to be a special kind of experience which reaches entities not otherwise accessible; yet it manifestly occurs and in our lives is psychologically and historically continuous with our other experience. This line is taken by Basil Mitchell in his response to Flew and Hare in the "University Discussion." [107] He agrees with Flew that theological utterances are intended as assertions. And he accepts the consequence that they must then be falsifiable. Of course, he says, the theologian recognizes that innocent suffering counts against 'God is loving.' Only, *so long* as he remains theologian, he does not take it as counting *decisively* against it. For his assertions are neither hypotheses open to constant revision nor tautologies irrelevant to experience; they are *commitments* to the person named by them. Confronted by evidence apparently contrary to his assertion about God, the theologian will therefore seek ways to explain this evidence to make it conform to his assertions—as one will do with any deep personal commitment. It cannot be fixed in advance how long the theologian—or anyone else—can keep this up without dishonesty and without qualifying his assertions into vacuous tautologies in the way described by Flew.

In another essay [108] Mitchell then suggests that the evidence that bears on the truth or falsehood of theological statements is religious experience. For example, that I do or do not experience the presence of God as a benediction upon life verifies or falsifies the assertion 'God is loving.' Clearly, such an experience does not verify my assertion in the same sense of 'verify' found in "the verifiability criterion." But why does it need to? As Mitchell points out, the demand

107. John Wilson, *Language and Religious Belief,* argues the same case notably.
108. Mitchell, "The Grace of God," *Faith and Logic,* ed. Mitchell, pp. 149–95.

that verification be an identical procedure for all types of assertion is a wholly unjustified metaphysical dogma.

But there is, it seems to me, a fatal difficulty. If "religious experience" means experience of some public event, then the occurrence or the nonoccurrence of that event will verify or falsify religious assertions in perfectly public fashion, and there is no need to make the detour over some special *sort* of experience. The move to "religious experience" usually, therefore, means making essentially private experiences the validater of religious utterances. Experienced contents that to someone observing me would seem unexceptional, *I* experience as the love or the chastisement of God. And if I say I experience the love of God, who is to dispute it? It is, after all, *my* experience.

But there is the crux of the problem. 'I experience what I experience' is indeed irrefutable. But it is hard to see what assertions, religious or otherwise, could be supported by this report. As soon as I identify my experience, as soon as I say, for example, 'I experience God's love,' I introduce a word or phrase for which, by using it to *identify* my experience, I claim a public meaning. If I say "I experience glom," and you ask, "What is glom?" and I respond, "This is glom," meanwhile sprinkling pepper in the air, 'glom' acquires the force to identify my experience. But if I respond, "Glom is what I am experiencing," glom' remains meaningless, and the object of my experience remains *unidentified*. Alasdair MacIntyre has put it perfectly: ". . . to name our private experiences in such a way that they can be . . . identified . . . is to introduce words which are used according to rules. And a rule is something essentially public. . . . So words like 'pain' and 'sensation,' which refer to private experiences, if any words do, are words in public language. It is not that we have private experience and invent words for them. But we learn the words and find their application in our experience." [109]

In general, if I say I have such-and-such experiences, you should take my word for it. But the words I use to say 'such-and-such,' here 'of God' or 'of God's love,' must, if my assertion that I have

109. MacIntyre, "The Logical Status of Religious Belief," *Metaphysical Beliefs,* pp. 167–211; see p. 197.

such-and-such experiences is itself to be meaningful, be governed by rules making possible public adjudication of sentences in which they occur. Thus my private experience may very well confirm me in my religiosity, but it cannot confirm my religious utterances, which is what we are discussing. Private religious experience cannot be the evidence relevant to the truth or falsity of theological utterances.

The next path that beckons is to develop a christological version of this appeal to religious experience. If all theological utterances are about Christ, perhaps the special experience that verifies them is "personal confrontation" with Him? Perhaps we should claim that God *can* be met, as Christ, so that this meeting is given as the event relevant to the truth of theological statements, and that while the one who meets God in Christ indeed cannot point Him out to others, this is only because the meeting with Him is a "pure I-Thou encounter." Most contemporary theology[110] has made this move, seeing the salvation of theology in the categories worked out by post-Feuerbach Hegelians. But this will not do either. R. W. Hepburn has made the decisive observation:[111] If I "purify" the "I-Thou relation" of all factual information *about* the one encountered, there is then no way to decide which person I encounter or even if it is a person at all. A personal encounter is not self-authenticating apart from impersonally verifiable assertions. If I meet Jones the plumber, that this person *is* Jones the plumber is an empirical assertion verifiable in the usual way. I always encounter a particular Thou—if I "encounter" anything at all—for example, the Risen Christ. But 'Jones the plumber' or 'the Risen Christ' is a description and therefore can be used only if certain facts obtain.[112] If I am to point out God to myself in the I-Thou encounter, I must have information *about* Him so as to be able to say, "This is He. This is not He." And these statements of information-about God or Christ will not be verifiable by an encounter that is supposed to be pure of all learning-about.

110. See the next chapter.
111. Hepburn, *Christianity and Paradox,* pp. 24–60.
112. This translates Hepburn slightly into our earlier idiom.

If I suddenly begin to speak as if to a person, but you as a third person see and hear no one (prayer!), you will ask; "With whom are you speaking?" If I respond, "With Jones," you will ask, "Who is Jones?" If I then respond, "The one with whom I am speaking," all is lost. And the case is not changed by postponements, so: "Jones is the all-present." "What does 'all-present' mean?" "That I can now speak with him." At some point we must step outside the direct personal encounter if the language in encounter is to be in any way adjudicable.

In our search for events or states of affairs relevant to the truth or falsity of theological assertions, we must therefore turn to what can be publicly pointed out. The obvious suggestion, for the language of Christian theology, was also made by Crombie: Jesus Christ as the Judge of the quick and the dead. The believer "looks for the resurrection of the dead, and the life of the world to come." [113] Crombie does not make much of the idea, but John Hick has developed it—or rather, an idea somewhat like it—as the main key to the logic of theology, under the rather odd name "eschatological verification." [114]

Hick sees faith as a fundamental "interpretation" of human existence and the world we exist in. The choice between religion and irreligion is analogous to that between the natural attitude and solipsism with respect to the reality of the other-than-me: no evidence or formal proof is either obtainable or needed. The believer is one who "sees in his situation as a human being a significance to which the appropriate response is . . . trust and obedience." [115] The believer "comes to terms" with himself and his world in terms such as 'creative,' 'God,' etc. The difference between the theist and the atheist is "the difference between two radically different ways of viewing and engaging in the experience of human life." [116]

Thus the issue between religion and irreligion is not experimental. No accumulation of evidence can establish or decisively refute either interpretation—though this does not relieve us of the inevitability of

113. Crombie, "Arising from the University Discussions," pp. 129.
114. John Hick, *Faith and Knowledge,* esp. pp. 109–63.
115. Ibid., p. 129.
116. Ibid., p. 139.

interpreting one way or the other. So far Hick has simply followed a familiar path. But now he goes on to assert, contra Flew, that theism is nevertheless a genuine assertion. For whereas naturalism interprets the world as complete in itself, religion interprets the world and man's life as "many-storied," so that man has a "spiritual nature" as well as a material nature. According to Hick, this means that the religious interpretation involves the claim that "some or all human personalities survive bodily death." [117]

As a consequence there *is* a crux between the religious and the irreligious interpretations of reality: If we do in fact survive death, this will verify the religious interpretation. And theism is, therefore, a genuine assertion.

But what will this experience of survival be like, and how will it verify one particular interpretation of predeath existence? Could we not invent any number of "interpretations" that included a survival claim but were not theistic? (This last question is not explicitly asked by Hick, but it seems to determine the continued development of his argument.) Hick's description of postdeath life as it is supposed to be predicted by the theistic interpretation is that it will be a life in which "the evidence for God's reality, instead of being systematically ambiguous, is wholly indicative of the divine presence. . . ." It will be a life in which the interpretation of life as mediating the divine presence will, while remaining an *interpretation* and so not demonstrable, be "the natural mode of apperception. . . ." [118]

What are we to say to this? That theological utterances will be adjudicated by the eschaton is the unanimous testimony of the theological tradition. And, indeed, the parable with which Hick counters Flew's parable about the garden beautifully expresses the true situation. "Two men are travelling together along a road. . . . All the time one of them is thinking of his journey as a pilgrimage to the Celestial City and interprets the pleasant stretches as encourage-

117. Ibid., p. 150. I have to say that this entire key section of the argument seems to me a mass of non sequiturs and unclarified language, e.g., "spiritual."
118. Ibid., p. 160.

ments and the obstacles as trials of his purpose. . . . The other believes none of this and sees their journey as an . . . aimless ramble. Since he has no choice in the matter he enjoys the good stretches and endures the bad. . . . During the course of the journey the issue between them is not an experimental one. They do not entertain different expectations about the coming details of the road, but only about its ultimate destination. And yet when they do turn the last corner it will be apparent that one of them has been right all the time and the other wrong." [119]

Yet Hick's more prosaic version of the analysis seems wrong at almost every point except the mere slogan of "eschatological verification." The poor reception that Hick's version has received is, I think, quite justified.[120] "Eschatological verification" is indeed the key to the logic of theological utterances. Thus the fundamental primitive confession of Christian faith was "Jesus is Lord." When this sentence is unpacked, it reveals a set of assertions about Jesus' future acts. That Jesus is "kurios," "Lord," means, in the summary language of the Creed, that "He shall come again with glory to judge both the quick and the dead." These future acts, if they take place, will be emphatically public and will verify in the most intersubjective way desirable the assertions of faith's confession that Jesus is Lord. Their failure to supervene would refute the confession. Thus Flew's demand seems to be satisfied simply by taking faith's talk about Jesus at face value.

Yet here we are already saying something quite different from what Hick says. And it is just at the point of the difference that the

---

119. Hick, *Faith and Knowledge,* pp. 150 f.

120. Decisive critiques of eschatological verification in Hick's version are given by Schmidt, op. cit., pp. 58 ff.; and Martin, op. cit., pp. 105–107, 117, 123. MacIntyre, "The Logical Status of Religious Beliefs," pp. 18 f., argues that if theological beliefs are eschatologically or otherwise verifiable, they are hypotheses and claim only provisional adherence—which is not how believers hold them. But he forgets that eschatological verification is verification at the *end,* of beliefs about the *whole* of life; so that if these are hypotheses, they are hypotheses on which we bet our lives—which is *just* what "faith" is.

Hick has also expounded his views in "Theology and Verification," in *The Existence of God,* and in *Philosophy of Religion.*

problems of Hick's analysis appear. The event that is, according to him, predicted by theological language, will be the experience of a religiously unambiguous life, a life in which the theistic interpretation will be as inevitable as faith in the reality of external nature is now. But we must ask what is to *happen* as a change from the present state of affairs. Hick seems to think of a decisive tip in the balance of evidence. But this will not do at all. For as he himself has insisted, rejection or adoption of a total "interpretation" is quite unaffected by evidence. The problem is that Hick has set up the whole matter in the framework of mere religious "theism" and its language. That language will surely be quite as indifferent to verification on the "other side" of death—what-ever that might be—as on this side. The occurrence of religious experience simply will not verify assertions about the putative object of that experience, not even when it is the experience of survivors of death.

It is not certain private characters of our experience, when we shall have survived death, that are predicted by Christian assertions, but certain public acts of Jesus. 'Jesus is Lord' predicts that a series of events dramatically appropriate as the conclusion of the story of Jesus, as already known to us, will settle the issue of our lives: that is, that those events will happen to and with us also, and that the involvement of each of us will be the dramatically appropriate issue also of each of our lives. The future event predicted by all specifically Christian theological assertions is thus, in terms of Jesus' own deed, "He will come again to judge the quick and the dead," in term of our life stories, "resurrection." It is *not* religiously unambiguous survival.

Four points in this proposal require further comment. The first is that the predictions whose fulfillment will verify our utterances about God are all predictions about Jesus Christ, a man already known to us. Otherwise, the notion of eschatological verification does not, after all, solve any of our old problems. For suppose we were to say simply that *God* (rather than Jesus Christ) will come, and that His coming will verify what we have been saying about Him. Unless we know enough about God so that we will be able to tell which coming is His coming, His coming will verify nothing.

It can only be utterances about a God who has been identified by a reference to some reality of this world—about which we can then make assertions meaningful in the ordinary way—which can be eschatologically verified.

The second is that the proposal introduces a new notion: "dramatically appropriate." We need this notion because 'He will come again to judge,' said about Jesus Christ, who died in Palestine centuries ago, poses some problems of meaning of its own. If Jones dies, and then after a lapse a person appears who claims to be Jones, by what criteria will we judge? That is, with what criteria for the truth or falsity of 'This man who now claims to be Jones is indeed Jones' will we operate? We must have some criteria, or the alleged assertions will be meaningless. Will we insist that the past Jones and the present Jones look alike before we pronounce them one? That there be continuity of memory? What *are* the criteria of personal identity? And even supposing that the usual criteria, whatever they may be, were all otherwise satisfied, would we *ever* be satisfied that this new Jones was the same person as our old Jones, in this case where death had intervened? What do we *mean,* 'This man who now appears as Jones is/is not the same as the Jones who died last year'? What do we *mean,* 'Jesus, who was crucified, will/will not come to judge the quick and the dead'?

The matter of personal identity is trickier than it first appears.[121] Let us suppose a person has left the room, and one has entered. Are they the same? In some cases it is clear that we will deny this: if the second person appears quite different, has no memory of the deeds done by the first person etc. In other cases the affirmation of identity is clearly called for: if, there is, for example, continuity of appearance and memory. But what if we should suddenly be presented with a case where there was perfect continuity of memory but great and inexplicable difference of appearance, or sex, or age, or race?

121. See Antony Flew, "Death," *New Essays* in *Philosopical Theology,* pp. 267 ff. For an interesting opening of the problem, see the debate reproduced by V. G. Aldrich as "Messrs. Schick and Ayer on Immortality," *Philosophical Reviw,* p. 47.

We would be quite at a loss whether or not to say 'This is the same person': that is, our presently established rules for using 'same person' simply would not cover the case. We would have to stipulate rules for the new case then and there—which would have to be done by simply stipulating: We will/will not call this person the 'same person' as the one who has just left the room.

How we will stipulate is a *decision* question.[122] A further specification of the way we use a key word of our language is demanded, and we must decide what specification we will make. Such a decision is a metaphysical decision; by it we decide what kinds of realities we will reckon with. In the present case our decision about how we will use 'same person' projects a vision of what man is or is to be. We do in fact make such decisions as we try to make increasing sense of existence; by making them, we step by step assume our posture toward the world.

It is clear that the claim that "this same Jesus," who was crucified so long ago, will come again is a case that our ordinary rules for 'same person' do not cover. It is a case where the claim must be *given* meaning by stipulating new rules for 'same person.' How will we decide? The issue is metaphysical; we will by our decision decide again how we will go at the world. If we are believers, we will posit a concept of personal identity consonant with the pattern of faith to which we are called.

What would such a concept be? Christian faith has a dramatic conception of man. A person is not a thing with attributes; a person is a *story*. It is for this reason that I suggest that personal identity be understood as the dramatic continuity of a story. Then dramatic appropriateness will be the criterion of personal identity and will be the rule for using 'same person' where more convenient rules about

---

122. "A queer, quasi-legal problem this, to identify two people as the same person. And a disturbing one: for we assume too easily that all questions about personal identity must be straight questions of fact, even though some questions about the identity of things are decision issues. . . . A decision issue is one in which what is at stake is: not what the facts are; but what we are going to decide correct verbal usage to be in the future, when the facts use thus and thus." Flew, "Death," pp. 271 f.

appearance and the like fail us. If a series of events fits Jones's story
as so far written, then the doer of those events is Jones.[123] If this
criterion is followed, the degree of certainty attainable in questions
of personal identity will, to be sure, vary with the degree to which
the person's or persons' life has an unique style and accomplishment. But this seems to me a *recommendation* of the proposed criteria.

We are able to make such judgments of dramatic appropriateness.
We say that the third act "somehow didn't fit" or that the play
"hung together" admirably. Aristotle pointed this out long ago. And
we are also able to say, "That just is/isn't the sort of thing Jones
would do," also where Jones is not a character in a play. These
judgments are after the fact. But, knowing the playwright to be
competent and to have a distinct artistic personality, we can also say
midway through Act II "I don't see how he's going to work this
out, but he will, and it won't be by having Jeddial be suddenly con-
verted either." We can predict *that* the conclusion will be dramatically appropriate and, in the individual case, delineate some limits of
what will be accepted as dramatically appropriate and what will not
be. Moreover, after the fact we can judge whether our prediction
was fulfilled: "He did it, the third act fits perfectly." Whether this
kind of prediction can ever be true about human existence outside
of the stage and books is, of course, the fundamental metaphysical
issue. Faith, which is exactly living life by its outcome and so with a
plot, is an affirmative decision on this issue.[124]

The appropriate mode of making predictions about history—that
is, about persons, about man-as-story—is to make predictions subject
to this criterion of continuity. Theological utterance is the making

123. This should not be taken as a particularly individualistic notion of
man. If, for example, in a tribal culture, the *tribe* acts, then personal identity is that of the tribe.

124. The suggestion is implicit that the one who has adopted the posture of unbelief has shut himself off from being able to use the correct criterion of personal identity. I do indeed think this. The problem of personal
identity will be insoluble for any unbeliever. My saying this is not an attempt
at apologetics; perhaps the correct view of the problem is to see it as insoluble.

of such predictions about Jesus and, insofar as His act is done on us, about ourselves.

The prediction *that* a history will conclude in a dramatically appropriate way and the delineation of *what* will be accepted as dramatically appropriate are independent of each other. Moved by confidence in the author, I can say during Act II of a play, "The conclusion will fit somehow," even when I am unable to see what a satisfactory conclusion would be. Moreover, after the fact I can judge whether my prediction was fulfilled: "I never would have thought of it, but it was of course what had to happen." If, therefore, I am asked for the events relative to the confirmation or falsification of a theological utterance, and refer to 'an event dramatically appropriate as the conclusion of Jesus' story,' this is a sufficient stipulation. By it alone the theological utterance is given meaning as an assertion; no specifications of physical confrontation or spiritual experiences are required.[125]

The attempt to delineate what will in fact be acceptable as a dramatically appropriate conclusion to the story of Jesus is a separate enterprise and the matter of theological eschatology. What will be said—whether, for example, a bodily appearance of Jesus is demanded, and what 'body' could mean in this context—depends upon other theological considerations. What is important now is to see that the events relevant to the truth or falsity of theological utterances can be stipulated independently of these problematical matters.

The third comment touches the phrases "the conclusion of the story of Jesus" and "the issue of our lives." It is clear that even if we

125. "It is natural for those whose conception of rationality has been modelled upon the natural sciences to insist that a final stand be made somewhere and the doctrine of grace be put to some decisive test. But the challenge has to be refused, because we are dealing with a . . . Person. That His activity issues in discernible differences I have been at pains to argue, but we cannot with confidence predict what these will be. The appropriate comparison is with other types of creative activity. It would not, for example, have been possible to predict what Shakespeare would make of the original story of Macbeth. . . . Nevertheless when confronted with the completed tragedy . . . we recognize them to be characteristic of their authors." Basil Mitchell, *The Grace of God,* p. 170.

could historically establish that Jesus had come back to life, this would in no way establish that the conclusion of His life will be the conclusion of ours: that is, that 'God is Jesus' is true. For even if we could know that He had come alive again and was now living, He might very well die again. And were He now suddenly to appear, however impressively, and deal with us, however decisively, nothing would establish that this was the *conclusion* of our stories. This is a hopeless muddle as long as the matter is thought of as Jesus having come back to life, being off somewhere now, and being going to "come back some day." It is hopeless so long as the "conclusion of our lives" is thought of as simply the last event: how would we ever know it to be the last? Only if the "conclusion of the story of Jesus" and "the issue of our lives" are both meant as ways of talking about *death*—and not about some "survival" after death—can they be meaningful expressions. Both are transcriptions of "Death and Resurrection." Here also we touch the problems of the next chapter.

The fourth point is that when the predictive element in an empirical hypothesis, whether scientific or everyday, is specified, we get something of the form 'If you do such and such, such and such will happen.' Thus, to take a famous example, 'This table is hard' predicts: 'If you hit it with your knuckles, they will smart.' The protasis of such conditionals is always, as here, something the inquirer is to do. But when the predictive element in theological assertions is specified, no such protasis appears. We cannot say, 'If you do such and such, Jesus will return.' Attempts that have been made, like "If we evangelize the world, the Kingdom will come in," are sub-Christian. Theological utterances do not, therefore, satisfy the *same* verifiability criterion as do empirical hypotheses. They satisfy *a* verifiability criterion. Theological language is *one of* the many descriptive assertive languages that interlock in our discourse.

The content of the basic onlook which, in *Christian* tradition, introduces 'God' into our discourse is: Jesus of Nazareth is my final future, on the day dated by death. Or: Jesus' story will be the exercitive and verdictive address to me which will finally settle the significance of my life. Moreover, when 'God' is introduced in *this* way, the things we say about God are not uncontrollable. We say that about God for which Jesus' story leads us to hope, and our hopes will be conclusively fulfilled or disappointed.

The things believers say about God do make predictions about future public events and do therefore satisfy a verifiability criterion. Many may think it necessary to judge the predictions fantastic and therefore to reject the assertions of faith. But that is another matter. Any analysis of theological language which evades the notion of verifiability is simply inaccurate as an analysis of the particular, actually used language with which we are concerned.

Theological statements are exercitive and assertive at once. They posit the future—and do so as statements of alleged fact. They are both value judgments and assertions; that is to say, they are eschatological.

A theological statement is therefore true if it in some way tells the story of Jesus Christ as the story of the end, and so the meaning, of our lives. It is thus judged by two partial criteria: First, it must correctly narrate the story of Jesus Christ; that is, if interpreted simply as a statement about this man, it must be correct in the ordinary way of statements about figures of history. Thus, 'God is loving' is correct taken simply as 'Jesus gave himself up.'

But by what criterion? How do we tell when the story of Jesus Christ is correctly narrated? One possible answer would be to say that it is the historian's task, working with the available records— the Scriptures—as data to be sifted, to discover the true story of Jesus—that is, to judge statements about him. Another answer would be the doctrine of the authority of Scripture, the position that the story of Jesus is correctly told when told in essential agreement with the version or versions thereof found in Scripture. Here we are again well into the next chapter.

Second, a theological assertion must tell the story of Christ as the conclusion of the actual lives of those to whom it is addressed. If no one can recognize himself in what is said, the statement fails. Issues arise here that lead again into the next chapter, and some lead beyond the scope of this book. Discovering *how* to tell the story of Christ so as to make plain its claim on its hearers is the regular and continuing task of theology. Here I wish only to make the point that the requirement of relevance and actuality is thus more than a general desideratum of theological utterance. It is not correct to say: "What he says is true but he can't make it understood." A statement in which those using it—whether as speakers or hearers—cannot find something about their own lives is simply *not* true in the sense of 'true' appropriate to theological statements.

Clearly, the criterion stated in these partial criteria is *functional*. It tests theological utterances by what they *do* to and for us in our existence. The performative-descriptive nature of theological utterance rules out any such strictly linguistic criterion as the inerrancy of Scripture or the infallibility of the teaching office. The theological tradition knows this functional criterion as the demand that theological utterance is adequate only if it "properly distinguishes Law and Gospel"—where "Law" means any word that makes us *seek* a future, and "Gospel" means the narration to us of that future.

V.

If all this is right, then we must make one last point about theological language—to lead again into the next chapter. This language works only on the assumption that a certain factual assertion about the past is true: that Jesus is risen from the dead. If He is only an item of the past, theology's basic onlook is false. Only if He is risen into the future, do the rules we have found to govern theological language form a consistent, workable set.

"On the third day He rose again from the dead." Clearly this is intended as factual narrative; it intends to recount a stretch of Jesus' story, and does so in a tone no different from that of "suffered under Pontius Pilate." Yet what this sentence claims is something quite beyond the possibility of historical knowledge. This bit of narrative is already a call for faith. To say 'He is risen' and to say 'He is Lord' are the same.

"He is risen" is the point where narration becomes gift and demand, the point where it becomes narration of the fulfillment of my story. "He is risen" is the union of narrative and proclamation, of tradition and kerygma. With this word the Gospel proclaims the identity of the Jesus whose story can be told as historical narrative and the One who will come as final judge. "He is risen" posits a union of present and future, of what is and the meaning of what is, of fact and value. To affirm statements in a language in which utterances about Jesus function as both performative of the final meaning of life and as factual narrative *is* to assert that Jesus is risen.

In general, talk about 'God' arises from positing eternity as the union of past and future, and so from evading the threat of the future, from evading the threat of death. Christian talk attacks this evasion and just so is itself constrained to speak of God. But where religion puts timeless being, faith puts an event, the Resurrection. This event is the union of what is available to us as the past with what we are called to as the future; it is the union of past and future in which we can live *for* something. The reality of this possibility is God.[126]

If we believe theological utterances are eschatological; the hidden logical hinge of every one of them is, therefore, "He is risen."

126. Introducing such fundamental *theological* considerations in so off-hand a fashion would be quite irresponsible if I did not express myself more fully elsewhere: cf. *God after God,* soon to be published.

6. Hermeneutics: Historicity

For most of this century the English Channel and the Atlantic Ocean have divided two philosophical worlds—and as a consequence seen a great deal of theological misunderstanding. Yet the underlying difficulties have been the same on both sides. In 1929, Rudolph Bultmann,[1] whose students now dominate German theology more than ever, wrote on exactly our problem: "What sense does it make to speak of God?"[2]

He flatly denied that it is possible to speak of God in "generally valid sentences . . . that are true apart from a connection to the concrete existentiell situation of the speaker. . . ."[3] This is so because we can speak so only of objects; such language operates, therefore, with "the subject/object schema"; and this schema is inapplicable to God, since we can find no standpoint outside of God from which to view Him as an object.[4]

1. For a nearly exhaustive treatment and a bibliography of the discussion that Bultmann has caused, cf. Günther Bornkamm, "Die Theologie Rudolf Bultmanns in der neueren Diskussion," *Theologische Rundschau,* 29, 1/2, pp. 33-141.

2. "Welchen Sinn hat es, von Gott zu reden?" Now in *Glauben und Verstehen,* I, pp. 26-37.

3. Bultmann, op. cit., p. 26.

4. Ibid., pp. 26-33.

Only *in* the meeting with God—that is, in faith—can we meaningfully say 'God.' Such language is completely "undenotable" and
"unsecured": that is, in our previous terminology, unverifiable.[5]
Such language is "nonobjectifying." It is used in the "concerned act"
of personal existence. The understanding that fulfills itself in such
speech is "existentiell" [6] that is, it is an act of personal choice which
is the very act of personal life. As such this understanding is available only to the one who chooses and can never issue in objectifying
descriptions.[7]

Yet Bultmann denies "that the nonobjectifiability of existentiell
decision means . . . its complete subjectivity, . . ." for decision occurs in the meeting of persons, in a situation in which the subject
transcends itself toward another—and it is this meeting which is
the reality bespoken by existentiell speech.[8] As examples of such a
language, which takes place as meeting and in which existence expresses itself directly, Bultmann therefore gives "I love you" or
"Please forgive me." [9]

There is also a language in which we speak *about* existence—
though here, too, as existence, not as an object. This is the existential
—as against existentiell—language of philosophy.[10] The paragraphs
above are a sample. God Himself can be bespoken only in existentiell speech. In existential speech we can only "develop the sense of
the *idea* of God and of faith in him. . . . But of God himself one
can only speak directly out of existence, in fear and trembling, in
thanksgiving and trust." [11]

The existentiell speech *in* which 'God' is proper is the speech of

5. Ibid., pp. 36 f.
6. All translations of *existentiell* and *existential* are misleading. Perhaps
this indicates that the possibility of making this distinction in German is a
vice rather than a virtue of that language. Anyway, I have chosen simply
to transliterate.
7. Bultmann, "Wissenschaft und Existenz," *Glauben und Verstehen,* III,
pp. 107–21. pp. 115 f.
8. Ibid., p. 117.
9. Bultmann, "Zum Problem der Entymythogisierung," *Kerygma und
Mythos,* II, pp. 179–208, p. 187.
10. Ibid., p. 187.
11. "Wissenschaft und Existenz," p. 120.

prayer, of praise and of that proclamation which is a direct challenge to the hearer's decision. In it no neutrally verifiable statements
about God appear. Theology must step out of this direct confrontation. But theology's existential speech can therefore only analyze
that human existence in which faith-in-God occurs; it cannot speak
of God Himself: that is, in terms of language, existential, theological speech does not *contain* the word "God." It speaks *about* the
word 'God.'

But language is always already given when we speak, and em-
bodies some specific ontological interpretation which is simply given
to our act of speaking; for example, it contains words like 'world'
and 'human.' Thus direct existentiell expression of the meeting with
God "as soon as it is spoken in words and sentences, appears in a
particular interpretation. . . ." Since this interpretation must itself
be the fruit of existential reflection, and since in any case my attempt to understand the witness to the meeting with God and to
make it my own witness in my language, will involve existential reflection, existentiell speech out of the meeting with God and existential, theological speech about existence so qualified can never be so
neatly sorted out in actuality as we have so far made it appear. But
the distinction is nevertheless fundamental for our understanding of
what we are doing when we use 'God.' [12]

Finally, since language is always already given, even direct existentiell expression must make at least implicit affirmations about
God. Thus even 'Our father . . .' calls God father; and when we
come to proclamation, we find ourselves necessarily making all sorts
of assertions about God's deeds and the like. Bultmann says that
such speech is "analogical": ". . . when we speak in this manner
of God as acting, we conceive the communion between God and
man as an analogue to the communion between man and man."

Bultmann does not really clarify what he means by "analogy."
But he insists that "God's love and care etc. are not images or symbols; these conceptions mean real experiences of God as acting here

12. Bultmann, "Das Problem des Verhältnisses von Theologie und
Verkündigung im Neuen Testament," *Aux Sources de la Tradition
Chrétienne,* 1960, pp. 32–42, p. 34.

and now." They are realistic speech and not images or symbols because uttering them is the very carrying out of the meeting with the one they name. We are justified and indeed required to speak so "since . . . we are not speaking of an idea about God"—in which case "God's love" would be a metaphysical symbol, a *chiffre*—"but of God Himself." [13]

Why can we never speak of God in "objectifying"—that is, verifiable—statements or even in neutral existential analysis? "God always remains beyond what we have once grasped: i.e., my decision of faith is only valid in that it is made always anew. [God] always stands before me as the *Coming One, and this his constant futurity is his transcendence.*" [14] Thus to call Jesus God is to say that the word about Him calls us to a final decision.[15]

Many of Bultmann's positions seem already familiar to us, and much of our previous discussion can simply be taken as repeated here. We have already attacked the central claim that the language of personal encounter needs no impersonal verifiability to maintain its grasp on reality. And the "analogy" that Bultmann proposes to substitute for verifiability we have also criticized, with negative results (supposing, that is, that Bultmann means anything specific by the term). The meeting with God as a person is not an analogous meeting with an analogously personal "person," but a meeting with a regular-type person, Jesus of Nazareth, in the way in which historical persons are ordinarily met, through the story about Him.

This summary critique, though correct and justified, would be superficial, for it is plain that the whole context of Bultmann's analysis is different. The context here is man's question about himself as existing, as *history*. Bultmann's concern for the operation of theological language arises from his work as an interpreter of the New Testament—that is, from his work as one whose task it is to interpret a historical document that claims to speak to us in the present about our God. His question is: How is this possible? And this is

13. Bultmann, *Jesus Christ and Mythology,* pp. 68 f.
14. Ibid., p. 121.
15. Bultmann, "Das christologische Bekenntnis des Ökumenischen Rates," *Glauben und Verstehen,* II, pp. 246–61.

also the question of this chapter: How does *historical* narration about God work? Since historical narration is the same as interpretation of the tradition, the thinkers with whom we will converse call this the "hermeneutical question." Bultmann has stated it so: "How is it possible to understand the documents of the historical tradition?"[16] We can specify: ". . . in respect of God?" This statement of the question has been improved by Gerhard Ebeling, who points out that we seek to understand, not words, but reality by means of words. Thus hermeneutical reflection is reflection on how words work to illumine reality;[17] and our question is: How do the documents of historical tradition bring God to understanding?[18]

II.

We continue with Bultmann:

To interpret a text is to make explicit—that is, state in language—what we have understood from the text.[19] But how *do* we interpret a text—that is, bring it to explicitly stated understanding? Bultmann begins simply: We go to the text with a question, a question that has some importance for us, or we would not ask it. Any text can be questioned from a variety of angles: aesthetic, economic, etc. Our choice of a way of questioning is determined by our interest—that is, by the direction of our own lives. Our putting of a question to a text therefore presupposes a certain interest in the matter of the text, which obviously cannot occur without a certain understanding thereof, which is thus a "prior understanding." This understanding

16. Bultmann, *Geschichte und Eschatologie*, p. 123.

17. Bultmann, "Wort Gottes und Hermeneutik," *Zeitschrift für Theologie und Kirche*, 56, 2, pp. 224–51, pp. 237 ff.

18. The most comprehensive, and in many ways generally satisfactory, development of the hermeneutic viewpoint is that of Hans-Georg Gadamer, *Wahrheit und Methode*. I could have developed the first two-thirds of this chapter in discussion with him, instead of Bultmann, Ebeling, and Ott. I chose not to in order to stay as close as possible to theology, and because to impose my theological criteria on Gadamer would have been to impose foreign criteria. My own dependence on Gadamer should be stated.

19. Cf. Bultmann, "Das Problem der Hermeneutik," *Glauben und Verstehen*, II, pp. 211–35, pp. 262 f., and his reference there to p. 31 and 32 of Heidegger's *Sein und Zeit*.

is interested understanding and so is part of the complex of choices and decisions that is our movement through life: it is existentiell.[20] So: "The possibility of understanding is based on this, that the interpreter has *a life-relation to the matter which comes to word . . . in the text.*" And this "life-relation" of the interpreter to what is said in the text is given "by the simple fact that author and interpreter live in the same historical world, in which human being plays itself out as a being-*in* understanding intercourse with objects and fellow-men."[21]

The question with which we approach the text can be the desire to understand human life itself: What is life about? Since the interpreter is himself human, and indeed is carrying out his human existence in the very act of existentiell interest which leads him to the text, the interpreter who asks this question of the text "concerns himself, in that he concerns himself with history, for his own possibilities, and seeks to win knowledge of himself. . . ."[22] The "prior understanding" which is the possibility of such questioning is existentiell confrontation with the problem of human life. We confront this problem simply because we do live and therefore must and do choose what our life shall be. Understanding is made possible by a seeking, uncertain prior understanding of human existence—here operating not in some aspect, like interest, for example, in economics—but as such, as concern for the interpretation of human life.[23]

Such interpretation is existential interpretation. We ask about a text: ". . . does an apprehension of human existence show itself in this text, which . . . proposes a possibility of understanding also for today's . . . man? Which . . . means a genuine decision also for him?"[24] To face such a decision in a text is existentiell understanding; to ask about it in this way is existential interpretation. Existen-

20. *Geschichte und Eschatologie*, pp. 126–33.
21. Ibid., pp. 126 f.
22. Ibid., p. 128.
23. Ibid., p. 128; "Das Problem der Hermeneutik," p. 228; "Zum Problem der Entmythologisierung," *Kerygma und Mythos* II, p. 191.
24. Bultmann, "Neues Testament und Mythologie," *Kerygma und Mythos,* I, p. 28.

tial interpretation has the task of bringing existentiell understanding to clarity—and so "holding it to itself." [25] The difference is between *hearing* and *asking*: "Did I understand?"

Existential interpretation is the genuinely historical use of history, for it corresponds to the essential nature of man's historical being.[26] "The historicity of human being is fully understood only when human being is understood as life in responsibility for the future and so as life in decision." [27] This is more fully expanded: ". . . everything which man does in his present . . . reveals what it really is only in the future. All is a venture. . . . This irreducible futurity is the historicity of human being, or rather, its temporality, in which its historicity is founded. . . . This futurity is . . . a coming forth out of a past" in that the past leads us into the situation of decision in which we face a future.[28] The past puts us in the situation of decision because it determines our choice, and yet does so ambiguously. For each must decide "what of his past shall be valid . . . and from what he shall free himself. . . ." [29]

Existential interpretation of a text therefore interprets the text as a question directed to the interpreter, who *is* in that he decides. Existential interpretation therefore uses the language appropriate to talking about the questioning, deciding, future-seeking character of life —that is, to talking about "existence." [30] Seeking this language is not a specifically theological task: it is done in that "profane reflection . . . which is the business of philosophical analysis of existence." And this reflection is nothing but "the clear and methodical explication of that understanding of being which is given with existence itself. . . ." that is, of the existentiell questioning about life

25. "Zur Problem der Entmythologisierung," p. 189.
26. The famous "demythologizing" is merely the negative side of existential interpretation and needs no special discussion here. What Bultmann understands by "myth" is speaking about the future which we are called to decide as if what is already actual could make the decision for us. Cf. "Die Christologie des Neuen Testaments," *Glauben und Verstehen*, I, pp. 245-67, p. 245.
27. *Geschichte und Eschatologie*, p. 102.
28. Ibid., pp. 168 f.
29. Bultmann, *Offenbarung und Heilsgeschehen*, pp. 14 f.
30. I.e., in *Existentialien*. Cf. Heidegger, *Sein und Zeit*, p. 44.

which leads us to concern ourselves with history in the first place.[31] Therewith the "hermeneutical circle" is closed: The entire enterprise of understanding and interpretation is possible only because we always already understand "in a way": that is, because we always just do find ourselves already living in a historically given world.

What about *theological* interpretation of history? How do we question texts about God? Here also understanding is possible because of an existentiell prior understanding which is simply given with our temporal existence.[32] In that we ask a text about God, we do somehow understand 'God.' "But does man know God, because he has a concept of God? No. He has only the God-question. . . ." The key part follows: ". . . and the knowledge that is contained in this question is basically none other than *knowledge about himself,* knowledge about what he is not and does not have. . . ." [33] The existentiell prior knowledge of God is given with existence in that it is identical with our existentiell questioning understanding of our own being.[34]

I wish here to state my general agreement with this development so far. But there is a conclusion that seems inevitable but that Bultmann never draws—for reasons that will appear later. The prior understanding behind, and the question put by, theological interpretation of a text is, we see, the same as that of existential interpretation in general. Must it not follow that all existential—that is, truly historical—use of history is, if pursued to the end, questioning about God? If only as a deepening of the God-question? And does this not also mean that the "only" in "only the question after God" is out-of-place—unless we are to attach the "only" to all historical understanding, which Bultmann clearly does not wish us to do? I want to draw all of these conclusions.

If we draw these conclusions, we can then go on to say: To question a text historically means to question it with reference to my own future—that is, with reference to the decision the text may call

31. Ibid., pp. 189–92. Cf. also "Das Problem der Hermeneutik," pp. 232 f.
32. "Das Problem der Hermeneutik," p. 232.
33. *Offenbarung und Heilsgeschehen,* p. 6.
34. "Das Problem der Hermeneutik," p. 232.

me to make. To question a text theologically is to question it about my *final* future, about what is to come of my life. And this is also the question about myself, about that final decision in which I am myself—for there must be a conclusion to my story if the occurrences of my life are to be a *story* at all, are to cohere as a life. Therefore the question about God is the presupposition of all historical questioning; and all historical questioning is implicitly the God-question.

The condition of our being able to question a text is the common history in which we and the text live. What would be the condition of our being able to question a text about God? Simply *that* there is any history and that there is history prior to all our questioning. And so again our ability to question history about God is the condition of our being able to question history at all.

Back to Bultmann. He asks the question: If genuine historical questioning is questioning about myself, does not this doom historical knowledge to hopeless subjectivity? Is objectivity possible here at all? In the sense that research,[35] using methods essentially no different from those of the natural sciences, can establish certain propositions about past occurrences, naturally it is possible. But such propositions are not yet history. Here Bultmann embarks on an ontological analysis of historical reality, of what is a "historical event": "Historical events and deeds are what they are . . . only together with their sense . . . historical phenomena are not what they are isolated and for themselves . . . but rather *in* their connection to a future. . . ." Thus, "History only reveals its sense when the historian, who after all, himself belongs in history, is aware of this and takes his part in history responsibly."[36] "Only the historian who is animated by his . . . responsibility for his future will be in a position to understand history. . . , to hear history's claim on him." Thus knowledge of history and knowledge of self coincide.[37] The final ontological consequence is that the subject-object division is inappropriate to historical reality: a historical "object" is itself only in that it poses a decision

35. *Historie.*
36. *Geschichte und Eschatologie,* pp. 133 f.
37. Ibid., p. 137.

for an existing "subject." [38] A historical event is real as a historical event in the challenge for my future which it poses to me.

Bultmann then says that insofar as the meeting with historical reality, thus defined, is not only existentiell confrontation but also existential interpretation, it too results in a presentation of history which neutrally says that such-and-such events represent such-and-such possibilities of existence, and which is therefore once again "objectifying." It is open to testing in discussion with other interpreters: that is, it is in some way verifiable.[39] This will count, of course, also for theological interpretation.

A certain tension is obvious between Bultmann's analysis of historical reality and the observations of the last paragraph. In particular, it is hard to see how or why existential interpretation of history should result in "objective," verifiable accounts, unless the research that establishes verifiable propositions about past events should have more specific importance for existential historical knowledge than Bultmann seems to give it—unless the kind of reality that this research uncovers should be an essential ontological determinant of historical reality. This point will occupy us later.

III.

The existentiell understanding of human life which truly fulfills man's historicity, and from which Bultmann's whole discussion in fact begins, is that which he finds posed by the New Testament. Existentially described: Man exists in that he meets others than himself, and in the decisions that these meetings pose to him. Thus his life is always future to him and can be fulfilled or lost in the decisions he makes. "In his decision he chooses basically . . . himself, as the one he truly shall and will be, or as one who fails his own true life." If he is to choose authentically, he must be free from the determination of the past, of his own past choices.[40] He must cling not to what he is, but to what will come, and precisely in its *in*deter-

38. Ibid., p. 133 f.
39. "Wissenschaft und Existenz," p. 115.
40. *Geschichte und Eschatologie*, pp. 49 f.

mination by what has been—and so he must live from that which he does not control and about which he has no guarantees. "That is 'faith': to open oneself freely to the future . . . the surrender of all security." Such existentiell self-understanding is "eschatological."[41] It is decision taken in meeting the One over whom we have no control, and over against whom the last decision falls, the decision of fulfillment or failure. Faith is decision for the insecurity of existence, in hearing God address me, in meeting the One whose address destroys my security.[42] Precisely so the believer is free: free "for genuine historical life . . . , for responsible decisions in the various meetings of life."[43] Thus the future that is at stake in the decision of faith—and so in all decision—is not "something which will come sometime in the course of time,"[44] but "futurity," the futurity of human life to itself, the freedom of authentic decision.

But how is this understanding and its existential explication historical? That is, why can it be won only through the tradition about a past event, Jesus of Nazareth? Perhaps the first proclamation of this understanding was somehow connected to Him, but why can it not now be proposed to existentiell affirmation quite without reference to Him?

Bultmann answers: Authentic historical decision is not an immediate possibility for man; he does not as he is possess the requisite freedom from himself, from his past. Precisely as we seek to fulfill our responsibility for the future, we seek to control the future and so to secure ourselves from it. And just so we remain determined by our past.[45] We must become free from our past. "But man cannot free himself from himself by his will; for in such an act of will he would remain the old man. He can receive freedom only as a gift."[46]

Therefore only a *proclamation* can free a man, a word spoken *to* him. For that I must give myself up in order to be myself is just

41. "Neues Testament und Mythologie," pp. 30 f.
42. Bultmann, "Die Krisis des Glaubens," *Glauben und Verstehen*, II, pp. 1–19, pp. 1–10.
43. *Geschichte und Eschatologie*, p. 51.
44. Bultmann, *Jesus*, p. 46.
45. *Geschichte und Eschatologie*, p. 179.
46. Ibid., p. 180.

what I cannot say to myself without perverting its existentiell meaning into the direct opposite.[47] I can receive the right to believe in God—that is, radically to receive my destiny from an other than myself—only from a word spoken *to* me which calls me to recognize God as the One addressing me.[48]

Eschatological existence is opened to me only by a word that poses a decision to me, and poses it as the decision between salvation and damnation, between authentic life and inauthentic life. Such a word must be proclamation; I cannot speak it to myself. It does not neutrally pose the possibility of authentic life, for me to weigh the pros and cons. The final choice cannot be so deliberated; the word that poses it is so purely existentiell address that it poses the possibility to me as my possibility—so that the speaking of this word is an event in which judgment and grace *happen*.[49] The eschatological proclamation challenges me to stop understanding my life from the past. It can make this challenge as my possibility because it is a word of forgiveness,[50] because it addresses me *as* one not bound by the past. The self-understanding posed by proclamation cannot be detached from the proclamation, because in it man understands himself *so* "that he learns to understand his present—as one qualified by the proclamation."[51]

But why does the word of eschatological proclamation have to occur as communication about a historical reality?[52] In order to *be* eschatological proclamation. For in being about a particular historical event lies the contingency of this message; since it is news about an event, it cannot be deduced or guaranteed; it can only be received when and if it comes. And precisely *as* contingent the proclamation can pose the eschatological decision—which is exactly that we give up all guarantees over against the contingency of the future. "The

47. Ibid., p. 181.
48. "Die Krisis der Glaubens," p. 10.
49. Bultmann, "Des Begriff des Wortes Gottes im Neuen Testament," *Glauben und Verstehen* I, pp. 268–93, p. 292; *Das Verhältnis der urchristlichen Christusbotschaft zum historischen Jesus*, pp. 25 f., note 79.
50. Bultmann, "Humanismus and Christentum," *Glauben und Verstehen,* II, p. 141.
51. *Glauben und Verstehen,* III, p. 30.
52. Ibid., p. 286.

word enters our world accidentally, contingently, as an event. There
is no guarantee, which we could rely on in believing." [53] "Only in
that an accidental historical event steps forth with the claim to be
the revelation of God, is man's claim already to know God broken."
Revelation is purely God's word *"in that* it is accidental." [54]

The same point can be reached in a different way. As the "paradoxical assertion that an historical event . . . is the eschatological
event," [55] the proclamation has the structure to which the paradoxical structure of eschatological self-understanding responds. The
Word is *"address* which is at the same time *communication,"* to
which corresponds "obedience, which is at the same time trust." [56]
The proclamation poses a self-understanding in which I am radically free *from* my historically given self precisely *for* genuine historical responsibility. It does this in that it is the eschatological
message in which the bondage to the past is set aside—as a communication about a past historical event.

Wherein is the eschatological proclamation news about *this* historical event Jesus—rather than some other? Bultmann's answer is
simply: Because this event "is proclaimed as such. . . ." [57] Jesus is
real as a historical reality in that as we hear of Him, a question is
posed about the future—this is the character of all historical reality.
It is the eschatological proclamation that in contingent fact is the
word that tells us of Jesus as a question about us. Therefore it is as
the eschatological event that Jesus is historically real. "Jesus Christ is
the eschatological event as the man Jesus of Nazareth *and* as the
word which sounds in the mouths of the men who proclaim him." [58]
That Jesus in particular poses this question, the eschatological
question, cannot be read off from the content of Jesus' life as research would describe it.[59] Insofar as existential interpretation finds
this question posed by Jesus, it is because we meet Jesus in texts that

53. "Welchen Sinn hat es von Gott zu reden?" p. 37.
54. *Offenbarung und Heilgeschechen,* p. 22.
55. *Das Verhältnis* . . . , p. 8.
56. "Die Begriff des Wortes Gottes . . . ," p. 288.
57. "Neues Testament und Mythologie," op. cit., p. 50.
58. "Das christologische Bekenntnis . . . ," op. cit., p. 257.
59. "Neues Testament und Mythologie, pp. 47, 50.

are themselves proclamatory.[60] That this proclamation about Jesus occurs is thus itself entirely contingent; nothing in the life of the historical Jesus necessitates it—as corresponds to its content.[61] Thus also the occurrence of the proclamation—marked in the proclamation as Easter—belongs itself to the contingent eschatological event.[62]

Let me at this point again record my basic agreement with Bultmann's argument—with certain reservations. We come now to the question to which Bultmann's answer is less helpful, and which is the source of those reservations: *How* does the eschatological proclamation talk about the historical event Jesus? Here the matter becomes complex. What follows is distinctly an interpretation.

The assertion that a historical event is the eschatological event is, we heard, "paradoxical." How so? Because confrontation with the eschaton—that is, with the final decision, with the reality of life's absolute futurity and insecurity—must in itself render all narratable past history existentiell irrelevant (even when that narratable past is confronted in existential interpretation). In the moment of eschatological decision the history of past decisions and the questions posed by them disappear before the historicity which is the pure present moment of future-positing decision.[63]

When, therefore, the meaningfulness in which a past event is truly historical is that it poses the eschatological decision, then the narratable course of that piece of past history is irrelevant to its historical reality. When the meaning of a historical event is eschatologically proclaimed, then what is proclaimed as meaningful is the event's pure givenness as a historical occurrence. All that needs to be said is *that* "the eschaton has happened in history." If that history is then narrated—that is, ". . . in the history of Jesus of Nazareth, who was born humbly . . ." —this is only explication of the "that."[64]

60. *Das Verhältnis* . . . , pp. 15–17, 20.
61. *Glauben und Verstehen*, I, pp. 208 f.
62. "Neues Testament und Mythologie," p. 51.
63. *Geschichte und Eschatologie*, pp. 30–49, 150 ff.
64. "Das Begriffs des Wortes Gottes . . . ," p. 292; *Das Verhältnis* . . . , pp. 2–14.

Thus the facts that research can discover about Jesus of Nazareth, the what and the how of His life, are not essential to proclamatory speech about Him. The eschatological proclamation asserts only that the eschaton has in fact happened as a historical event—as a reality of *the kind* about which research can discover facts.[65] This minimal reference to the Jesus of the past is, however, essential to the proclamation; by it the proclamation maintains itself as news about a historical contingent event and so is "legitimized" as contingent proclamation.[66]

Turning to the history of Jesus in the full sense, of the event as interpreted, with its meaning, this is either the Jesus of the eschatological proclamation or the Jesus of some other existential interpretation of the tradition about Him. Such interpretation depends on the knowledge of past facts gained by research.[67] Since what we know of Jesus is primarily His preaching, existential interpretation will be an interpretive repetition of His message: Bultmann's own Jesus, or the Synoptic Gospels insofar as these are not direct proclamation, are examples. Jesus' preaching was an eschatological message, and its repetition can therefore lead into existentiell confrontation with Jesus and His eschatological challenge. Yet even this genuinely historical contemporization of Jesus' historical reality as the witness to the eschaton is not eschatological proclamation in the sense of our discussion (and so it is not *God*-utterance). For no historical event is proclaimed *as* the eschaton; Jesus Himself is not proclaimed as the final event.[68]

And when the history of Jesus—also in this full sense—*is* proclaimed as the history of the end, then its significance, too, is exhausted in *that* it is so proclaimed. All that need be said is that the historical Jesus is the end happening—even when 'historical' has its full sense.[69] This is because of the narrative content also of existen-

65. *Das Verhälthis* . . . , pp. 9–17.
66. "Der Begriffs des Wortes Gottes . . . ," p. 292.
67. *Das Verhältnis* . . . , p. 15; *Jesus,* p. 9.
68. *Das Verhältnis* . . . , pp. 18–26.
69. Ibid., pp. 23–27.

tially interpreted history, because it too depends on research into the facts of the past, and so is the story of past decisions and possibilities.[70]

The mode of the historical reality of the Jesus Christ of the proclamation is thus also specified. In that Jesus is proclaimed as the eschatological event, He is historically real as an event that can never be past but "remains always present—*in the proclamation.*" Faith is faith in the Jesus Christ who is personally present as the proclamation.[71] "Jesus speaks and is this word of the Christian proclamation. . . ."[72] Thus, "The word of the Christian proclamation and the history which it communicates . . . are one." The Resurrection, the purely contingent event of the historical event Jesus being the eschatological event, is then ontologically specified as the first occurrence of the proclamation; Jesus "rose into the proclamation." [73]

For all the subtlety and frequent truth of these last analyses, one cannot feel satisfied. It is doubtful that Bultmann's history-dissolving concept of eschatology is adequate. Bultmann appeals to Paul, who refers to Jesus' life not at all and speaks only of the "crucified and Risen Lord," and to John, for whom the bare fact of Jesus "coming" is the salvation event.[74] Yet "Crucified" is certainly a bit of biographical data, in which for Paul, Jesus' whole work was summarized; and John did after all write a gospel, with whatever peculiarities. It is quite right that "The combination of historical account and kerygmatic christology in the Synoptic Gospels does not have the point of legitimizing the kerygma, but rather of legitimizing the history of Jesus as messianic by putting it in the light of

70. One way of getting at the difficulties of Bultmann's position would begin at this point. When related to the proclamation, research and genuine history collapse into one—thereby Bultmann annuls at the decisive point the distinction on which his whole analysis is built. And what is really accomplished by calling "paradoxical" the relation between this new "history" and the proclamation? Cf. Bornkamm, op. cit., pp. 134 ff.

71. Ibid., p. 25.

72. "Der Begriff des Wortes Gottes . . . ," p. 289.

73. *Das Verhältnis* . . . , p. 27.

74. *Geschichte und Eschatologie*, pp. 30–50.

kerygmatic christology." [75] But if the narratable history of Jesus is kerygmatically irrelevant, why did it need to be kerygmatically justified?

In any case, the position that results is untenable. For Bultmann, when Jesus' history is to be told as about God, as eschatological occurrence, it is reduced to the "that." In the proclamation we meet the Christ who lives in the event of the proclamation; to do this we do not need to learn about the historical Jesus. This is a christological version of the claim that direct language of personal encounter, which occurs here in a meeting with Christ, is informative apart from any impersonal verifiability. This claim we have already rejected. In general, the whole problem of verifiability recurs in the discussion of hermeneutics as the problem of the relation between the "Jesus of historical research" and the "Christ of the proclamation." Our previous discussion will give us guidelines here, too.

In terms of our present discussion, we can make the point by noting that the mere statement *that* "God has acted in history" must be, in its pure formality, existential speech and not existentiell speech— and so not really accomplished speech about God by Bultmann's own criterion. The statement *that* "a historical event has occurred" does not bespeak a historical reality; it only ontologically analyzes a historical reality otherwise evoked by narrating it. Existentiell speech about history would have to be narration. [76]

This problem stretches far back into Bultmann's thought as we have discussed it. Bultmann gives no account of *how* the proclamation gives us the eschatological existence we cannot otherwise acquire. What is the linguistic operation of this event? We may surmise that Bultmann can give no account, because he will not admit the kind of narrating utterance that actually confronts us with a contingent event.

Gerhard Ebeling summarizes the discontent that all feel here by asking how the eschatological proclamation can be understood, if it

---

75. *Geschichte und Eschatologie*, p. 13.
76. Cf. also Gerhard Ebeling's remarks on this point in *Theologie und Verkündigung*, pp. 68 f.

is supposed to be talk about history which, however, narrates no history.[77] That is indeed the problem, and we turn to Ebeling's discussions.

IV.

According to Ebeling, Bultmann's great contribution is the strictness with which he holds the correlation of faith to the proclamation, to the Word.[78] Ebeling's investigations of what happens when we speak, of the nature of the "word-event," are intended to clarify this correlation.

What utterance is supposed to do is interpret reality. It is the function of the word to illumine, to bring reality forth from darkness and indetermination, to bespeak reality as what it truly is. There are many ways in which this happens, of which description is but one. But in no case is the event of illumination a mere recording of how things already are: "The depth of this event of interpretation is first grasped, when we see that as a bringing-to-truth it is at once a discovering and changing of reality."[79] To bespeak reality as what it truly is is to call it to its true self, to call it to what it must and shall be. Perhaps we may clarify this for ourselves so: The choice of a word is always an evaluation—and so the positing of a fulfillment.

Thus the decisive question about any utterance is not so much what it records as what it accomplishes, what future it "opens."[80] The decisive question is: What will or can be different because this word is spoken? It is important to note that Ebeling intends this analysis to be essential: it applies also to those utterances that are indeed recordings of how things are: they, too, open the future inso-

77. This is the pivot of controversy in the long settling of accounts with Bultmann which is the content of *Theologie und Verkündigung*.

78. *Theologie und Verkündigung*, pp. 26 ff, 35.

79. Ibid., p. 15.

80. Ebeling, *Das Wesen des Glaubens*, p. 250; "Wort Gottes und Hermeneutik," *Zeitschrift für Theologie und Kirche*, pp. 224–51, p. 245.

far as they are *acts* of recording.[81] This point will become important later.[82]

The basic model of the word is, therefore, the spoken word, the event of one person addressing another. For it is what uttering a word accomplishes that is essential. If we begin, not from "propositions," but from the structure of the situation of speaking, which is always a speaking-to, we see that the "power of the word-event is that it is able to touch and change us in our existence, in that one person communicates something of his own existence to another. . . ." The function of the word-event is fundamentally the challenge to become other than I am which an existence other than I poses in addressing me.[83] The word is most purely word, therefore, as the address in which one man involves his life with that of another, in which he pledges himself to him—in which a *promise* opens a new future.[84]

We can now formulate the function of the word as the illumining of existence. The word occurs in order that man may come forth again as man.[85] My true humanity is brought to light in the event of address and response. The secret of human being is that it ". . . is a being called to from elsewhere, an existing in answer and as answer. . . ."[86]

Inasmuch as man lives in time, his identity with himself is questionable, since it is his identity with his past self and his future self. He experiences the question whether he will confess his past and decide for his future. "To identify oneself with one's past deeds means to be responsible for them. To decide for one's future means to be responsible for it. . . ." Thus I have my identity with myself only in this question and answer, and ". . . existence is in its very

81. One should note here how close the "existential" and "analytic" schools often come. "What we need to do for the case of stating, and by the same token describing and reporting, is . . . to realize that they are speech-acts no less than [performative utterances, wishes, etc.]. . . ." Austin, *Philosophical Papers*, pp. 236 f.

82. Below pp. 203–5, 208–9.

83. *Das Wesen das Glaubens*, p. 248 f.

84. "Wort Gottes und Hermeneutik," p. 246.

85. Ibid., p. 246.

86. *Das Wesen des Glaubens*, p. 145.

basis a word-event." [87] "The word—that is clearly man himself.
. . ." [88]

In this question and answer, the conscience, as "the occurrence of being questioned and called out to answer is both the call and the hearing of the call, both the accuser and the accused." [89] The fundamental word-event in which man is man is the soundless voice of conscience, of man's questionability to himself.[90] Indeed, insofar as the world is given to us as reality that concerns us, with which we deal as we find our way through life, the character of questionability, of being a problem for us, belongs not only to our existence but to the world in which our existence is given us. Thus the world's insistent presence to us is already a word-event.[91] "The world as the reality which concerns us is, even if not understood, already the call and question of God." [92] With the last two words of this citation we are in the next train of thought.

In the realm of human existence and its world, in the realm of historical reality, "being and understanding, existing and meeting, what one has and what counts for" are inwardly related and so also "what one is and what one is not yet, the past and the future." [93] In this direction of what has already come to be to what will, or must, or shall be, historical reality is constituted. Ebeling puts it this way: "That is real which has a future." [94] In the correlation of existing and meeting, having and counting as . . . , we see also the word-character of historical reality: That is real which has a future—and it has a future in that it is spoken, in a word that aims at something.

These analyses clarify a vast area of our problem. Simply looking at language as something that is done, as an act that changes things, is the decisive step. But there is one point toward the end where

87. Ebeling, "Theologische Erwägungen über das Gewissen," *Wort und Glaube,* pp. 429–46, p. 440 f.
88. *Das Wesen des Glaubens,* p. 250.
89. "Theologische Erwägungen . . . ," pp. 436–40.
90. Ibid., p. 443.
91. Ebeling, "Elementare Besinnung auf vorantwortliches Reden von Gott," *Wort und Glaube,* pp. 349–71, pp. 369 f.
92. *Das Wesen des Glaubens,* p. 255.
93. Ibid., p. 158.
94. Ibid., p. 158.

some clarification is perhaps needed. We should not press too hard Ebeling's language about the "soundless voice" of conscience and reality. Whatever can be soundless, surely not a "call" or a "voice."[95] The conscience does not, I think, "call" at all; it is—just as Ebeling began by saying—"the occurrence of *being* called [my italics]. . . ." But the questioner is always someone other than I. The address in hearing and responding to which my identity as a human being occurs, is always the voice of someone else—in the simplest and most literal sense.[96] We should interpret the conscience as the possibility of being spoken to, which is given with our spoken-to humanity.[97] So also the world, as reality that concerns us, is indeed there for us as a word-event: but not because reality somehow of itself speaks soundlessly to us; but because it has been presented to us by others bespeaking it to us, and so is present to us only as already interpreted in language.

Indeed, as Hans-Georg Gadamer has most fully explicated, the world is there for us as the *world* only in that we meet reality as bespoken reality.[98] That we live in a world is given with the givenness of language. "The thereness for us of the world is constituted as language. . . . To have a world means: to relate oneself to the world. But relating oneself to the world requires that one frees oneself from what meets one out of the world sufficiently to represent it to oneself as it is. To be able to do this is both to have a world and to have language."[99]

It follows that human existence as word-event always presupposes already occurring word-event. We exist as human only in the tradition of speech—which is altogether Ebeling's view also.[100] Thus

95. Heidegger, *Sein und Zeit,* pp. 272 ff., and our linguistic tradition to the contrary. Ebeling's language here comes directly from Heidegger.

96. Thus a *pure* phenomenology of existence is impossible. Everything remains unclear until I record the empirical fact that someone has spoken to me—and begin from there. We must make this nonphenomenological assertion in order to do justice to the phenomenological results.

97. I am certain, from direct conversation, that this interpretation follows Ebeling's intention.

98. Gadamer, *Wahrheit und Methode,* pp. 415 ff.

99. Ibid., p. 419.

100. Cf. below pp. 180–81.

also the beginning of that tradition, the word that is evoked by no preceding word at all, cannot be understood by an analysis of human existence or of the world—an understanding that it seems to me Ebeling does somehow try to achieve. Rather the occurrence of that word is the miracle of the creation of man: "And God blessed them and said to them. . . ." The cultural tradition as a whole, the contingent fact of language being given, is the locus of creation. Reality is "questionable," etc., only because it is always given as already interpreted in language. The questioning power of the world depends, therefore, on a prior word-event, and so on the original address of God, who opens the conversation.[101]

If we turn Gadamer's argument around, we may also say that we can now understand why creation is creation of the world—why we do not merely confess "I believe in God . . . who has created me." If the givenness of speech opens our humanity, it opens that humanity as being-in-a world. For language has no independent existence over against what it says—that is, over against the givenness of a world.[102]

And the ontological difference between God and man is that God speaks before being spoken to, that He is in himself questioner and responder. God is ontologically specifiable as a *conversation*—which brings us again to the doctrine of the Trinity. It also follows—and here we definitely are led by our interpretation of Ebeling to turn some of his statements around—that our temporality is not the basis of our living by the word. Rather, our being addressed and called to answer is the basis of that character of our existence we call temporality. It is because I am questioned about what will become of me that my relation to what I will be is a matter of decision and risk, that it is history and not only organic development, that I am temporal in Bultmann's and Ebeling's sense. So also tradition is the condition of temporality, not vice versa.

These reflections on tradition lead us back to our exposition of

---

101. To this whole complex, cf. the essay by Franz Mayr, "Philosophie im Wandel der Sprache," *Zeitschrift für Theologie und Kirche*, 61, 4, pp. 439-91.

102. Gadamer, op. cit., pp. 419 ff.

Ebeling. He distinguishes between the event of the word and the given reality of the language we use to speak. The language I speak is the tradition of speech by which my act of utterance is made possible. "Languages are . . . structures of tradition grown up through centuries, in which the whole many-leveled reality of historical life has stored itself. . . . All speech depends on this previous givenness of language. . . ." Learning a language opens reality as such to me; the language makes possible the word-event by which reality is interpreted and understood. "Indeed we *live* from this, that reality is opened to us by language. . . ." [103]

The language I speak is my relation to reality. And it is a particular, materially determined relation to reality, determined by the history in which this language has come to be the particular language it is. In the various languages radically different modes of meeting with and understanding reality have their subsistence.[104] "With language, with its concepts . . . and syntactical possibilities, determined forms and contents of thought are given, a cultural living space which embraces the one who lives in it. . . ." The specific possibilities of understanding my life and the world I live it in, the specific possibilities of decision in which I face the future and in which I exist as a historical being, are given by the language I am taught.[105]

As the tradition of language makes the word-event possible, so word-events create language: ". . . an extraordinary word-event *creates* language, i.e., it creates new possibilities of bespeaking and understanding the reality which concerns us. . . ." [106]

So far, it seems to me, so good. But I think we can, quite in Ebeling's sense, go farther. Tradition, as "a structural element of human being," [107] brings us, it seems to me, the cultural heritage in a double way in one act of handing on: The tradition at once narrates to us the matter of our heritage and in that same act of narration initi-

103. *Das Wesen des Glaubens*, p. 251.
104. Ibid., p. 251.
105. Ebeling, *Die Geschichtlichkeit der Kirche und ihrer Verkündigung als theologisches Problem*, p. 17 f. Cf. also "Theologische Erwägungen . . . ," p. 443.
106. *Das Wesen des Glaubens*, p. 252.
107. *Die Geschichtlichkeit der Kirche* . . . , p. 31, and in general pp. 31 ff.

ates us into the language by which the matter of our heritage is interpreted, so as to be reality which concerns us, which poses decisions and risks for our existence—which is indeed our *heritage*. Thus the tradition-act which is someone telling me "Julius Caesar was a dictator" at once and as the same act proposes an alleged fact and drills me in the word 'dictator' by which the fact becomes for me a reality over against which I have possibilities of decision important also for my own life. So also a decisive event, in so far as it is language-creative, at once enters the tradition as narrative content and enriches the tradition by the language in which it can be confronted as its true self. The historical tradition and the linguistic traditions are the same or, rather, live always in the same act of handing-on. And both, in their unity, lead back to God as the first speaker.[108]

From here we can then move on to some of the deepest insights of Gadamer—insights that we will simply appropriate.[109] The possibility of understanding any writing is traced by Bultmann to the "fact that author and interpreter live in the same historical world. . . ."[110] But what does that mean? It means, according to Gadamer, that my life is always already determined by the living *tradition* of which any specific writing is but a part. If the hermeneutical circle means that I always already understand, in a way, the matter of the text that I interpret, this is so because interpretation of a text is an act of further appropriation of the living tradition by which I always already live.[111] Past and present are always already mediated by the tradition of language; the language in which I now interpret I received from the tradition constituted by all past utterances.[112] Thus "understanding is not so much an undertaking by

108. It is perhaps time for me to register the hope that no one will take these speculations about God as the initiator of the speech tradition as attempts to prove His existence. The formal resemblance of the argument to Thomas' proofs is intended. The invalidity of Thomas' proofs as proofs detracts not at all from their exemplary value as ontological analyses.

109. My criticism of Gadamer may be inferred, by those who know Gadamer's book, from my criticism of Ott on pp. 201–5 below.

110. Cf. above, p. 201–5.

111. *Wahrheit und Methode,* pp. 250–90.

112. Ibid., pp. 361–82.

the subject as a penetration into the tradition-event in which past and present continuously mediate themselves."[113]

Vice versa, the prior understanding which I bring to the text and by which the text is opened, is not a fixed entity somehow given with human nature: it is given by the very tradition of which the text is a part and in the very continuing act of understanding the tradition of which understanding the particular text is again a part. "The anticipation of meaning which guides our understanding of a text . . . , is determined by our participation in the tradition. But this participation is, in our relation to the tradition, continuously developing. It is not simply a presupposition. . . . We produce it ourselves, as we understand and so participate in the tradition-event. . . ."[114]

With this understanding of the hermeneutical circle as tradition, a persistent confusion also is eliminated. The distance in time between the text and us is not a hindrance to understanding, to be "bridged over"; it is the very condition of understanding. For if it is from the tradition that we receive the necessary prior understanding, then only as the matter of a text has had time to work in the tradition can we approach that text with an appropriate prior understanding.[115]

We return to Ebeling, and at what is for him perhaps a decisive point. He concludes from his analysis of the word-event that where the word-event fully succeeds, there it must be God's word that occurs. The highest function of the word would be to open the possibility of truly having a future. "But where could such a word be found?"[116] Such a word would call us forth to our humanity itself, would bring our reality to its truth.[117] Such a word would illumine and make us clear to ourselves.[118] It would be the word-event by

113. *Wahrheit und Methode,* p. 275.
114. Ibid., p. 277.
115. Ibid., pp. 275-90.
116. *Das Wesen des Glaubens,* p. 250.
117. "Wort Gottes und Hermeneutik," pp. 246.; *Die Geschichtlichkeit der Kirche . . .* , pp. 15 f.
118. *Das Wesen des Glaubens,* p. 255.

which my identity with my past and future would occur, by which I would be myself, by which I would be whole—it would be the event of salvation.[119]

This word that is really word, "this . . . word which truly illumines and opens a genuine future, is usually not to be found. Men deny it to each other. . . ." We deny it to each other because it can occur only as a *promise,* which calls the hearer to rely utterly upon the promised future. It can occur only when "the speaker promises himself . . . , pledges himself and his own future for the future of the other. . . ." Only God, only the word "through which God comes to man and promises Himself to him," can do this, for only God *has* His own future so as to be able to promise it. The only true word is the word that calls forth faith as total reliance upon a promised future.[120]

Thus God and the word-event belong together.[121] The word of God is not a mysterious, special sort of word: it is "in respect of its word-character perfectly normal, natural, oral word occurring between one man and another." The distinction is in what happens: If the word succeeds, if it occurs as life-giving word-event, it is God's word. If it occurs as spoiled, killing word-event, it is man's. The question is whether man the liar or God who is truth comes to word.[122]

Indeed, "God meets us as word." [123] His revelation of Himself to us is a word-event. To understand this, we must see that we are here concerned not primarily with the informative, but rather with the "historical" function of the word: one person addresses another and so presents himself to him, and thereby also calls him to come forward and answer.[124] The meeting with God is accomplished by and as the word-event of His word—a meeting is always a word-event. True God-utterance is not, therefore, only communication

119. "Theologische Erwägungen über das Gewissen," p. 442.
120. *Das Wesen des Glaubens,* pp. 253 ff.
121. "Wort Gottes und Hermeneutik," op. cit., p. 246.
122. Ibid., pp. 244 f.
123. *Das Wesen des Glaubens,* p. 101.
124. "Elementare Besinnung auf verantwortliches Reden von Gott," p. 370.

about God; it is an event "in which God Himself is communicated." [125]

True speech for God is speech in which the speaker makes himself "responsible for God before the world," through which "God and the world meet"; [126] it is "address, promise through which God is *proclaimed into* the world [my italics]." [127] And since God is there for us as a word-event, God-utterance is inherently dependent on tradition. "For God is not a phenomenon given in direct meeting. . . . If we had not heard of God, if He had not been proclaimed to us . . . , how would we ever get the idea of a doctrine about God at all? God's givenness is His historicity." [128]

Christians confess that this true word-event, God's word, occurs as the Gospel,[129] as the proclamation that points to Jesus as "the Witness and Basis of faith." [130] "Genuine, fulfilled word-event" occurs when "one man is able to promise God to another man" because of Jesus.[131] It is as Gospel that we can speak of God.

Here we can pose two questions. One is that to which we found an unsatisfactory answer in Bultmann: What is the relation between the Gospel, the true and saving word-event, and the events of Jesus' life to which it refers? The other is: What is the relation between this word-event and that which otherwise occurs? We will discuss the second question first, since it is Ebeling's form of the question about the particular operation of our God-language as a part of language as a whole.

V.

What Bultmann calls the existentiell character of speech about God, Ebeling puts so: The speaker's own commitment to what he says is a necessary element of the saying of it. The speaker must by

125. *Das Wesen des Glaubens,* p. 106 f.
126. Ebeling, "Weltliches Reden von Gott," *Wort und Glaube,* pp. 372–80, p. 374.
127. Ibid., p. 380.
128. "Elementare Besinnung . . . , op. cit., p. 354 f.
129. Ibid., p. 247.
130. *Das Wesen des Glaubens,* pp. 116 f.
131. Ibid., p. 255.

his speaking wager "his own existence on the existence of God." Any and all attempts at "proof" (we may, I think interpret this to mean "verification") of what we say about God is an attempt to evade this wager: thus, "Speech about God has so much the character of pure assertion, that there can be no sure protection against its being misunderstood as pure caprice. . . ." [132] Yet if this were all that could be said, our speech about God would be only for the religiously gifted; it would make no binding claim on those we address. Indeed, if every relation to reality as otherwise given were missing, speech about God would not be understandable at all. [133] We must therefore ask how God is meaningful within our ordinary experience of reality.

"In . . . reality as it confronts me, God confronts me as the questionability thereof . . . ," at the moment when the question-ability of that reality which concerns me becomes my own questionability as a person. God meets me when I experience the questions and problems that are the matter of my own existence as *given me* with the world in which I, without my doing, simply find myself placed. [134] In particular, in birth and death the radical questionability of life is given. [135] We may, perhaps, interpret Ebeling's statement so: I experience the world as a question directed to me by an other.

We have already identified the conscience as the occurrence of this being questioned. The voice of conscience is not, says Ebeling, the voice of God. But it is the "condition of the possibility of understanding what is meant by the word 'God.'" The conscience seeks the word that would accomplish my identity with my past and my future, my wholeness as a person: that is, it raises the question after the word of God. [136]

In our dealings with reality, God, therefore, occurs for us as a

132. "Elementare Besinnung . . . ," op. cit., p. 363 f.
133. "Theologie und Wirklichkeit," *Wort und Glaube*, pp. 195 f. These are apparently the questions of our last chapter. Ebeling has a form of Flew's dilemma; cf. p. 196.
134. "Elementare Besinnung . . . ," pp. 365–69. Ebeling calls this the experience of "passivity." God announces Himself in what Heidegger calls the *Geworfenheit* of existence.
135. *Das Wesen des Glaubens,* pp. 100 f.
136. "Theologische Erwägungen . . . ," pp. 441 f.

question. And that means He occurs for us as a word.[137] The Gospel, the particular witness of Jesus Christ, is the word in which God happens to us. But, as question only, all word-event is God's address: "In reality as questionable, the word-event which God initiates is already underway. . . ." [138] And so, "The world as reality that concerns us is . . . already the call and question of God. Therefore the human word is, in its deepest basis, answer. . . . Speech is . . . an echo to God's question." [139]

The word-event which thus occurs in all speaking, and which comes finally from God, is not the true word-event which saves. It rather fixes us in the questionableness of our identity with ourselves, in our falsity as men.[140] It is—and here we encounter a concept that we will make decisive for this whole chapter—not the Gospel which makes alive but the *Law* which kills.[141] Yet this Law, this deadly word-event which occurs apart from the Gospel, is the condition of the Gospel's meaningfulness. Ultimately, therefore, "the hermeneutic location of talk about God [is] the distinction between God and God." [142] It is what happens as the movement that occurs in the tension between the God of the Law and the God of the Gospel.[143]

The Gospel is "beneficently related to the word-event which has always already occurred from God and which touches uncomprehending man as the Law that kills." [144] The Gospel, the word of God, speaks of what the Law has already spoken of. It does so because the Gospel "is concerned for real men," [145] and the reality of sinful man occurs precisely in hearing the Law. Thus the word of God, and so our words about God, are precisely the illumination

137. *Das Wesen des Glaubens,* p. 255.
138. "Elementare Besinnung . . . ," p. 369.
139. *Das Wesen des Glaubens,* p. 255.
140. "Theologische Erwägungen . . . ," p. 445.
141. "Wort Gottes und Hermeneutik," p. 247.
142. Ebeling, "Der hermeneutiche Ort der Gotteslehre bei Petrus Lombardus und Thomas von Aquin," *Zeitschrift für Theologie und Kirche,* 61, p. 319.
143. Ibid., pp. 319–26.
144. "Wort Gottes und Hermeneutik," p. 247.
145. Ebeling, "Die 'nicht-religiöse' Interpretation biblischer Begriffe," *Wort und Glaube,* p. 141.

of our reality as we live it. Indeed ". . . talk of God . . . aims at nothing other than to speak of our reality . . ." so, that our reality is apprehended and dealt with in such a way as to bring it to its fulfill-ment.[146] "Because God and the world come together in the word-event, this coming together is itself an event: the event of God and the event of the world. Only then is God really spoken of, when God as an event, and therefore also the world as an event, come to speech. . . ."[147]

Against certain tendencies in Ebeling, we must insist that reality speaks to our conscience in this way only because of our participa-tion in the speech event which is the prior of all our experience, and that the voice of the Law is not a soundless voice of conscience but the oral, normal address of our fellows. If we keep this clear, then it seems to me that all this is both correct and helpful. Showing the existence-illuminating character of God-language will not by itself suffice to describe its particular function: we simply refer here to the conclusion of our last chapter, that God-utterances also predict a certain future event. An important part of the current continental debate [148] is therefore simply omitted here: whether the relevance of God-utterances to the question which man is to himself is by itself the verification of those utterances.[149] But this aside, we have here surely a far more penetrating description of the event of speech about God than any we have yet encountered.

In particular, the introduction of the concepts of Law and Gos-pel [150] is essential to the clarification of the whole matter of this chapter. We will take this opportunity to develop this somewhat: The event-character of the word (1), the correlation of the word-event to time (2), and the word-character of historical reality (3), all acquire their final expression in these concepts: (1) The word,

146. "Theologie und Worklichkeit," pp. 199 f.
147. "Weltliches Reden von Gott," p. 380.
148. Cf. Wolfhart Pannenberg, "Die Frage nach Gott," *Evangelische The-ologie,* 25, 4/5, pp. 238–62.
149. I have discussed this question in its own terms elsewhere: "Gott als Antwort," *Evangelische Theologie,* 26., 7, pp. 368–78.
150. The Lutheran theological tradition, from which they are drawn, has reflected far more persistently on the *workings* of proclamation than has any other tradition.

understood as Law and Gospel, is understood by what is accomplished. The Law is any address that breaks my satisfaction in what I already have become and am, which demands that I live for someone or something. The Gospel is the pledge to me of one for whom I may live, the promise of what I am not yet but will be. (2) These concepts understand what the word accomplishes as the unity of past and future: The Law is any word that ties the future to the past, to what precedes it. Its pattern is: If you do so and so, such and such will happen. The Gospel is the word that allows us to own our past from the future. It is a promise, it speaks of what will be by God's act, in spite of what we have done and become. (3) That the Gospel speaks to the one addressed by the Law gives the unity of past and present, gives the possibility of history. Here also we grasp the tradition-character of the word-event. That God's word is both Law and Gospel means that it is a future-opening challenge posed by the past: that is, that it is tradition.

VI.

Back to Ebeling and to the question: What is the relation between the Gospel, the saving word-event in which talk about God authentically occurs, and the story of Jesus which is its narrative content? Ebeling puts the question so: Why must the word that reaches its goal in faith be the particular word that comes explicitly from the Christ-event? Why is faith's self-understanding dependent upon understanding proclamatory utterances which refer to a past event? Then Ebeling immediately restates the question in subtle and revealing fashion: "What does the past event which the proclamation brings to speech contribute to understanding that at which the proclamation aims?" [151] Here we can already see the form of Ebeling's answer: The narration of the story of the "historical Jesus" is necessary for *understanding* the proclamation as proclamation— that is, as the word-event in which salvation occurs, in which God happens.

The tradition of speech in which believers are able to speak of

151. *Theologie und Verkündigung,* pp. 30 f.

God—as more than a desperate question—is the tradition of christo-logical proclamation, of speech in which in one way or another Jesus is said to be the eschatological event. Some such utterances give Jesus titles: so "Jesus is the Christ." Others are "christological narrations": so "Jesus is risen." [152] In all such, Jesus is proclaimed as the event about which the question of existence asks, about which the word 'God' asks.

Now what happens if this eschatological language is not under-stood? And not just certain eschatological expressions, but the whole point of talking eschatologically? What happens if the hearer is just not in that situation of being bothered about the unity of his own life, in which such language can bring his reality to word? What happens if we say, "In Jesus, God is at work," and the word 'God' seems pointless? Then, "How does the proclamation come to understanding as proclamation?" This is the problem to which Ebeling finds that Bultmann gives no answer—and cannot because he refuses to allow any relevance to the content of Jesus' story.[153]

In this situation, understanding the proclamation requires that we inquire into the point of talking eschatologically; in Ebeling's terms, into its "necessity." We must ask *why* we talk this way; in Ebeling's terms, we must inquire into the "basis" of the kerygma, into the rea-son for making such utterances.[154] "Not-understood proclamation . . . must let itself be questioned about the basis of the proclama-tion. . . ." [155] Now since the proclamation with which we are con-cerned is an account about Jesus, this question about the basis of proclamatory speech is a question about Him; it is a question about what happened with Him to make this kind of language needful, to give it point.[156] The event that makes our situation one in which eschatological christological proclamation has a point must itself come to word.[157]

This question is then a question directed, in one sense, behind the

152. Ibid., pp. 140 ff.
153. Ibid., pp. 31, 38, 49, 64.
154. Ibid., pp. 49 ff.
155. Ibid., p. 45.
156. Ibid., pp. 48 f., 64.
157. Ibid., pp. 50 f.

proclamation itself to the event about which the proclamation speaks, and which is the basis of the proclamation's significance. It asks: What happened back there before the proclamation? Ebeling shares Bultmann's rejection of trying to get behind the word-event of the proclamation in order to substantiate the proclamation, to "show historically" that the proclamation is believable. But he argues that a recourse to the historical Jesus is nevertheless necessary and legitimate in order to interpret the proclamation, as the way in which the proclamation itself makes itself understandable.[158] "What is it that makes the proclamation be the word-event in which 'God' is not just an unintelligible chiffre . . . ? If the question into the historical Jesus helps here, then its point is not to go around behind the word of proclamation, but on the contrary to question more deeply into this word so as to experience it from its very basis. . . ."[159]

Thus telling what happened back there with Jesus is the way in which the proclamation makes itself intelligible as proclamation. As part of the work of proclaiming, we must ask: What happened back there? And, Ebeling asserts, we must pursue this question with the best historical technique we can muster. Here we encounter the significance of historical research for theology. It is a principal concern of Ebeling's to work out this significance.

The significance is at first negative. Research into the "historical Jesus" is a threat to the proclamation. For all historical research rests on critique of the tradition. Thus in the present case the historical Jesus means, simply, the real Jesus, as distinguished from the at least possibly perverted account of the tradition—which in this case is precisely the proclamatory tradition.[160] Thus historical research into Jesus necessarily assumes that Jesus may have been different than the proclamation makes Him out. Moreover, the historical account of Jesus necessarily excludes much that is essential to the proclamation. It excludes post-Easter interpretive elements. It excludes

158. *Theologie und Verkündigung,* pp. 28 ff., 55, 62, 71.
159. Ibid., p. 77.
160. Ebeling, "Die Frage nach dem historischen Jesus und das Problem der Christologie," *Beiheft 1* to *Zeitschrift für Theologie und Kirche,* 56, pp. 14–30, pp. 16 f.

all those events that the tradition says happened after His death: Resurrection, Appearances, and Ascension! "Death is the boundary of historical statements." And it excludes 'God.'[161] But what if *this* Jesus is the real Jesus?

Moreover, the historical Jesus is a relativized Jesus, in two ways: He is the historically "conditioned Jesus, who is very far from us . . . and whose strangeness will become clearer the more rigorously we investigate Him historically." And our historical grasp of Jesus is itself historically relative, it sees Him from one of many possible standpoints. But how are we to *proclaim* this Jesus?[162]

We may ask: If critical historical research is a threat to the proclamation, why must our question about the event of Jesus be done as historical-critical research? Ebeling has two answers here. We may summarize his main answer so: Historical-critical research simply *is* the way in which we now grasp past reality. How others may have done so is irrelevant. The historical-critical method expresses the modern spirit, "for only with the breakdown of traditional western metaphysics . . . did the historicity of existence come fully to consciousness. When . . . the fact of historical change, of historical conditioning . . . became clear, the freedom, but also the necessity . . . , was given to consider history in its pure historicity, i.e., objectively from a distance."[163] Therefore, "One cannot object that the proclamation does not speak of Jesus from historical interest and as an historical phenomenon—though this is true. But it speaks of God in relation to Jesus, who was an historical phenomenon. This is so decisive for the proclamation that it must be held to it, even though the way in which this must today be done was unknown to the original proclamation."[164] For *us* to refuse to con-

161. Ibid., pp. 17 f.; *Theologie und Verkündigung*, p. 54. On the point itself, see the thought of Peter Brunner, perhaps as presented in my article "The Doxological Concept of History in the Theology of Peter Brunner," *Zur Auferbauung des Leibes Christi: Festgabe für Peter Brunner*, pp. 181–200.

162. "Die Frage nach dem historischen Jesus . . . ," pp. 19 f.

163. Ebeling, "Die Bedeutung der historisch-kritischen Methode," *Wort und Glaube*, pp. 1–49, p. 33.

164. *Theologie und Verkündigung*, p. 62.

sider a historical phenomenon historically would be dishonest, which is prohibited also theologically.[165]

Moreover, it is precisely existentiell confrontation with the text that requires that we investigate it historically. Historical-critical method and existential interpretation are not opposed. "On the contrary, precisely the procedure that critically makes the documents transparent in their historicity and therewith in their distance from the present . . . creates the necessary presupposition for . . . letting them say something to us. . . ."[166] The historical-critical method is precisely the practice of "self-criticism by the interpreter with respect to all discoverable possibilities of self-deception about what the . . . text intends."[167] Ebeling demands that the rediscovery of and emphasis on the existentiell, nonobjectifying character of the word-event must prove itself by clarifying also "the proper place of objectifying thought, as this is proper to, before all, modern science."[168] The informing function of the word is not its essence, but it cannot be ignored.[169] It is historical-critical method by which this demand is fulfilled in theology.

Thus proclamatory speaking is both bound to historical-critically derived narration of Jesus' story and threatened by it. It therefore follows that either "the question of the historical Jesus destroys christology or the question of the historical Jesus must prove identical with the christological problem. . . ."[170]

The second of these alternatives cannot be realized so long as research into the historical Jesus poses only the questions: What facts are to be discovered? How are they to be explained? But a deeper understanding of historical reality indicates that the more comprehensive question must be: What has come to speech in this event?[171]

165. *Theologie und Verkündigung*, p. 61.

166. "Die Bedeutung der historisch-kritischen Methode," p. 36.

167. Ebeling, "Diskussionsthesen zur Einführung in den Studium der Theologie," *Wort und Glaube*, pp. 447–57, p. 451.

168. Ebeling, "Verantwortung des Glaubens in Begegnung mit dem Denken Martin Heideggers," *Beiheft 2, Zeitschrift für Theologie und Kirche*, pp. 119–24, p. 123.

169. "Elementare Besinnung . . . ," p. 370.

170. "Die Frage nach dem historischen Jesus . . . ," p. 16.

171. *Theologie und Verkündigung*, pp. 55 f.; "Die Frage nach dem historischen Jesus . . . ," pp. 20 f.

Let us interpret this question so, reaching back to earlier discussion: What language-creative word-event has occurred as this event?

If research sets itself to answer *this* question, then all the critical techniques of historical method, as well as its concern for "the facts," retain their right. What has, in fact, come to speech can only be settled by careful method.[172] But now the possibility exists that the proclamation will prove to be the appropriate answer[173] to, and "interpreting handing-on" of, what research discovers was said by the Jesus-event. At least the possibility exists that the historical Jesus and the Christ of the proclamation will prove identical. Whether it will in fact be so depends, of course, on what research into the texts shows to have come to word in Jesus.[174]

Ebeling has several statements of what he thinks research shows came to word in the historical Jesus. For our purpose the most direct is all we need. In Jesus, *God* came to speech. The witness and fate of Jesus was the word-event that is the basis of our needing and being able to proclaim a message in which 'God' appears.[175] For the call to decision which Jesus' message and fate were, created the existentiell situation in which eschatological proclamation had a point.[176] So also now, the meeting with Jesus, accomplished in the word about Him—as the meeting with persons of history is always accomplished—qualifies our situation eschatologically; the handing-on of the word that He was creates the situation in which the proclamation has a point, in which it is intelligible. The proclamation itself does this; through the witness to the historical event Jesus, the proclamation makes itself understandable.[177]

More specifically, the word of the historical Jesus brings God to word in that it is at once a word that assures our identity, our wholeness, and a word that makes the questionability of our reality final. That is, the word that happens with Jesus is Gospel, and it is

172. *Theologie und Verkündigung,* p. 56; "Die Frage nach dem historischen Jesus . . . ," pp. 20 f.
173. *Theologie und Verkündigung,* pp. 51–82.
174. "Die Frage nach dem historischen Jesus . . . ," p. 21.
175. *Das Wesen des Glaubens,* pp. 64–91.
176. *Theologie und Verkündigung,* p. 75.
177. Ibid., pp. 79 ff.

Law. "That Jesus is experienced as assuring word means that he is experienced as Gospel, and so the basis of faith. . . . In [so doing] . . . he meets us where we are, in the unsureness which is the essence of sin. Jesus verifies the reality which concerns us. He makes us certain of how it stands with us in it. He makes the Law to which we are . . . fallen unambiguous." [178] The word that came and comes to speech in the historical Jesus strikes the conscience as Law and Gospel.

In this existentiell situation the proclamation of Jesus as Himself the eschatological event is meaningful. The "eschatologically qualified situation" in which eschatological proclamation of Jesus makes sense is faith (indeed, Ebeling's preferred formulation of what came to word in Jesus is that *faith* came to word in Him). [179] Jesus is the "basis" of faith in that the word-event which He is makes faith as a way of existence possible and necessary. [180] Such directly proclamatory utterances about Jesus as "Jesus is Lord" or "Jesus is risen" or "God is at work in Jesus" are thus faith's confessional response to the historical Jesus. [181] Specifically Christian God-utterance is the confessing proclamation which is the life of faith.

The train of thought we have followed has been put together from various discussions in Ebeling's works and leaves out much that is important for him. It is, therefore, a construction. But it seems to me a train of thought that successfully negotiates many of the most difficult points in our whole problem area—until the very end. There, it seems to me, Ebeling—or at least Ebeling as here interpreted—comes to grief.

It follows from Ebeling's position that the christological proclamation is not itself the ground of faith. Rather, the proclamation takes place, and is only meaningful, as the confession of already occurring faith—faith that has its basis in what comes to word in the *historical* Jesus. "The historical Jesus" is, according to Ebeling—and he is correct [182]—Jesus up to the Resurrection. But now, if the Gos-

---

178. *Theologie und Verkündigung,* p. 81.
179. "Die Frage nach dem historischen Jesus . . . ," pp. 21 ff.
180. *Theologie und Verkündigung,* p. 32.
181. Ibid., pp. 45, 72, 75, 80 f.
182. Though cf. below pp. 218–27.

pel comes already to word in the historical Jesus, then the Resurrection does not belong to the narrative content of the Gospel, to its witness to Jesus. Only the briefest glance at the New Testament will show that, on the contrary, the Resurrection is the central narrative content of the Gospel. The "news" was precisely that one had risen from the dead.

It seems to me that we should agree with Ebeling that both Law and Gospel occur as the event of the *man* Jesus. In what He did and said and what became of Him, God came and comes to word. The Gospel can indeed occur, and faith be founded, without such specific eschatological predications as "Jesus is Lord" or "God is in Jesus." The narrative of what happened with the man Jesus *is* the call to faith: it is the event of the word of God, the Gospel. The use of such language as 'God' or 'Lord' is an act *of* faith; it is confessional response to the word of and about the man Jesus. But the narrative of what happened with the man Jesus is the Gospel only as the narrative of the conclusion of our stories and therefore as including "and on the third day He rose again from the dead." In the narrative of "the historical Jesus," in the story of the not-yet risen man Jesus, the Gospel does not come to word. Prior to the Resurrection, no one had heard the Gospel in the full sense. And in an account of Jesus that leaves out the Resurrection, no one now hears the Gospel.

If these criticisms are correct, there must be an essential difference between the *man* Jesus and the *historical* Jesus. There must be a difference between what happened with Jesus and what any historical research—even perfected research—could discover to have happened with Him. There must be a permanent difference between what came and comes to word in the story of Jesus and what can come to word in any methodically secured version of that story. And this means further that there must be a necessary mode of narrating the past informatively other than research—or indeed than any effort to recall.[183] Ebeling never seriously considers the possibility of other modes of bespeaking past reality—so that our enthusiastic agreement with him at every step before the last only commits us

183. To this last, cf. below p. 231.

to holding that objectifying recollection is essential to our apprehension of what happened with the man Jesus, not that it is the whole of that apprehension.

The suggestion immediately presents itself that what comes to word in the historical account of Jesus is the Law, and that the *Gospel* first comes to word in the proclamation of Jesus as risen, as the conclusion of life. Perhaps by following this suggestion we will also find *why* we cannot abstract from the informing function of the word, a point to which Ebeling gives no theological answer. The suggestion lies ready in Ebeling's own work. For he explicitly asserts that the "secular disciplines," [184] to which history must certainly belong, "are themselves activities in man's carrying through of his existence . . . ," [185] and that their function is that of the Law.[186]

Our rejection of the final step in Ebeling's argument requires us to revise his concept of historical reality. Before we can go on to test this suggestion, we need, therefore, further investigation of the nature of historical reality—which we will do in conversation with Heinrich Ott and Wolfhart Pannenberg.

First, however, there is an important question to which also in Ebeling we have found no answer. How does utterance *work* to open or bestow a new self-understanding or mode of life? This question has been a concern of Ernst Fuchs, to whom we turn next.

VII.

Fuchs develops in detail the analysis of human being as being that finds itself in language.[187] In the language into which I am born, I

184. *Philosophicae disciplinae;* the passage occurs in an interpretation of Thomas' *Summa Theologica,* I,I,1.
185. "Der hermeneutische Ort der Gotteslehre . . . ," p. 316.
186. Ibid., pp. 316–18.
187. In developing this one theme from Fuchs, I am selecting drastically. Much of what we have discussed with Ebeling could have been taken up with Fuchs, and perhaps more besides. I have used Ebeling because I am much surer that I know what he is saying. One has the feeling that Fuchs would be saying something marvelously important if he were saying anything at all. In the following I do not always attempt to speak Fuchs's own language; this would necessitate disproportionate length.

am given the "self-evidencies" of my life, the relation to reality from which I always begin, which I do not need to decide. Yet language is also the possibility of the word that challenges all self-evidencies, that poses the decision for the future. Language incorporates past agreements in fixed apprehensions—and precisely so opens the world, which means that it is always ahead of us, giving the possibility of what we are not yet, of what will fulfill our life. Just this challenge to the future, given in the past, is "being," and it appears only in language.[188]

Thus the question of what I *am,* or am to be, of my self-understanding, is the question of what I have to say. The question is "whether and for what a man has a word, when it comes to his own life."[189] My existence has a clear meaning when it is clear if and when I am to speak.[190]

The relation to reality which is given with our common agreed-upon language is, insofar as I make this language my own, my relation also to myself. Therefore the question of existence is whether I speak this common language as my particular possibility, which means that I question and choose, rather than simply accept its self-evidencies. To do this is to seek new agreement, to participate in the birth of the new language. Thus only new language can be the language of self-understanding, where it is the clarity of my existence that determines when and if I speak.[191] Or we may say the same thing so: The question of existence is to whom I hearken, in the confrontations in which I am made to seek, and perhaps to find, new possibilities of communication.[192]

The new language of self-understanding is the language of *love,* in which as we speak to each other the needed word is there. Precisely as I love I know when and to whom to speak: that is, I under-

188. Fuchs, "Das Problem der theologischen Hermeneutik," *Zum hermeneutischen Problem in der Theologie,* pp. 116–37, pp. 128 f.; *Hermeneutik,* pp. 63, 68 ff., 132 f., 142.; "Was ist existentiale Interpretation? B," *Zum hermeneutischen Problem . . . ,* pp. 91–106, pp. 103 f.

189. Fuchs, "Was wird in der Exegese des Neuen Testaments interpretiert?" *Beiheft 1* to *Zeitschrift für Theologie und Kirche,* pp. 31–48, p. 35.

190. "Was ist existentiale Interpretation? B," pp. 103 f.

191. *Hermeneutik,* pp. 111, 134–40.

192. Ibid., p. 143.

stand myself.[193] Vice versa, as I understand myself—that is, am freed from bondage to the self-evidencies—I am free to recognize and respond to my neighbor's true need. And that means to speak the word that will in turn go before him to open a possibility of true existence.[194] The loving word *is* the act of love. Love "appears as word," for love is communication.[195]

Thus a true, language-creating word-event is a permission, not a command. It calls forth what is right in our being. It grants freedom,[196] for it is the "nevertheless" to the way things are in which we are free from our past history for our future history.[197] It is the language of self-renunciation, of renunciation of the attempt to find the basis of life in what we have already become.[198] And the freedom we possess as the "nevertheless" to history is exactly freedom for the word, freedom to say what ought to be said.[199]

We cannot speak this language of love and freedom, of self-understanding, by ourselves.[200] As the language of love, we can speak it only with each other.[201] More particularly, we speak it as we come into language-building agreement [202] with Jesus.[203] For it is *His* new language; what happened in His existence is that love was spoken, and so spoken as to draw us into agreement with this speaker: [204] "Jesus was that particular loving one who made everything depend on our coming to see His path." [205] We do not,

193. "Was ist existentiale Interpretation? B," pp. 103 f.; *Hermeneutik*, p. 271.

194. *Hermeneutik*, pp. 70, 111.

195. Fuchs, "Jesus und der Glaube," *Zeitschrift für Theologie und Kirche*, 55, 2, pp. 170–84, pp. 178 f.

196. Fuchs, "Der Sprachereignis in der Verkündigung Jesus, in der Theologie des Paulus, und im Ostereignis," *Zum hermeneutischen Problem in der Theologie*, pp. 281–305, p. 283; *Hermeneutik*, p. 143.

197. "Was wird in der Exegese . . . ?" pp. 47 f.

198. *Hermeneutik*, p. 189.

199. "Was wird in der Exegese . . . ?" pp. 35 f.

200. "Was ist existentiale Interpretation? B," pp. 96 f.

201. Ibid., pp. 104 ff.

202. *Einverstandnis*.

203. *Hermeneutik*, p. 229.

204. "Jesus und der Glaube," entire; *Hermeneutik*, pp. 246 f., *Ergänzungsheft*, pp. 11 ff.

205. Ibid., p. 13.

indeed, simply adopt Jesus' language—that is, repeat His self-understanding. As we seek from *our* given language with *its* self-evidencies to come to agreement with Jesus, the new speech that occurs is our language of self-understanding.[206]

We are bound to Jesus as our helper in authentic utterance [207] because we do not sustain the question about our true selves,[208] we do not make the word of faith entirely our own [209]—and this by the very nature of faith as a transcending of history in history.[210] As an "attitude" within history, faith cannot succeed. But it can hold us in communication with the one who speaks the new language, and that is enough: "what is to be said, Jesus will say Himself." [211]

The possibility of our speaking the language of self-understanding depends on its being spoken independently of us, on the historical distance between us and Jesus, which guarantees that this language is always already spoken before we try to speak it. We are dependent, that is, on this language being historically communicated to us. And that in turn means that we are dependent on the texts that tell of Jesus and instruct in speaking His language.[212] "We live from the language won by the witness of faith which is passed to us as the New Testament. . . ." [213]

The paragraphs above are in Fuchs's view the result of "existential interpretation" of certain texts, the Scriptures, which instruct in the language of self-understanding. Existential interpretation inquires what happens when we understand the text, and so brings to word the relation between the self-understanding of the interpreter and that of the text, brings to word the way in which the text questions the self-evidencies of the interpreter's language. Thus in the

206. *Hermeneutik,* p. 280.
207. Fuchs, "Zum Predigtentwurf," *Zum hermeneutischen Problem in der Theologie,* pp. 349–51.
208. *Hermeneutik,* pp. 144 ff.
209. Ibid., p. 210.
210. "Jesus und der Glaube," pp. 176 f.; "Was wird in der Exegese . . . ?" p. 48.
211. *Hermeneutik,* pp. 146 f.
212. *Hermeneutik,* pp. 146 f., 125, 115 f., 140, 153; "Jesus und der Glaube," pp. 176 f.
213. *Hermeneutik,* p. 271.

present case it brings to word the difference between our word and the text's, and the need of help which arises therefrom. It is clear that existential interpretation is itself therefore an essential phase of the communication of the language of faith,[214] if the knowledge of sin and grace be supposed essential to such communication.

Thus existentiell and existential interpretation demand each other in the communication of Jesus' language. Existentiell communication of Jesus' language is confession of Jesus as the one with whom we seek agreement, to whom we hearken.[215] But precisely the attempt to communicate what "hearken" may mean is existential interpretation.[216] The relation is once formulated: "The decision to keep silent or speak is the criterion of having understood. If I am able to make this decision, I have understood. . . . At this point of self-examination existential interpretation wins its . . . unique power. It is to be used precisely with texts which require that I also be able to speak—or perhaps be silent—and which therefore are fully understood only when I submit myself to this test." [217] So existential interpretation is itself an existentiell act and turns of itself into existentiell communication.[218] It is precisely existential interpretation that confronts our existence with the text's understanding of existence, so that in the confrontation our existence acquires clear meaning.[219]

So far Fuchs. If we follow him—as, *insofar,* I wish to do [220]— then we can say that the proclamation gives us a new mode of existence in that how I exist and what I have to say are the same. This communication of language takes place as existentiell and existential address at once. My existentiell prior understanding and the existentiell address of the proclamation are both already given in some spe-

214. *Hermeneutik,* pp. 141–45; "Was ist existentiale Interpretation? A *and* B," pp. 85 f., 92–94, 99.

215. *Hermeneutik,* pp. 143 f.

216. Ibid., pp. 144 f.

217. "Was ist existentiale Interpretation? B," p. 96.

218. "Das Problem der theologischen Hermeneutik," p. 132; "Was ist existentiale Interpretation? A *and* B," pp. 69 f., 104 f.

219. "Was ist existentiale interpretation? B," p. 103.

220. My critique of Fuchs is—besides that he is deliberately obscure—the same as of Ebeling.

cific interpretation of reality. When then what the text is about is what it is to be and I so question the text, then existentiell question and address are directed at the rightness of these interpretations and so occur as existential interpretation. Let me anticipate what I will make of this.[221] The proclamation communicates to me a story to tell, the story of Jesus; and in the confrontation with the way in which the proclamation tells this story as a story about *me,* I come to a way of utterance in which Jesus' story *is* about me. The work of the proclamatory word is at once its direct narration and its language-creating impact.[222] And to understand the proclamation means—as is indeed true of all understanding—to acquire language. To pick up Gadamer once more: ". . . the hermeneutic conversation [with the text] must, like all conversation, work out a common language. . . . This work is identical with the accomplishing of understanding. . . ."[223]

VIII.

Heinrich Ott, Jürgen Moltmann, and Wolfhart Pannenberg all seek to overcome the problematic of the Bultmannian position by radical ontological elimination of the dualism that runs through it and emerges as the various polarities of: facts and meanings, research and truly historical apprehension, history and eschatology, historical Jesus and Christ of faith. Ott and Moltmann attack one side of the dualism; Pannenberg, the other.

Ott's question is the question of the particular reality of history. He says that Bultmann made the decisive step to an adequate interpretation of historical reality by showing that the scheme of knowing subject and known object is inadequate, and by positing instead

221. Cf. below pp. 239–40. What Fuchs does with this insight is another matter.
222. "Linguistic form and tradited content cannot be separated in hermeneutic experience. If every language is a way of seeing the world, it is so . . . through what is spoken in this language. . . ." We must "acknowledge the oneness of language and tradition. . . ." Gadamer, *Wahrheit und Methode,* p. 417.
223. Ibid., p. 365.

"*confrontation* and the *understanding* decision which arises in it as the reality of all historical being." Moreover " 'confrontation' and 'decision' are so understood that in them both the knower and the known . . . each are constituted anew. . . ." [224]

Yet Ott claims that Bultmann is inconsequent. Bultmann continues to reckon with "objective facts," with objects of neutral research as a realm of reality over against the reality of meaningful, interpreted events.[225] Thus arises a dualistic conception of time and history. On the one hand there is the time of before and after, of succession. This is the dimension of natural occurrences and the realm of neutral research into facts about the past. It is the realm of objects. On the other hand there is the dimension of the true historical event, of existentiell decision. As distinct from the time of before and after, this time has no succession and is exhausted in each pure present of decision; thus true history cannot be narrated.[226]

Ott tries to overcome this dualism by roundly denying that "there are any objectively ascertainable facts at all," and so taking over the qualities of sucession and so of narratability—which "facts" preempt for Bultmann—for meaningful, interpreted history.[227] More cautiously, he says that the objects of neutral research are not "what really happened" but are rather only a particular abstraction therefrom. Detached research is, of course, necessary. But it only provides raw material for understanding. And only with *understanding* do we apprehend reality. "Only with interpretive investigation of history do we begin to know what really happened." [228]

Ott seeks to establish this thesis by showing that the world of "objective facts" is a particular "ontological project" belonging to a particular existentiell attitude— "subjectivism." This is the way of existing in which the existing person secures himself against the challenges and threats of the reality in which he lives by ab-

224. Heinrich Ott, *Geschichte und Heilsgeschehen in der Theologie Rudolph Bultmanns,* p. 154.
225. Ibid., pp. 24, 41 f.
226. Ibid., pp. 116–38.
227. Ott, *Die Frage nach dem historischen Jesus und die Ontologie der Geschichte,* p. 12.
228. Ibid., pp. 12–21, 33.

stracting from its meaning for his existence and reducing it to existentiell neutral objects of observation and manipulation—thereby also positing himself as an independent subject [229] (this does not, of course, mean that every historian is personally a subjectivist).

Asking in what ontological project objectivizing research occurs is indeed an essential step. But I wish to propose a different possible answer. The world of neutrally ascertainable facts does indeed open to research in an ontological project; historical research is indeed the activity of a particular mode of existing in and toward the world. But this in no way means that there are no such facts, or even that they are in any pejorative sense an abstraction from reality—for *all* modes of reality rest upon an original existentiell project, Ott's reality-as-confrontation included. It in no way means that objective research strips its objects of meaning for the existence of the researcher—if the objects of research are indeed discovered by a particular existentiell attitude, they must carry some meaning. It only means they have their own particular meaning. The notion that the object of empirical research in no way challenges the future of the researcher is a misunderstanding of the whole nature of empirical research.[230]

The question to ask is *what sort* of meaningfulness facts about the objectivized past—as such—carry, what sort of challenge they pose to the future of the researcher. The question to ask is about the justification and necessity of the ontological project in which empirical, objectivizing, historical research occurs.

What way of meeting with reality could it be that objectivizes reality and so consists precisely in renouncing all claims to find my

229. Ott, *Die Frage* . . . , pp. 17–20.

230. "The translation . . . from historic present to object of historical research, from history which is in motion and can be influenced by one's own knowledge and decision to looking back over a motionless past history, occurs at the point of the existentiell historicity of the historian. The objectivizing, researching, relation to the past history is therefore itself an eminently existentiell, historic, and history-making relation." Jürgen Moltmann, *Theologie der Hoffnung,* p. 220. It is remarkable that Moltmann also makes no use of this insight.

future and the justification of my life in the reality already given to me—that is, in the story of the past—and just *so* is an existentiell, future-meaning confrontation with that reality? It could indeed be subjectivism. But it could also be repentance.

In repentance I apprehend the given reality of life with no illusions of finding any justification or meaning for the future in it— and precisely so have hold of just that justification and meaning. When I seek in repentance to understand my life as I now possess it and as I and my fellows have made it, I begin with the confession that there are no direct lines from that life to any future fulfillment, that as I am given by the past I am cut off from my future. Thus I am bereft—and freed—of all reason to twist the story of the past in accordance with my dreams and decisions. The way is open for the empirical study of history. Yet I do not thereby simply reject the known past—that is, the known story of my life and of my fellows —as irrelevant to my search for the meaning of life. For the meaning of my life is grasped precisely *by* my confession that my past does not lead to fulfillment—a confession that responds to the message of forgiveness, that grasps the meaning that God gives what has been done, in spite of itself.

Thus empirical research is to begin with a possibility of faith. *Apart* from faith, the existentiell project behind historical research is, I suggest, secularized repentance: that is, a form of what theology has called "civil righteousness," that honesty and rectitude in facing the reality of life to which *all* are called.

The existentiell decision in which empirical research in general— historical or otherwise—becomes possible is the tentative entertaining of all knowledge of how the world is. An empirical assertion is one I am prepared to alter or abandon if the predictions of future events derived from it fail. The ethos of empirical investigation is radical affirmation in the life of thought of the insecurity of the future.[231] Empirical investigation of history is thus abandonment of

231. It is a fine irony that philosophers of existence, who call for such openness, also lament the dominance of "objectifying science," which is about the only place where this openness now occasionally occurs.

the attempt to bind the future by the past; from this viewpoint, too, it is secularized repentance, civil righteousness.

Moreover, as soon as we recognize that objectivizing research is also existentiell confrontation of a particular kind, the abstract contrast between relatively unreflected life from a tradition and scientific research into the tradition is broken. We are in a position to recognize that the apostles' deference to the tradition about Jesus and a critical theologian's worry about the historical Jesus can have exactly the same function. All effort to *remember* how it was is objectivizing, for this effort establishes the past as a reality distinct from the present life of the rememberer. Only in a purely mythical apprehension of reality would this effort be entirely lacking, would the past be entirely unproblematically enacted in and for the present. Whether such a purely mythical understanding has ever occurred, I do not know. It has, at any rate, never occurred in Christianity—the existence in primitive Christianity of that very odd phenomenon, the Gospel-tradition, is the proof. Indeed, there has been something like historical research in Christianity from the beginning—see the prologue of Luke's Gospel. All efforts to remember how it was spring from the same existentiell project, from civil righteousness.

Civil righteousness is, of course, deeply ambiguous. Ott argues that objectivizing consideration of the past is the self-assertion of the subject, and therefore sin. Here it is argued that it is repentance, whether in faith or as civil righteousness. Both are right. The act of objectivizing remembrance is ambiguous; as I perform it I can never ascertain which description applies. Nor do I need to. For we live, here also, by forgiveness.

We are on the verge of being able to introduce again the decisive concept for this whole problem—the concept of the Law. But we must wait a little longer. We return to Ott's analysis of historical reality, which we will in large part affirm—with the qualification that "objective," "neutral" investigation is also meaningful, future-opening confrontation with reality, and so included by the analysis.

According to Ott, the only reality of the past is the meaningful "image" of the past which arises in interested, interpretive confrontation with the tradition. He denies that this position is either idealistic or relativistic, for the final image is fixed by God's view of human history and by faith's participation therein. Thus the "historical Jesus" of interpretive historical investigation—there is on this basis no noninterpretive historical investigation—and the Christ of the proclamation have the same sort of reality and are known in fundamentally the same way. They differ only in belonging to difference "layers" of historical reality.[232]

Before we can make much of this, we will have to translate it into terms of *language*. Then it will be: Historical reality is *narrated* reality, as the being spoken of what meets me. The final story is fixed by God's judgment of human history, which faith *hears*. As to what the difference between the interpretively remembered Jesus and the Christ of the proclamation might be, Ott gives little help—"layers" is meaningless. We will turn to this question shortly. With this translation we carry through a fundamental ontological turn, which is necessitated by the tendency of the whole path of thought we are on. I can do no better here than to cite Franz Mayr: " 'Being' has been interpreted in western thought . . . on the model of the particular being as this 'appears' to a 'seeing.' But there is another starting point . . . by which being is understood from hearing what is said about it by someone, whether by gods or men." [233]

We may suppose that Ott would accept our translation, since his analysis of historical reality continues: It is the very nature of historical time to be neither undifferentiated succession in the past nor a pure present of meaningful confrontation. Neither is the "then and there" of the past irrelevant to my decision here and now, nor does its relevance for my here and now abstract from its concrete reality "then and there." A "then and there" of the past counts for a here and now exactly as what it was then and there. "Time is *qualified succession*. It is the continuing occurrence of meaning." And it is language that constitutes this meaningful mutuality of successive

232. *Die Frage nach dem historischen Jesus* . . . , pp. 24–32.
233. Mayr, "Philosophie im Wandel der Sprache," *Zeitschrift für Theologie und Kirche,* 61, p. 456.

events in time. "Time and word belong together. The word . . . *narrates* [my italics] what has occurred in time and thus lets it live *on* in time. Its function is re-presentation. . . . In the word what has been is present and real; in the word what is coming announces itself." [234]

To this one can only say: Just so! Yet one addition must be made: The word narrates not only what has been; in order to do this, it narrates what *will* be. We must not lose sight of the fundamental character of speech as the mutual challenge in which those who meet open the future to each other. When this is joined to the present insight that historical reality is what can be narrated, we see that the primary historical use of language is narration to another of what is to come—that is, prophecy. The successive events of time are a story, so as to be narratable, only in that they are seen from a conclusion: a story is a story by virtue of its conclusion. With this secured, we can put in the final piece which Ott does not: Time is plot. 'To be temporal'='To be a story.' 'To be temporal'='To await a proclaimed conclusion.'

Yet clearly only what *has* happened can be narrated, unless we are to invent our own future—which is the serpent's temptation. Thus the true word is narration of the past as the opening of a future. And the saving word, the word that makes historical, plotted life possible at all, will be the narration of a past occurrence as the conclusion of life. [235]

Finally, if historical reality *is* historical in that it is narrated, then Jesus is the saving, eschatological event in that His past story is narrated as the conclusion of the story of human life. Here we have the final clarification of the key concepts in the conclusions of the previous chapter.

Yet a new problem arises. Ott rightly emphasizes that the "there and then" of a past event is not absorbed in the here and now of its

234. Ott, *Objektivierendes und existentielles Denken*, p. 130.
235. Ott: "We exist in a network of meaningfully inter-connected events precisely because we are again and again confronted with the End." *Eschatologie*, p. 63.

narration and the decision that responds thereto. Yet it is hard to see how Ott can avoid this if the objects of disinterested research are not true historical reality. Supposing they are, I see the matter so:

The *content* of the proclamation is that "salvation happened then and there as Jesus"—and so prior to the occurrence of the proclamatory narration of Jesus' story. How are we to reconcile this with our present insight that historical reality—and so also Jesus—is what it is in that it is narrated? Clearly the proclamation's assertion about Jesus, that He is the salvation-event prior to the proclamation, can be true—according to the insight into historical reality's word-character which the proclamation itself forces on us—only if Jesus' then and there and our here and now are narrated together in a word, in narration and response, which occurs prior to the proclamation. We are led again to the doctrine of the Trinity, to the description of God whose divine reality in Himself is precisely speech and response, conversation. Jesus' story is our involvement in address and response of the Father and the Son in the Holy Spirit. To describe historical reality as we have done *is* doxology of the triune God.[236]

We can now introduce the concept of the Law, departing decisively from Ott. I assert: All history is real as said, as narrated. The existentiell meaning of the word in which Jesus is *proclaimed* as the eschaton is indicated by calling this word the Gospel. The existentiell meaning of the narration of history *as such* is that it is God's *Law*.

To see this last, we pick up earlier results: Language is given prior to our speech. The miracle of its givenness is the miracle of God's primal address to us by which we are called to human existence. The tradition that brings us language and the tradition that narrates to us the past—and that continues when we in turn interpret the tradition—are the same. Thus it is God who addresses us in the narration of history. And we have now learned the existentiell content of this address: By it we are called into ever more desperate

236. To this see Jenson, "The Doxological Concept of History in the Theology of Peter Brunner." My great indebtedness to Brunner precisely at this point must be acknowledged.

self-assertion and into repentance, in complete ambiguity. The word from God that does this is God's *Law*.[237]

This ambiguity of the work of the Law is overtaken by the proclamation of the Gospel. This brings us back to a particular stretch of history-as-such, to the "historical Jesus." It was and is the *Law* that comes to word in the story of Jesus insofar as this is not proclaimed: that is, what comes to word in the "historical Jesus," in Jesus' existence prior to the Resurrection, is the Law. It is Jesus in the event of proclamation—that is, Jesus' life *including* the Resurrection—in whom the Gospel came and comes to word.[238]

Now we can say: The "truly historical" Jesus is exactly an object of "objectivizing" historical research, inasmuch as such research is also a mode of meaningful confrontation. Also an interpretive narration, such as Bultmann's Jesus, maintains its authenticity as confrontation precisely by fidelity to the results of research. The proclamation is proclamation of this Jesus; it includes the remembrance of his past story—the difference between earlier uncritical remembrance and modern researching remembrance is at this point irrelevant.[239]

237. In this development we are taking up Bultmann's intention. Ott says that the dualism he fights in Bultmann has "doubtless its final basis in the dualism of Law and Gospel. . . . One can only record this basic decision. . . ." *Denken und Sein*, p. 8. So also we simply record that Ott does *not* see this dualism as necessary to the movement of the Gospel—and that we do.

Moltmann points in the same direction by identifying "guilt" and "death" as the driving forces of our interest in history; cf. Moltmann, *Theologie der Hoffnuug*, pp. 243 ff. But he sees no other way than the Gospel of dealing with the guilt and death incarnate in history. Cf. below, pp. 213-16.

238. Whether the Lutheran character of this solution is a recommendation must be left to the reader. I am led to it by what seems the logic of the matter. That the logic of the matter lands me with Luther is for me a satisfaction. For it does seem that the view taken here is closely related to Luther's own view. Cf. Hans-Walter Krumwiede, "Usus legis und usus historiarium," *Kerygma und Dogma*, 8, 4, pp. 238-64.

239. "At the beginning of all historical hermeneutic must stand the resolution of the abstract opposition between tradition and research, between history and knowledge thereof. . . . We will do well not to conceive the historical consciousness . . . as a radical novum, but as a new factor within that which has always constituted man's relation to the past." Hans-Georg Gadamer, *Wahrheit und Methode*, p. 267. As soon as we recognize the existen-

The reason the proclamation is and must be proclamation of the very Jesus who is a possible object of research, is that the Gospel is what it is only *as* the end of the Law. To be Gospel, our proclamation must, in the very narration that is the Gospel, also bring the Law to speech: that is, the Gospel narration must be a historical narrative about the historical Jesus. Here is the necessity of narrating "how it was" with Jesus as one tells the Gospel—whether this be done relatively naively or relatively scientifically. It is the necessity of the Law to the Gospel.

Why does the Law thus adhere in the Gospel? Because the preaching of the Gospel is addressed to man as he really is. Man lives in response to that address of God which has always already called him—and in the case of alienated man that address is the Law. Only in that the Gospel narrative is also a Law narrative is there a man there to whom it is addressed: that is, only in that the Gospel is about the historical Jesus—who *can*, at least, be researched —is it about us. Or we may put it so: The prior understanding which I bring to, and by which I am opened to the proclamation and the texts of the proclamation, is the understanding of myself as guilty, in which the tradition holds me in that it is also the tradition of the Law.[240]

All history is real as said, as narrated. That all true telling of history has in it at least the possibility of being researched, means that what is said in the telling is *Law*. The telling of *Jesus'* history is sometimes also *Gospel* because the telling of this history has in fact occurred as proclamation, as eschatological address. We thus affirm

---

tiell function of research, we can recognize the obvious fact that " . . . research is itself not only research, but mediation of tradition." Ibid., p. 268.

On this point, see the whole splendid discussion on pp. 250–69 of this work.

It is also most interesting that Gadamer (p. 311) sees juristic interpretation as the model of all historical knowing. Thus he, too, interprets the central reality of all historical knowing as lawlike—though of course not necessarily as God's law.

240. Thus the answer is yes to *both* questions that Gadamer puts to Bultmann: "Is man as such . . . moved by the question of God? Or must one say that only from God's initiative does human existence experience itself as moved by the question of God?" *Wahrheit und Methode*, p. 314.

Bultmann's position: *That* this proclamation occurs is precisely the miracle of the Resurrection. But since all historical speech is narrative, we can now see that Easter, the beginning of the proclamation, must itself be a narratable part of the proclaimed story—which is at least unclear for Bultmann.

Also the eschatological history-telling includes a story of past events. This inclusion is the proclamation's address to the lives of its hearers. The truth of this story of past events is therefore essential to the existentiell validity of the proclamation. Historical knowledge of what really happened with Jesus cannot establish the truth of the proclamation—the pure contingence of the occurrence of the proclamation, of Easter, prevents this. But research could reveal that the historical story of Jesus was inappropriate to the proclamation—that Jesus did not, for example, proclaim the coming of the Kingdom—and so refute the proclamation. The proclamation is essentially threatened by its own historicity—which matches the relation of Law and Gospel perfectly.

IX.

We may now draw some consequences of our insight into the law-character of historical narration as such. If this is Law, and the proclamation is Gospel, then the move from narration of how it was with Jesus to proclamation, to narrative of His story as the conclusion of ours, cannot take place in the course of the effort of historical recollection. For the Law and the Gospel are related antithetically. The Law does not lead to the Gospel; it is *overcome* by the Gospel. Whether the effort of remembrance be the effort of direct remembrance (as in the case of some, at least, of the apostles) or of the maintaining of a relatively naively accepted unbroken tradition, or the work of historical-critical understanding of texts, it will never lead of itself to proclamation, to God-language. In traditional terms, exegesis is not the whole of theological reflection.[241] A step beyond

241. This is the locus of dogmatic theology as an enterprise distinct from exegesis.

the attempt to understand the tradition is needed. What is said in proclamation can never be wholly supported from the texts.[242]

All God-utterance about history is prophecy; it tells Jesus' story as the story of the future. Yet this prophecy is also about the past. It tells Jesus' past story as the future; it does not create its own story and is bound to tell Jesus' story historically accurately. It is so bound because it is prophecy directed to men as they are, because it is Gospel that fulfills and overcomes the Law.

It further follows that, both in theology and out, what we have followed Bultmann in calling "interpretation" is not one single activity. Insofar, on the one hand, as *all* historical narration essentially is "interpretation"—that is, insofar as it springs from and is made possible by a life interest and has a meaning for the narrator—that meaning is precisely the discovery that the past does not open a consummating future, that the tradition does *not* provide the meaning of its cultivator's life. The historian's insistence on distance and disinterest—an insistence from which all the pleas of the hermeneuticists have not been able to move him—is precisely the appropriate grasp of the existentiell meaning of the effort to understand the tradition. Such "interpretation" is not, then, "application" to the present. It is the—painfully meaningful!—renunciation of application.[243]

242. Cf. the third criterion.
243. Cf. Heinz Kimmerle, "Metahermeneutik, Applikation, hermeneutische Sprachbildung," *Zeitschrift für Theologie und Kirche,* 61, 2, pp. 221–35. The interpreter is indeed led to the text by a living relation to its matter, a relation mediated through the tradition; and an existentiell dialogue may well be continued outside the specific historical-critical investigation. "But this is not the mark of the strictly scholarly historical-critical work on texts. This rather gets under way in that the historian puts the strict systematic of his procedure between himself and his object, that if there was a dialogue he treats it as broken off, that he puts his 'living relation to the matter of the text' in suspension. . . ." And (p. 229): "If this view is right then the broken-off dialogue cannot be taken up again without further ado once the scholarly work of understanding is concluded. If the object of understanding is so deeply alienated in the process of being worked on in scholarly fashion, then the end-result of this understanding is also alien."
This is exactly my view, except that I see this suspension as itself one basic interpretation, as itself an existentiell decision, so that the relation between scholarly understanding and "extra-scholarly dialogue," i.e., in our

Insofar, on the other hand, as we do seek meaning for our lives in the tradition, insofar as we apply it, *this* "interpretation" is always more than an understanding of the tradition—in any reasonable sense of "understanding." And the "historical reality" which is bespoken by such interpretation is not "what really happened" by itself —whether this clause be taken in the empirical historian's sense or in Ott's sense. It is "what really happened" plus what is *going* to happen. Apart, therefore, from prophecy there is no such thing as language that tells or evokes that "historical reality" in which I can find the meaning of my life. All deliberate interpreting of history is prophecy, whether we will or not.[244]

With the assertion that the proclamatory narration of history is prophecy, we come to a concept adopted by Jürgen Moltmann for the same purpose. I can only agree: "The apprehension and interpretation of past history is then no longer archeological but . . . eschatological. These narratives of history come under the class of prophecy—prophecy which looks back but intends the future. . . . The sense of history [is to be] awaited from the future and grasped as a commission to the present. . . ."[245]

According to Moltmann, Christian speech about God is always eschatology; it is speech about the God who is always future, who is met in His promises. It has a different logic from the logic of description of what is now the case. Eschatological utterances find their truth, not in corresponding to reality as it is given, but in contradicting it. "They do not result from experience, rather they are the condition of the possibility of new experiences. They do not seek to illumine the reality that is there, rather the reality that is coming. They do not seek to copy . . . the reality that is there but to lead the reality that is there into the change which is promised and hoped

present case, the use of the text in proclamation is not exclusive, as for Kimmerle, but dialectical as Law and Gospel. But even so, the use of the text in proclamation comes to be a reflection distinct from understanding the text as such, contra Bultmann and with Kimmerle (p. 230).

244. Thus Christian theology was born from the coincidence of *tradition* and *prophecy* in the primitive Church. Cf. Ernst Käsemann, "Die Anfänge christlicher Theologie," *Zeitschrift für Theologie und Kirche,* 57, pp. 102–85.

245. Moltmann, *Theologie der Hoffnung,* 238 f.

for." Eschatological utterances *make* reality historical,[246] by opening up that difference between what is and what will be in which
reality as history occurs,[247] by uncovering the future possibilities.[248]
The theologian is called, not to interpret the world, but to change
it.[249]

The hermeneutic principle of eschatological utterances is, therefore, the commission to the reader to call the world to its future
in the coming of Christ and to hopeful labor in and for the world.[250]
The point is not to seek objectively to ascertain what is permanent and fixed in a chaos of change; precisely the new and the
awaited are the key categories. "In place of passionless consideration . . . steps empassioned awaiting and engaged commission for
what is coming. In place of the question about the permanent essence and eternal source in times past . . . steps the historical question about the future and its preparations and annunciations in the
past." [251] Study of the past has the task of probing the possibilities
of future fulfillment which lay in past events, possibilities realized
and possibilities lost. We study the past to see how it needs, and will
be fulfilled in, the coming Resurrection.[252]

Here we come a long way forward. It is a decisive step when
Moltmann locates the possibility of talk about God in the identity of
the crucified Jesus with the coming lord, an identity asserted by the
proclamation of His resurrection. Making this identification is a
promise, for in it the reality of death that was is identified with the
reality of life that is to come. The resurrection of Jesus is the promise of His own coming as our future.[253]

Yet there is a disturbing tone: Moltmann always lets the kind of
knowing which is knowing how things now are, appear only in a
negative role. God, who reveals Himself in promise and commis-

246. Moltmann, *Theologie der Hoffnung,* pp. 11 ff.
247. Ibid., pp. 74–84.
248. Ibid., p. 30.
249. Ibid., p. 79.
250. Ibid., pp. 260 ff.
251. Ibid., p. 238.
252. Ibid., pp. 246 f.
253. Ibid., pp. 75 ff.

sion, does not, according to Moltmann, prove his deity "over against the question man already has about God." [254] Moltmann presses theological utterance against an exclusive alternative: "The truth of the promise . . . does not lie in an *adaequatio rei et intellectus* . . . rather in the specific *inadaequatio intellectus et rei* in which it places the hearer." [255] Why must the second exclude the first? We hear that Christian theology can have nothing to do with the ways of thinking that rule in "the positive sciences." [256] In particular, Moltmann urges that historical research as a "positive" science must simply be overcome: It is closed to the future in that it takes its own horizon for absolute.[257] This last is exactly what we have seen *not* to be the case.

Moltmann is suspicious of historical research insofar as it is "positive," that is, as it seeks an *adaequatio rei et intellectus*. The general concepts that such a historian must use to grasp historical connections are alleged to be, by reason of their generality, bound up with specific ways of interpreting reality, and "therefore stand in the carrying-through of a philosophical knowledge of the world as history." [258] But precisely such a philosophical understanding of reality-as-history makes " 'history' into a new concept for 'universe' or for 'reality in its totality' "; so that "a new cosmos-concept is formed and history is no longer understood historically." [259] Modern consciousness of history arises precisely from the experience of the crisis of all stable order and tradition, in the experience of history as the permanent crisis of all certainty.[260] Our historical study has been the attempt to grasp what survives the crisis; it has been "anti-crisis research" and thoroughly conservative. Our historical concern has been to find an end of history, and so to *make an end of* it.[261]

Moltmann describes historical study as a sort of historical-epis-

254. Ibid., p. 202.
255. Ibid., pp. 106 f.
256. Ibid., p. 82.
257. Ibid., pp. 247 f.
258. Ibid., p. 225.
259. Ibid., p. 243.
260. Ibid., pp. 210 ff.
261. Ibid., pp. 238 f.

temological self-righteousness, the attempt to secure our own lives by finding by ourselves the end of our destiny. This is no doubt a possibility, and one we constantly realize. But it is not the only possibility of historical concern as the search for *adaequatio rei et intellectus*. Research can also be openness to the future—indeed, it must be. Nor is it just to deny that it often actually has been. To be sure, historical research as resistance to crisis and historical research as openness to crisis are always inextricably tangled as we actually go to work. But this is the ambiguity characteristic of civil righteousness: it is always also self-righteousness. To exactly this ambiguous reality the Gospel is bound.

X.

Back to Ott. Having argued that the objects of objectivizing speech about history are not the objects of theological narration of history, Ott asserts that all genuine speech about historical reality—and so about God as acting in history—is purely existentiell. Ott distinguishes two fundamental types of statement: those of the objectivizing sciences and "hermeneutical" statements to which the statements of "faith" belong. The first are verified by "neutral testing," [262] and the knowledge they communicate springs from "distanced observation." [263] Statements of faith are verified by the changes in existence they evoke; existential interpretation is the way of showing what effect in existence such a statement should have.[264]

Ott insists that such "hermeneutic" experience is knowledge, "hermeneutic knowledge," which occurs in "historical meeting"

262. Ott, "Existenziales Interpretation und anonyme Christlichkeit," *Zeit und Geschichte: Dankesgabe an Rudolf Bultmann*, 1964, pp. 367–97.

263. Ott, "Der Begriff der *fides implicita* in der Sicht evangelischer Theologie," *Korrespondenzblatt des Collegium Canisianums*, 99, 3, pp. 5–16, p. 8 f.

264. This is an improvement on Ott; he himself calls existential interpretation itself the "verification"—which is most misleading. "Existenziales Interpretation . . . ," pp. 367 ff.

with someone and in the "dialogue" by which such a meeting occurs.[265] Thus "hermeneutical" language is cognitive.

Whether this claim can be maintained depends, of course, on what you are willing to let 'knowledge' mean. But it is clear that Ott's sharp distinction of hermeneutical utterances from those verifiable by observation means that the former cannot be *informative*. And that causes the problem: Ott rightly insists that "the matter of faith and theology, the Gospel, is intelligible; it is intended to be understood; it must be communicated also to those who do not yet believe." [266] But he does not appear to have considered that for such common intelligibility a language is required whose usage rules are generally available; and if a cognitively significant language is to be generally intelligible, then believer and unbeliever must be able together to describe Jesus Christ in order that both may understand, and in the same way, by *whom* the believer is "addressed."

Ott indeed says that objectifying, informing language is necessary. But he gives it no significance for the logic of hermeneutical language. Thus he claims that all theological statements which seem to be neutrally verifiable—for example, "Jesus was crucified"—are in reality "integrating meaning-elements of the indivisible contact with God," to which we come "solely through the personal confrontation itself. . . ." [267]

Thus Ott continues Bultmann's view of existentiell theological language. But with elimination of Bultmann's dualism, the matter becomes even more problematical. We must insist that the making of statements about Jesus which are verifiable quite apart from existentiell affirmation of the proclamation about Him, is essential precisely to the existentiell significance of the proclamation. As Ott does it, it is hard to see what can differentiate preaching and theology from talking in tongues. Objectivizing speech may well be "subjectivism," and this may well be the original sin. But the attempt to regard our theological speech as simply distinct from

265. "Der Begriff . . . ," pp. 8–11.
266. "Was ist systematische Theologie?" p. 31.
267. Ott, *Dogmatik und Verkündigung*, pp. 35 f.

objectivizing speech is Corinthian enthusiasm, and must end in the same strange sounds that were made in Corinth.

XI.

Wolfhart Pannenberg's concern is exactly to show that our talk about God is not enthusiastic or sectarian. He says that the distance involved in making objectifying statements about what has happened is the very condition of language, of persons coming to an understanding with each other on the matter at hand.[268] Indeed, it is precisely the unlimited future-directedness in which we come to speak of God that gives us the distance over against the reality around us in which it can be a world of objects for us.[269] And the claim to universality which is made for the Christian God must prove itself by the relevance to all reality of what is said about Him.

Like Ott, Pannenberg wants to overcome the dualistic split between existentiell historicity and the objective course of events.[270] Where Ott makes existential confrontation with the text absorb the historical question about what happened, Pannenberg claims that objective historical research is itself the way to the meaning for us of the past.

He sees the matter so: The demand that texts must be interpreted in the sense of their writers has produced both our present awareness of the gulf between the text and ourselves—and so the hermeneutic question about their existentiell meaning for us; and the awareness of the varying motivations of writers and therefore of the difference between the past event itself and the witness to it—and so the historical question about what "really" happened. The separation, and even hostility, of these two ways of questioning texts about the past is irremediable so long as historical research treats the texts only as documents of *particular* past events. For then the meaning

268. Pannenberg, "Hermeneutik und Universalgeschichte," *Zeitschrift für Theologie und Kirche,* 60, 1, pp. 90–121, pp. 114 f.

269. Pannenberg, *Was ist der Mensch?* pp. 9–11.

270. Pannenberg, "Heilsgeschehen und Geschichte," *Kerygma und Dogma,* 5, 3, and 4, pp. 218–37, 259–88, p. 218.

of the texts for us now is not sought by historical research and must indeed be separately questioned.[271]

But properly the hermeneutic question should be absorbed by the historical. For as Bultmann himself says, true understanding means not only questioning the text but facing the questions that the text directs to the interpreter. But if the interpreter is to allow the text to do this, he must expose himself fully to what the text is in itself, and so to the particularity of the *back-then* of the text. And "If the historical distance of the *back-then* is preserved, then the connection between what happened then . . . with the present can hardly be found other than in the connected course of history itself which joins then and now. . . ."[272] The bridge cannot be the word of tradition and the proclamation *as such,* for the word is always in fact a word *about* something, in this case, the historical occurrence back then. The notion of a "pure word-event" is a vicious abstraction.[273]

We must "look for the connection through the course of history of the present with the past situation from which the text comes. I.e., the texts can only be understood *in the connection of the whole of history* which binds the past with the present, and not merely with what is now at hand but with the present horizon of future possibilities; for the meaning of the present will only be clear in the light of the future."[274] Only, therefore, in the context of *"universal history"* is the hermeneutic task of bridging the then of the text with the present life of the interpreter finally soluble.[275] And only when historical research broadens to universal history does it absorb the hermeneutic question—as it must if that question is to be answerable.[276]

"Only in the horizon of a world-history can the individual event be considered in its full meaning."[277] The consequence is that his-

271. "Hermeneutik und Universalgeschichte," 90–95.
272. Ibid., pp. 102 f., 116.
273. Ibid., pp. 112 ff., 116 f.
274. Ibid., p. 116.
275. Ibid., p. 118.
276. Ibid., p. 44.
277. "Heilsgeschehen und Geschichte," p. 280.

torical research always depends upon some projected outline of history as a whole, upon some conception of reality-as-history,[278] on the basis of which the historical material is questioned. The historian brings a projected conception of history as a whole to the texts; the documentary evidence speaks for or against this conception and precisely in so doing is historically cognized. Thus the historian's preconception of history as a whole makes specific research possible; and specific research verifies, modifies, or disqualifies the historian's preconception.[279]

The question arises: What *sort* of projected conception of history as a whole is suitable to historical research? It must be one in which the *end* of history is envisaged—for otherwise history is not envisaged as a whole—and yet not in such a way as to hide the openness of the future and the contingency and unpredictability of events. This is possible, says Pannenberg, if the end of history is understood as known *"proleptically,"* so that "in reflection on the proleptical character of our knowledge of the end of history the horizon of the future would be kept open and the finitude of human experience preserved." History must be envisaged as a "whole, given as such by an end which has become accessible in an anticipatory . . . way. . . ." [280]

Thus Pannenberg's fundamental hermeneutic contention is that objectivizing historical research, if done against an adequate projection of history as a whole, itself discovers the existentiell meaning of past history. Applied to the history of Jesus, this analysis of historical research means that critical examination of the available evidence in pursuit of the question "What happened?" within a projected view of history suitable to such examination, must itself lead to knowledge of His meaning for us. If Jesus is indeed the revelation of God, then "the history of Jesus, at which the researches of the historian aim, encompasses the revelation of God in itself and pre-

278. "Hermeneutik und Universalgeschichte," p. 109.
279. "Heilsgeschehen und Geschichte," pp. 281 ff. Pannenberg is here dependent on Collingwood.
280. "Hermeneutik und Universalgeschichte," pp. 110, 120 f.: "Heilsgeschehen und Geschichte," pp. 280 ff.

cisely as an object of research is only grasped in its true character when seen in this its uniqueness. . . ."[281]

In order to hear the witness of the New Testament as a unity and as the basis of faith, it is necessary to go behind the various different witnesses, including the biblical, to the *event* to which they witness. Such a proceeding is historical-critical research. What can be learned about this event will then necessarily be the criterion of the adequacy of the various witnesses, including the biblical.[282] The "Christ event is not value-free in itself and only clothed with one or another significance by a kerygma distinct from itself. . . . the Christ event carries its significance . . . in itself."[283] The meaning of the Christ-event is God. Thus it must be possible to discover by historical research "that in Jesus of Nazareth God has revealed Himself."[284] If the events of biblical history "are apprehended in the historical connections to which they belong, they speak their own language, the language of facts. God has demonstrated his deity . . . in this language. To apprehend this we need add nothing to the revelatory facts . . . beyond what can be found in them."[285] Between theological assertions and the assertions resulting from historical research into the biblical history, there is no essential distinction.[286]

Events of the past "speak" a meaning in this way only, of course, when they are not torn from the historical connections to which they belong; only when considered within the context of tradition in which they occurred.[287] For the Christ-event, this context of tradition was the Jewish apocalyptic. The key is the Resurrection.[288] "For a contemporary Jew, insofar as he shared the apocalyptic expectation, the event of the resurrection needed no interpreting. . . .

281. "Heilsgeschehen und Geschichte," p. 275.
282. Pannenberg, "Was ist eine dogmatische Aussage?" *Kerygma und Dogma*, 8, 2, pp. 81–99, pp. 89 ff.; *Grundzüge der Christologie*, pp. 15–24.
283. "Was ist eine dogmatische Aussage?" p. 91.
284. "Heilsgeschehen und Geschichte," p. 278.
285. Pannenberg, *Offenbarung als Geschichte*, p. 100.
286. "Was ist eine dogmatische Aussage?" p. 91.
287. Ibid., p. 91; *Offenbarung als Geschichte*, p. 100.
288. *Grundzüge der Christologie*, pp. 61 ff.

If *such* a thing had happened, there could be no doubt what it meant." [289]

Seeing history as it was seen by the tradition within which the Resurrection occurred (if it did), that Jesus rose meant: (1) The end of the world is occurring; the resurrection of the dead and God's final judgment are at hand.[290] (2) Jesus' pre-Easter claim that God's final judgment over every man is spoken in His, Jesus', word, has been confirmed by God Himself.[291] (3) And therefore God is revealed in Jesus' word and destiny.[292] The last point must be more fully developed.

Apocalyptic created the idea of a universal history, corresponding to the universal claims of the God of Israel.[293] In a conception of historical reality as made up of discrete stories, a god whose reality was experienced in historical events could only be one of many gods. Only the whole of history can be understood as the revelation of the one God.[294] But history will be a whole only at its end.[295] Therefore God's self-revelation can happen "strictly speaking . . . only at the end of all history." [296] Thus it is possible to speak of God's having revealed Himself only if the end of history has been anticipated, only if an event has occurred which "although it has occurred once in the past, at a specific time, always is yet before us as our last future." [297] But if Jesus is risen from the dead, this is just what has happened: the Resurrection and the Judgment have happened ahead of time. "With the resurrection of Jesus the end of history has already happened for Him, although we others still await it. Therefore . . . the God of Israel has conclusively demonstrated his divinity in the fate of Jesus and is now revealed as the one God of all men." [298]

289. *Grundzüge der Christologie*, p. 62.
290. Ibid.
291. Ibid., pp. 62; 47–61.
292. Ibid., pp. 64, 218–86.
293. *Offenbarung als Geschichte*, p. 96 f.
294. Ibid., p. 17.
295. Ibid., p. 104.
296. Ibid., p. 98.
297. Ibid., p. 143.
298. Ibid., pp. 104 f.

The argument is tightly worked out. And parts of it seem solid. Within the apocalyptic project of history as a whole, the resurrection of Jesus—if it happened—must indeed have meant the revelation of God. Pannenberg is also right in insisting that the historian must consider past events in the context of the tradition in which they stood. He is also right in saying that the historian must himself work with a projected conception of history as a whole. But it has not yet been shown that the conception of universal history with which we now investigate the past must be the same as the conception with which the principals of particular past events experienced those events, and from which we now understand the meaning of those events for them. Therefore it has not been shown that the meaning that our investigation discovers an event had for its principals must be the same as the meaning that our investigation will find in it for us. Indeed, in most cases the two conceptions of universal history *cannot* coincide, since the historian must investigate many different civilizations. Pannenberg's argument that if Jesus did rise from the dead, historical investigation must discover that this event means the revelation of God is, therefore, valid only if in this particular case the conception of universal history within which the event occurred must, for some reason, necessarily also be that with which we now study the past.

This is exactly what Pannenberg asserts. Only with a knowledge of the anticipated conclusion of history can we conceive history as a whole without binding the future, and so cogently investigate the course of history. But this is exactly that "understanding of history . . . which is to be read from the history of Jesus in its relation to Israelite-Jewish tradition." Indeed, the biblical tradition is the source of the whole notion of universal history.[299] Only if history is thought of as ruled by the absolutely free yet faithful God can its continuity and contingency be simultaneously understood: ". . . events which are in themselves contingent are, as it were, connected backwards, are related back to what has been. Through such retroactive relating continuity is created ever anew. So God's faithfulness

299. "Hermeneutik und Universalgeschichte," p. 121.

expresses itself." The Christian idea of God is properly indispensable to historical research.[300]

The biblical understanding of history as a whole is thus the only one adequate to historical research.[301] And where the biblical understanding of history is really lost, there the apprehension of reality as history and of man's historicity cannot long survive. For if God does not carry the continuity of history, men must; but men are a plurality of individuals and cannot found history as a unity.[302]

If we temporarily let this last argument stand, then the one question that remains is the factual one: Does historical investigation, working—as Pannenberg insists it must—with the biblical conception of history as a whole, find that Jesus in fact rose from the dead? I will omit Pannenberg's detailed analysis of the state of the records—which, I may say, seems compelling—and give only the results:[303] (1) "In view of the age of the fixed traditions handed on by Paul, and in view of Paul's nearness to the events, the supposition that appearances of the risen one were really experienced by a series of members of the primitive Christian congregation, and not perhaps invented in later legend-formation, is historically well-based."[304] (2) All attempts to explain their experiences as illusion, wish-fulfillment, or the like lack any basis at all in the documents.[305]

So the key point: How then *will* the historian reconstruct the events that led to the rise of primitive Christianity? What possibilities the historian will consider will depend on what conception of historical reality he brings to the data. In particular, if he knows in advance that the dead do not rise, the issue is settled.[306] But within the biblical conception of history (which is, again, the only one finally adequate to research), resurrection must be a meaningful idea.[307] Moreover, the biblical conception of history preserves the

300. "Hermeneutik und Universalgeschichte," pp. 285 f.
301. Ibid., pp. 280 f.
302. "Heilsgeschehen und Geschichte," pp. 321 ff.
303. *Grundzüge der Christologie*, pp. 85–102.
304. Ibid., p. 87.
305. Ibid., pp. 93 ff.
306. Ibid., p. 95.
307. Ibid., pp. 79 ff.

contingency and uniqueness of the individual event which is the object of historical research; it breaks the metaphysical dogma that nothing can have happened differently than what happens now—that a dead man cannot have risen.[308]

Thus the situation is: The documentary evidence makes it probable that certain people did have experiences that they took to be experiences of a risen Jesus. Resurrection is a meaningful notion, and we do not know in advance that it cannot have happened. There is no evidence for any other interpretation of their experiences. Pannenberg concludes: If the rise of primitive Christianity is, in view of the available evidence, "only understandable if viewed in light of the eschatological hope for a resurrection from the dead, then that which is so named is an historical event. . . . An event which can only be spoken of in the language of eschatological expectation is to be asserted as having historically occurred." [309]

Pannenberg is aware that historical research can lead only to probabilities, to assertions held pending further evidence.[310] Thus historically mediated assent to the occurrence and meaning of the Resurrection is not yet *faith*. Faith is trust in and commitment to the God who is revealed in the—historically ascertainable—Resurrection. It is directed therefore to the future fulfillment of the promise the Resurrection makes: that we, too, shall rise to life with God.[311] Yet before I can trust this promise, I must be able to take it seriously, which means in this case, since the promise is made by an alleged historical event, that I must find that allegation historically probable.[312] Knowledge of God's revealedness in Christ is not faith as trust; it is that *in* which we trust.[313] Thus, for Pannenberg faith is not a factor in the logical and hermeneutical problematic, which

308. "Heilsgeschehen und Geschichte," pp. 259–67.
309. *Grundzüge der Christologie*, p. 95.
310. Ibid., p. 103.
311. "Heilsgeschehen und Geschichte," pp. 277 f.; *Offenbarung als Geschichte*, p. 101.
312. I cannot find that Pannenberg has anywhere in writing made this last point quite so clearly. I base this on the continuation of the passages just cited and on personal conversation.
313. Ibid. See especially the footnotes on pp. 277 f. of "Heilsgeschehen und Geschichte."

concerns the knowledge *prior* to faith. So also, because the Resurrection is the historical *anticipation* of the end, final verification of the statement 'Jesus is risen' can only come at the end of all things. Verification by historical research can do no more than provide the basis for expecting such verification.[314] But again, the expectation of this final verification is not part of the specifically historical and hermeneutical problematic.

Pannenberg's hermeneutical proposal is complete: Cogent and objective historical research must find it probable that Jesus rose from the dead. It must also discover that this event means, in itself and so also for us now, that His word and fate is the revelation of God. Therewith the hermeneutical problem is absorbed by historical questioning.

This proposal clearly shares many concerns with the present study: Both insist that our proclamatory talk about Jesus must be informative in some sense related to the way in which the sciences are, and therefore it must be in some way verifiable. Both insist on the narratable, course-of-events character of the history in which God is revealed. Above all, both see Christ's final coming and resurrection as the key to the logic of theological language.

I may express my agreement with Pannenberg so: Man talks about God in that man's existence is a questioning, in that he finds himself only in the future.[315] Thus Pannenberg continues the fundamental insight we have traced through Bultmann and Ebeling. Yet at the same time he holds to the informing function of Christian language about God. The result is that he conceives the future from which we live, not as abstract "futurity," but as the concrete conclusion of history—whereby also history becomes not "historicity" but what I have called "a story." Thus we are agreed that Christian language about God is meaningful only within a projection of the total story of human history.

Yet at the same time the divergence is sharp. More radically than

---

314. I again cannot find that Pannenberg has clearly made this point in print; but it belongs to his position.

315. Cf. here, besides the foregoing, "Die Frage nach Gott," *Evangelische Theologie*, 25, 4/5, pp. 238–62.

any other, Pannenberg develops a monistic view of history and proclamation: Distanced, objectivizing historical-critical research results in assertions that just *are* eschatological proclamation. Accurate description of Jesus' particular human path *is* identification of Him as the eternal Son.[316] The investigations of the present study, on the other hand, lead to replacing the Bultmannian dualism of facts and existentiell meaning with the even more radical dualism of Law and Gospel.[317] Because it is so close and yet so opposed, Pannenberg's proposal is the final test for the proposal made here.

Pannenberg's hermeneutic holds together or falls apart with the question: Is it ascertainable (not ascertained) by historical research that Jesus rose from the dead?[318] I do not think it is. This objection is not based on the claim that only that can have happened in history which is like what happens now, so that we can know in advance that a dead man cannot have risen—though a good case might be made for this claim.[319] My objection is not a material objection. It is rather that 'Jesus rose from the dead,' if understood as it must be to correspond to the logic *of the witness in fact given* by those who experienced His appearances, is not verifiable or falsifiable by historical research and therefore is not a sentence that can appear—as either affirmed or denied—in a report of research into the events in question.

We encounter in the sources primary testimony that asserts: "Jesus was alive after his death." This is—to say the least—unexpected. What do we do when we encounter such an unexpected testimony in historical sources? We say: If this testimony is accurate, then as we continue to examine the sources we will find such-and-such traces in the sources (other, of course, than repetition of the witness itself); if it is inaccurate, we will find such-and-such different traces. We form the hypothesis: "This testimony is accurate," and derive from it predictions about our future experience with the sources. If these predictions are fulfilled, the hypothesis is so far con-

316. *Grundzüge der Christologie*, pp. 354 f.
317. Thereby fulfilling Bultmann's deepest intention.
318. Pannenberg insists on this himself. *Offenbarung als Geschichte*, pp. 141–43.
319. See Van D. Harvey, *The Historian and the Believer*, pp. 68–101.

firmed; stating this confirmation is then the same as asserting the content of the testimony as our own historical assertion.

But from the statement: "The witness of those who said 'Jesus rose from the dead' is correct," no predictions can be derived for what, other than repetition of this witness itself, we will find in the sources. And this is not due to the accidental state of the tradition or to some other material factor—which would be logically irrelevant. What the witnesses say is of such a character that verification in the rest of the tradition is in principle impossible. Two factors are relevant here: (1) The witnesses make it clear that the visibility, audibility, and tangibility of the risen Jesus coincided exactly in time and space with their experiences of the risen Jesus: that is, the witnesses were not able, and did not intend to be able when asked, "What do you mean, 'risen'?" to say, "Look over there and you will observe such-and-such happening" (we will make a vital modification of this in a moment). The witnesses speak precisely of appearances, not of meetings. But then there *can* have been no occurrences other than the occurrence of the experiences of the witnesses themselves, of which trace might now be found in the sources. (2) The witnesses claim that the Jesus whom they experienced was living the reality of life-beyond-death. But since neither they had, nor do we have, experience of that life, we are not able to say what would be the further consequences in our world if Jesus were indeed risen in this sense (and not merely resuscitated).[320]

I do not say that 'Jesus is risen,' whether uttered by those who experienced His appearances or by us, is informatively vacuous. I do not say that the experiences of the witnesses were "religious experiences" in the sense of the last chapter. 'Jesus is risen' does indeed predict an intersubjectively indicable event and is therefore informative. It predicts that He will come to final judgment of all men. But since this event is predicted for after any given historian's present (*qua* historian), and since the character of the experiences the wit-

320. "If the reality of Jesus' resurrection is mediated . . . to us only in the mode of missionary proclamation and if this mode of information seems to pertain to the reality of the Resurrection itself, we must ask if the necessity of this sort of statement . . . is not based on the character of the event itself." Moltmann, *Theologie der Hoffnung*, p. 170.

nesses claim to have been of the risen Jesus prevents any other predictions about intersubjectively observable characters of the tradition or the world being drawn from this claim, a historian *qua* historian simply cannot weigh the claim. This is not unusual: he cannot weigh the claims of the natural sciences either.

What *can* we expect from historical investigation of the Resurrection? Pannenberg is right in saying that when I encounter the claim that Jesus rose, I must, if I am to take it seriously, look into the matter historically—with whatever degree of historical consciousness and technique I possess. As we have already argued, the proclamation's binding to history that can be investigated is its binding to our reality. Moreover, such investigation might have discovered that the tradition about Jesus' appearances was entirely legendary in its literary form or paralleled in mythical accounts; or it might have found basis in the sources for explanations of those appearances in terms of delusion or the like. That investigation does not produce such results is, just as Pannenberg says, necessary to our being able to credit the Resurrection. But the most that can appear in a researched version of the Resurrection events is: reliable sources make it probable that certain persons experienced appearances of Jesus as risen, and there are no grounds for explaining these experiences in terms of delusion or the like.[321]

Such a result may indeed be regarded as a certain historical confirmation of the Resurrection. Yet the statement of the Resurrection *itself*, 'Jesus is risen,' cannot be affirmed or denied in a report of historical research. And it is this that is, it seems to me, necessary to make Pannenberg's hermeneutic work. If the Resurrection, and so Jesus' meaning for us as God's revelation, is not historically verifiable, then the attempt to abolish the dualism of research and proclamation fails. Pannenberg takes us straight to the decisive point, and in the debate with him the final decision is made. We have now to work out the consequences.

The particular Resurrection that the proclamation affirms has not proved, after all, accommodable by historical method. I doubt,

---

321. It seems to me, as to Pannenberg, that this is indeed what investigation discovers.

therefore, that the proclamation's projection of history as a whole is that with which historical investigation does, or should, work. It is that which we *proclaim*. To adopt this conception and to affirm that Jesus is risen come to exactly the same thing—so that 'Jesus is risen' is analytic within the proclamation's vision of history. Empirical investigation cannot work with this projection, for to use it is to affirm as having occurred an event that cannot be discovered empirically. What *can* be said is that the proclamation's vision of the whole of history is the only one that claims to know the end of history and yet, because its vision of the end is anticipatory, does not stop empirical investigation of the past *also* being done, which indeed demands it, as we earlier established.

Historical investigation must indeed work with a projection of history as having a goal—but the existentiell decision in that project is precisely renunciation, renunciation of the claim to *know* that goal, or better, renunciation of the claim to know the connection between that goal and the past events that are the object of the investigator's concern. The historian who is also a believer *believes* in the continuity of past reality and future goal, of what he has become and what will become of him: that unity has been enacted for him as the unity of death and resurrection in the life of Jesus. But it has been enacted *as* that which is to come, as the End. And therefore also the believer does not *know* what that unity is like: that is, he cannot use it as a principle in research or speculation.[322]

I suggest that the historian works with a *secularization* of the proclamation's vision of history. History is done under the Law, not the Gospel. While the impact of the Christian idea of God—which is explicated as the proclamation's vision of universal history—is indeed essential to the investigation of history, for the reasons Pannenberg gives, it is as the *absent* God, who determines our existence exactly by not being known, that God rules here. The God of the modern experience of history is the unknown God, the God of the Law. This is the ultimate reason why the Resurrection, which *is* the Gospel, cannot be affirmed within the historian's version of the past.

322. Cf. Moltmann, op. cit., pp. 179 ff.

But if the Resurrection cannot be discovered by historical investigation, how can we claim to know that it has occurred? We can agree entirely with Pannenberg that appeals to "intuition," "the eye of faith," etc., fail; the believer has the same organs as anyone else.[323] We spoke of the proclamation's narration of history as *prophecy*. The proclamation narrates the story of Jesus as the story of the End. Doing this prophetic act is the same as adopting the proclamatory projection of history as a whole, and so is the same as making the affirmation 'Jesus is risen.' We *prophesy* that Jesus is risen. Or rather, 'Jesus is risen' is not so much a content as a mark of believing prophecy, of telling of Jesus as the End; it is the New Testament "Thus saith the Lord. . . ." Nor do we leave the realm of information with such prophecy: this prophecy is subject to the control of historical investigation, since it is exactly the historical Jesus whose story we prophesy as the End, of whom we by so doing say, "He is risen."

What is the justification for telling prophetically the story of Jesus —that is, saying He is risen? We do this in response to a *command* to do so, the command to proclaim the Gospel which is addressed to us in the proclamation of the Gospel when we hear it. Either this command enforces itself on us or it does not.[324] Thus the affirmation of the Resurrection depends upon the continuous tradition of the *act* of living proclamation—upon Paul having witnessed to someone in Corinth, and he to . . . , and so on to us. The tradition here in question is not the handing on of the content 'Jesus is risen'; it is the tradition of *doing* telling Jesus' story as the story of the End. This is the true special tradition of the Church, and only in it is it *obedience* and not fantasy to say 'Jesus is risen.'[325]

To say 'Jesus is risen' is response to a command. It occurs, that is, in a word-event in Ebeling's sense. If the hermeneutic question cannot be absorbed into the historical, then the distinction of the event-character of the word from its statement-character retains its justifi-

323. "Heilsgeschehen und Geschichte," pp. 267 ff.
324. In a dogmatic treatise we would here speak of the Holy Spirit.
325. Cf. my article, "An Hermeneutical Apology for Systematics," *Dialog,* 4,4.

cation. We therefore retain earlier results [326] that were challenged by Pannenberg's proposal, and build further: The event of saying and hearing the proclamation belongs to the reality as historical event of that which is proclaimed. Thus the beginning of that proclamation, the Resurrection, itself belongs to the story to be narrated. It is in this situation that when in obedience to a command we say, 'Jesus is risen,' we claim also to *describe* an event that has happened. And this is not a claim that our existentiell projects are real because we project them: it is the claim we take up by speaking the Gospel; and the Gospel is at every step an attempt at accurate statement of the facts about us as we have become, as we are by the Law; the Gospel is narrative of the historical Jesus and of the historical us. Moreover, 'Jesus is risen' will be eschatologically verified—or it will not be.

Thus we are back with historical research. This, too, we have seen, is interpretation. Thus the same structure is found here as in the Gospel-telling of Jesus: the act of narrating belongs to the reality of what is narrated. What, then, is the difference? The difference is the difference of the Gospel and the Law.

The Gospel binds the past to the future. It is *promise:* it says what will certainly be, and permits us to own what has been and what has come of us freely, as those whose destiny is posed and not decided by the past. The Gospel is forgiveness: it is the true word which ever and again grants us the future as *God's* future, which because it is God's is unconditionally ours and so frees us from seeking our destiny in what is in our hands, that is, in the past.

The Law, on the other hand, binds the future to the past. Its pattern is: "If you . . . then . . . ," where the apodosis is a determination of our future, and the protasis is something in our control, that is, something past to that future. The Law throws us back on ourselves and on the past and so opens the future as a future without promise. It therefore opens the past as a past without hope. Precisely so it opens it as an *object,* and creates that distance to what we have done and to what has happened to us in which specifically human existence is possible, and in which the Gospel can speak to us.

326. Cf. above pp. 206–7.

Finally, if all historical reality is interpreted, bespoken reality, and if the word in question is Law *and* Gospel, so that interpretation is interpretation-as-Law or interpretation-as-Gospel, then historical reality is irreducibly ambiguous and at odds with itself. History is the history of damnation and the history of salvation at once; its very essence is self-contradiction. The reconciliation is *eschatological;* it awaits the final judgment of God, who will finally decree what history has meant and been.[327] This judgment of God which will reconcile Law and Gospel, death and life, is now beyond our ability to capture in a formula; it is beyond our imitating other than by the act of repentance, by the act of flight from the Law to the Gospel. Yet we may live by that decision, we may repent and flee to the Gospel, for the eschatological decision has already been enacted for us as the unity of death and resurrection in the life of the man Jesus.[328] It is in that flight that the unity of past and future, Law and Gospel, occurs for us, that reality opens for us as history.

327. Hegel's only real fault was that he confused himself with the last judge; but that is quite a fault.

328. Cf. Moltmann, op. cit., p. 206. "Then it comes out that this world cannot bear" the Resurrection and the new world created by the Resurrection. "The dialectic which will carry this contradiction must be an apocalyptic dialectic. The reconciling synthesis of cross and resurrection can be expected . . . only in the totality of the new being."

7. Exhortations

We were impelled down the path of this study by the feeling that Christian talk about God rang increasingly hollow. What have we accomplished to alleviate this feeling?

We could say that we have discovered that God-utterances do function, and what that function really is—so that if in our preaching and praying we pay careful attention to how such utterance really works, we may hope that our talk will function smoothly and efficiently, and that the impression of mal- or nonfunction will be lifted. And it would not be simply wrong to say this. Yet it is clear that a multitude of problems hide in that "really." We are very close to the vicious circle of: "Theological utterance is just fine if one sees how it really works." "How do you tell how it really works?" "By thinking how it would have to work to be just fine."

The possibility of this circle points to an insight from the beginning of our way: every philosophical analysis of a body of language is in fact a proposal. If this is generally true, it is true also in the present case. Chapters 2 through 6 of this book constitute a proposal by the author to the reader: "Come, let us speak so, that 'God' is used in such-and-such connections and in those only." This proposal

234

has been worked out in a confrontation between the self-understanding of classical Christian theology and the cultural forces—natural science and the historical attitude—that evoke the emptiness of our God-talk as we in fact usually do it. What is proposed is that if we wish now to talk responsibly about God, this is how we must do it. I put to the reader, therefore, a decision: the decision whether to embark on the language activity described.

But this is still unsatisfactory. It was not our purpose to *invent* a language which people might choose to *begin* to speak. It was our purpose to examine the utterance about God of *Christian faith*—for its function and the legitimacy of that function. And Christian faith is a given reality of history, given moreover as a continuous reality from a specified past date to the present. We are thus in the position of having to say at once that our description of a way of speaking is the proposal of an improvement—and so new—and that it describes the logic of a standing tradition of speech.

The solution to this puzzle—or, rather, the insight that the puzzle is artificial—is indicated by "tradition" in the last sentence. "The language of Christian faith" is not a fixed entity; it is precisely a tradition. A tradition subsists *just as* the tradition-event in which given language, used to answer new challenges, issues in new language. The continuity of language is the event in which, as I seek understanding with him to whom I *now* hearken, the agreements that regulate the language I already have are questioned so as to lead to new agreements, new bonds of common apprehension. The consideration of a proposal such as that of this book should be just such an event, which *is* the continuity of a historically given language.

Yet in the case of faith's language, this is still not the whole answer. We do not speak in faith merely because we speak in a way that *grows out of* the past language of faith. The claim that we proclaim the same faith as believers before us clearly involves a continuity besides that of the tradition of language. This is: the new person in the search for understanding with whom new Christian language is spoken, is always the same Jesus, presented in the proclamation of Him as the coming one who is always new. It is in responding to and passing on this proclamation of Jesus that faithful language is always new. And therefore it is always also the same. What 'same' means in "same Jesus" is the bond of the proclamation to that Jesus who is an object of recollection and research.

That this is so, that Jesus is indeed now present in the proclamation as the one who is never passed by, is of course a version of the central affirmation of faith: "He is risen and will come again." This assertion will be verified—or not—by the end of the human story and only thereby. The motive for making this assertion now is not therefore already accomplished verification but obedience to a command as a word-event in which I find myself existing. So also the claim to speak anew now from the one same Christian faith is always a claim which will only be verified in the fulfillment. I can now make this claim only as a commitment, as a wager of my own existence.

From an uncommitted viewpoint, the situation is, therefore: That the language policy described in this work is a possible consistent policy of cognitive, informative speech is shown—or not shown—by the analysis that proposes it. But that the described language is the language of *Christian faith* is a verifiable, but at present an unsupported, hypothesis. It must only be clear that this last is true of *all* attempts to think how now to speak responsibly of the Christians' God.

The decision about the adequacy of any proposal therefore can be made only from within the tradition of faithful speech. An analysis such as that in this book must be tested for its faithfulness by the believers, by those who live in and by the tradition of believing language. We ask, as a question asked in carrying out our existence within the tradition of faith: In responsibility both to the proclamation as we have heard it from the tradition and to present reality as best we can apprehend it, is this the way we must speak? And even this formulation is artificial, for neither a living tradition nor presently apprehended reality are entities that we can weigh from outside. What actually happens can only be that *in* our determination by the Church's tradition, we try to understand such a proposal— and then see what comes of this understanding for our future talk about God. I say "we" because this counts also for the author of the proposal.

This last is, of course, simply what is true of theological proposals in general—only that when language specifically is discussed, it is good to make it explicit. We are thus signaled that our analysis of the language of theology is itself materially relevant to theology. And this must, of course, be so. For if, as we said at the beginning, the criteria by which we decide what to say and what not to say about theological language are themselves in part theological, then any actually proposed analysis must involve theological commitments. So we can now say: Whether the language policy here proposed is that which faith seeks must be decided as theological questions ought always be decided, by the authority of the Bible as it works within the continuing tradition-event which is the history of the Church's proclamation. The reader is asked: Is the proposed policy biblical? That is, if we speak so, will we be speaking as we must to answer the prophets and the apostles?

II.

My hope that God-talk done as here described will not ring hollow is given by the analysis itself, in which the language-building and destroying presence of natural science and the historical apprehension is the constant partner. That the talking described here is that proper to *Christian faith* is a theological decision which reading believers must make with me—or against me. In responsibility to this hope and to the circumstances that it is hope in a *proposal,* I must, after all, conclude with some "practical" homiletical reflections on our performance of talking about God—with, as it were, therapeutic suggestions for the disease of theological pointlessness.

First, let us talk of God matter-of-factly. Our utterances containing 'God' must all be, at least implicitly, informative statements about the man Jesus of Nazareth and what He has done and will do. If we find ourselves about to say something about God and are in any doubt that this is so, let us keep silent. Let us resolutely avoid all talk of God as of a being "out there" somewhere. But let us even more resolutely avoid all talk of God as the "principle" or "force" or "immanent reality" of something-or-other.[1] If we want to say that God is "love," then let it be clear in every turn of our discourse that by "love" we mean neither a great Lover out there nor that prime nonesuch, love-in-general or the "principle of love," but *Jesus'* love, what He did and will do.

This is not a mere exhortation to be "christocentric." There is a way of talking about Christ or "Jesus"[2] where He too loses his matter-of-factness. The "Jesus Christ" who is simply the God of popular theism with more distinct features and emotive attachments is no improvement. Nor is the spooky "Jesus" who hangs about bothering people at their work. And to baptize spirituality-in-general as "Jesus" or "Christ" changes little: 'Jesus is love-in-general' is even hollower than 'God is love-in-general.' Let our rule be: We will say about "Jesus" only that to which historical research into the life of the man by that name could be in some way relevant.

Let us follow these rough rules: If we are about to say something about God that if pressed we will have to explain in terms of "analogy," "picture," "symbol," or the like,[3] we will not say it. If we are about to say something about God that "only believers can understand," we will admit that we do not understand it either, and not say it.

Next, let our talk of God *be* a word-event. Whenever we are about to say 'God,' let us stop and ask: Suppose my utterance is affirmed by my hearer, what step in his life will that affirmation be? If we are not sure that it will be any step, let us keep silent. Let us understand uttering 'God' as an act of violence performed upon the hearer, so that, for better or worse, if he hears, he must come from the experience of hearing a different man than he went in. Let us speak the Law as executioners and the Gospel as friends at the cell

1. If we *must* choose between orthodox theism and the way-in-there "love" that *Honest to God* has popularized, then in the name of the modern, secular world, let us by all means choose the former. I do not mean by this to say anything against Robinson's often witty critique—only against his positive proposals.

2. This can often be recognized by pronunciation, e.g., "Jeesus."

3. Except, of course, as all speech can be so described.

of the condemned. If we are to speak of God, let us remember: We will be commanding, blessing, cursing, complimenting, and insulting our hearers.

Here is the terrible and almost complete failure of our preaching. Our preachers do not proclaim absolution: they say, "Go home and tell God about it and He will forgive." We do not *bring* the good news: we say, "The good news is in the Bible. Read it diligently." It must be clear: Such preaching does not say anything about *God* at all. For God is real for us only as the word-event in which we then and there, as speakers and hearers, are condemned and rescued.

Together these recommendations clearly involve a rule of parsimony in talking about God. Let us say 'God' only when we absolutely cannot avoid it. This is not a recommendation of retreat to silent inwardness. The point is to speak always so that the truth of our lives occurs in our speaking—and to speak of *Jesus Christ* so that in *this* speaking the truth of our lives is uttered. If we do this, then ever and again we will not be able to avoid 'God'—until the day when Jesus confronts us, and all our truth will be uttered in an utterance of 'God' that will take all eternity.[4]

Finally, speaking of Jesus matter-of-factly, *and* so that this speaking is the act of our existence, means speaking eschatologically. It is only in that we tell about Jesus as about the end of our human story that a transforming word-event can occur as factually informative narrative. Let us use many future tenses. And when we use past tenses, then let us do so in the context of the one particular past tense statement: 'He rose.'

No doubt it is this recommendation that is most likely to be misunderstood. Eschatological speech so easily becomes mythology. Let us work this out a little more fully.

If we come to speak in response to the proclamation, we acquire a new story, Jesus' story, to tell about the conclusion of our lives, *and* the language that so construes reality that in it we are able to understand our lives as having a conclusion. Existentiell and existential interpretation occur together in mutual necessity.

But this way of putting it is oversimplified. Better: I acquire the

4. Origen!

story of Jesus and am driven to *seek* the understanding of life, the language, in which I will be able to tell this story as the conclusion of my own. I do not simply *acquire* this language. Rather, that I be able to grasp my own life as leading up to Jesus' story of death and resurrection is the *goal* of faith. What moves me to this search is the promise, itself a part of the story, that the search will be successful. The part of the story that makes this promise is the Easter story, which belongs to the existentiell narration precisely as an existential qualification of the story as our story at the end. Resurrection is thus the part of Jesus' and our story that comes *after* death only as a particular existential qualification *of* death. The proclamation interprets death as the occasion of fulfillment rather than of absurd termination. What the proclamation gives me is the permission and possibility of speaking of the life that ends, of death, in a language that so construes reality that it is possible to speak of fulfillment.

It is tempting to say that the proclamation allows us to experience death itself as fulfilling confrontation with God in Christ; but this would return us to positions we have already rejected. What we must say is rather that the proclamation interprets death as the occasion of *Jesus'* final act of addressing us in judgment and affirmation. And this interpretation indeed includes language about *after* death —for Jesus will then speak as the one who died and now lives, and who calls us—also and especially then!—to *answer*. Death is the occasion of Jesus' call to us to answer—that is, *to live*. And this will not be a private, as it were one-at-a-time, "experience"—any more than any other event of call and answer, of language, is private. *We* will speak and answer. And this final word-event—as accomplished word-event the achievement at last of love—will never end. It *is* the end.

This gives the last in this series of exhortations. The language of faith is never achieved. We speak faithfully when we respond to, and ourselves make, the promise of that utterance in which we will one day speak the meaning of life in God. Let us now, therefore, speak of God in fear and trembling and in reliance on forgiveness: "Here, Lord, is what we must say. If we misspeak, forgive us."

Index

241